Understanding the world economy

Global issues shaping the future

Tony Cleaver

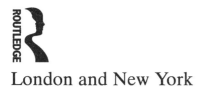

London and New York

First published 1997
by Routledge
11 New Fetter Lane, London EC4P 4EE

Simultaneously published in the USA and Canada
by Routledge
29 West 35th Street, New York, NY 10001

© 1997 Tony Cleaver

Typeset in Times by Keystroke, Jacaranda Lodge, Wolverhampton
Printed and bound in Great Britain by Hartnolls Ltd, Bodmin, Cornwall

British Library Cataloguing in Publication Data
A catalogue record for this book is available from the British Library

Library of Congress Cataloging in Publication Data
Cleaver, Tony, 1947–
   Understanding the world economy: global issues shaping the future
/ Tony Cleaver.
      p.   cm.
   Includes bibliographical references and index.
   1. International trade. 2. Economic development. 3. Debts,
External. 4. Environmental economics. 5. Foreign exchange.
I. Title.
HF1379.C55   1997
337—dc20   96-9862
                                                                CIP

ISBN 0–415–12815–3 (hbk)
       0–415–12816–1 (pbk)

Understanding the world economy

Understanding the World Economy gives an up-to-date account of how the world economy is changing. The text follows themes from one side of the world to the other, examining the economic forces at work and the impact they have on us. Looking forward to the new century, the book argues that as trade and finance become increasingly globalised a worldwide perspective will become vital to economists. The broad range of topics covered includes:

- international trade and finance
- economic development and growth
- foreign debt
- environmental economics
- exchange rates and currency union

Key theories are illustrated in contemporary real-world settings and explained in jargon-free, non-technical language.

The book will give a comprehensive introduction to students new to the subject whose interest goes beyond their own national economy.

Tony Cleaver is Secondary Head of The English School in Bogotá, Colombia. His career has involved teaching in schools, colleges and universities in the UK, Singapore, Chile, the Netherlands and Colombia.

Contents

Preface

This book has grown out of a series of lectures and seminars that were given at Durham University from 1991 to 1994 to undergraduate and postgraduate non-economists. The content of the following pages to some extent reflects their needs, but perhaps derives more from my own interests and understanding of what issues are becoming of increasing importance in any debate on economics.

From the beginning, one of my central interests has been to widen the scope of an introductory text to embrace the experiences of a broad selection of countries. In part, the international focus of the book comes from living and working in five different parts of the globe and realising how frustratingly difficult it is to learn economics without a strong national – typically US or UK – bias. English is an international language. Millions of students around the world are introduced to economics and business administration in this language but international examples of economic principles in action tend either to be absent from the more popular textbooks or come right at the end when dealing with the analysis of foreign trade. It is as if the rest of the world is far away from most class and lecture rooms. But in international schools and universities in cosmopolitan centres such as Singapore, Rotterdam and Buenos Aires the rest of the world sits down right next to you. For students such as these, I hope the global outlook of this book will be welcome. For those engaged in studying the Theory of Knowledge for the International Baccalaureate diploma, the Introduction may be of particular relevance. It attempts to explain what distinguishes economics from other academic subjects and why it rewards effort in mastering its discipline.

But this book is not only for those with a cosmopolitan upbringing. We are all world citizens now. What breaks in the news in one nation today most other nations find out about only seconds later, thanks to the telecommunications revolution. The more we are aware of world events, therefore, the more important it becomes to understand the economic principles which underly them. It turns out that what drives government policies and dictates the business environment in Durham is surprisingly similar to that which impacts on Bogota. Privatisation of public utilities, for example, has been debated and implemented in both places – hence the emphasis on 'The World Economy'. Only ten years ago it can be argued there was no such thing. There were at the very least three worlds: a first world of industrialised, high-income, market economies; a second world of autarkic communist bloc nations; and a third world of poorer, less-developed countries. Although always a contentious classification, this view of humankind was common enough to make the 'Third World' a fairly standard term of reference when discussing the fortunes of low-income, non-communist countries.

Such an easy, tripartite division of the world cannot be defended today. The transformation of the former Soviet and East European command systems into emerging market economies has caused the second 'world' to disappear, and it has never been easy to separate all other nations into rich and poor – still less today now that average incomes in some fast-growing countries of the latter group rival those traditionally classified in the former. Although still a long way from being a single, unified marketplace, therefore, it is the argument presented in these pages that the world economy is now recognisably one.

No single country or bloc of countries can successfully isolate themselves from economic realities elsewhere, as the former COMECON partners once attempted. The differences between command and market economies are analysed in chapter 1 and the path of transition of the former into the latter is examined in chapter 2.

The international transmission of economic ideas, government policies and their consequences, for good or ill, are considered in chapters 3 and 4. The post-war Keynesian orthodoxy and how it has been superseded by deregulating 'supply-side' economics is here explained. These are policies which were once identified with Britain's Margaret Thatcher and are now being implemented by governments all round the globe.

Analysis of the increasing division of the world economy into regional trade blocs is begun in chapter 5. The gains from trade and, specifically, the North American Free Trade Agreement as it impacts upon Mexico are considered. Brief reference is also made to strategic trade policies as practised by Japan.

Closer economic integration is pursued with reference to the European Union (chapter 6); and the implications of a single European currency (chapter 8) follow after the analysis of money and banking.

Global money, the world trade in oil and international debt are all related. Each deserves a chapter. The rapid changes taking place in international finance have revolutionised modern banking practice and have left governments, and traditional economics textbooks, struggling to keep up. I have tried not to get too left behind. The analysis of oil, meanwhile, provides a fascinating application of the microeconomics of demand, supply and price, and of the theory of the firm. This chapter could well serve as an introduction to the principles of economics for students of business administration, since so many important issues flow from it. The chapter on international debt returns again to analyse the impact of unregulated markets in the world economy.

Two themes of increasing importance come towards the end of the book: the growing part played in the international arena by a few, dynamic, Asian economies and the export-promoting strategies they have employed; and, finally, examination of the economics of the environment. The world economy shares a world ecology and these two perspectives urgently need to be brought together if we are to understand what it means to conserve the planet.

The book closes with a final review of global issues to be faced in the twenty-first century.

An explanation is required for the diagrams to be found enclosed in this text. Most are quite unlike those found in any other economics book. I must thank students at Durham, and particularly those of the 'Use Your Head Society' for introducing me to this form of mental shorthand. They taught me that ideas do not need to be laid down sequentially on the printed page to convey a coherent message – in fact our brains may not work most efficiently that way. I thus attempt to summarise the arguments presented in each chapter in these 'mind maps'. Ideas flow out in different directions: key concepts are circled and linked to others forwards, backwards and sideways. Symbols and illustrations help imprint certain features in the mind. Please note that these maps are in no way definitive: the reader can no doubt improve on them since my brain has been channelled over the years to think in a rather rigid way! Nonetheless I hope that each diagram succeeds in some way to illustrate a number of the more important points and thought processes developed through the book.

Finally, thanks are due to colleagues without whose help this book would not have been written. All weaknesses in this text are undoubtedly mine; any strengths, however, are drawn from two institutions: Chris Marsden, Head of Educational and Community Relations at British Petroleum in London confirmed me in my post as BP Fellow at Durham University, encouraged me to publish and gave me complete academic freedom to follow my own interests in this regard. To all friends at the Department of Economics at Durham, I owe a great debt for the welcome and warmth offered to me – and especially to Rodney Wilson and Peter Johnson for their daily support, advice and guidance whilst I was in this post. The world economy keeps on changing, but I have found the company of certain economists an enriching and enjoyable constant. Muchisimas gracias.

T.C. Bogota, 1996

Introduction

Economics is not always easy to get on with. It is not that the subject matter is dry, soulless and confusing – just that many textbooks seem to present it that way.

The reality is that people actually care passionately about economic issues. Too passionately: there have been more revolutions, killings and 'disappearances' caused by disputes over rival systems of economic organisation than due to disputes of any other kind. Nonetheless, students do not usually turn to economics books for stimulating reading or to resolve problems in passionate debate.

So there is a dilemma in studying this subject. People know intuitively that economic affairs are important and that more knowledge in this field is desirable; but, at the same time, many complain after long hours of study that what can be gained from mastering all the difficult analysis involved seems to be very little. In the jargon of the textbooks, the rate of return seems to be too low to fully repay the investment.

This is a justifiable complaint. Students live very crowded lives. An hour or two's study in the evening has a very real *opportunity cost* – you lose the opportunity to do so many other entertaining things; take three months out of a year to cram in a course of study and the sacrifice is enormous – the pay-off had better be worth it; extend that course to cover two or three years and we are talking about what seems a lifetime.

Time is very precious. As Einstein knew, it is not a constant. It flies by faster when you are a student; it slows down and crawls along as you get older and are presented with fewer life-changing decisions. An economist might wryly remark that there is diminishing marginal utility involved here: the more years you consume, the less precious each one seems!

What it all amounts to is that newcomers to economics are understandably impatient to learn how to use the subject to unlock some of the mysteries, conundrums and injustices of everyday life. For those with eyes to see, such problems are all around us – on the streets, on the television, in the newspapers. Will the poor always be with us? Is unemployment *natural*? Why are prices rising? Doesn't anyone care about the environment? These are difficult questions, every one; all good reasons for turning to economics.

The very first book ever written on the subject was *An Inquiry into the Nature and Causes of the Wealth of Nations.* It is a good title. These things are all worthy of study – providing you gain in learning, not confusion.

This book is an attempt to help. It does not promise to provide the solutions to all or any of the world's problems – if these solutions were so easy to come by they would already be in place – but it is designed to make some of the ideas, theories and arguments more accessible to the general reader. If you can understand these a little better you can then understand why certain politicians, business executives and other practical people put into effect some of the policies they do. You should thus be able to argue with a little knowledge – rather than with a lot of prejudice – why you think certain actions are right or wrong.

But beware: a little knowledge is a dangerous thing. Complex problems can easily be oversimplified. Reducing issues of world importance to a few pages is necessary to begin with – this is a taster in economics, after all – but further understanding requires commitment to longer study. Quick, short-term returns are necessary to keep investors happy and 'hanging-on in there', but long-run profits and sustainable growth are not bought so easily. A textbook or two may be necessary – and, hopefully, you will in time be able to see through the dry logic into the passionate implications of what this subject is all about . . .

ECONOMICS, SOCIAL SCIENCE AND THE THEORY OF KNOWLEDGE

Let me emphasise at the beginning one particular feature of economics that is common to all forms of learning, whether it be science, languages, art or whatever. This is perhaps more obvious in economics than in many other subjects, but it is true for all: *we can never know anything with absolute certainty.* Do not deduce from this that economics is therefore not worth bothering about. Just because 'final answers' are unattainable, that knowledge is a time-consuming pathway without end, it does not mean we might as well give up at the start. Be assured that a certain amount of profit can be gained fairly quickly and, if you invest your time wisely, returns can magnify with compound interest as you go along.

Economists know only too well the fallibility of their science. Like weather forecasters, we make predictions about what we think might happen. Since there are so many variables to consider, so many things that can change, we have to assume that some will remain constant (in the 'short run') and base our predictions on what is expected to happen to others. Past experience helps. If we observe that every time in the past when a wind blew from the west it brought rain then we can induce a general law that can be applied to the future – it will rain when the west wind blows next, assuming all other things remain the same.

With the weather, of course, just as in economics, we can never be absolutely sure. Storms from a totally unexpected quarter can blow all our calculations adrift. Things never stay constant for very long.

The analogy with meteorology can be pressed too far, however. This is because it can never be emphasised enough that economics is first and foremost *a social science* – the product of a set of analytical tools that attempts to make sense of society. It concerns itself with different issues than, say, sociology, anthropology, history, etc., but its subject of study is very much the same: humankind – and economics shares with these other disciplines, therefore, the same difficulty of applying scientific methodology.

This assertion – that economics is essentially a scientific inquiry into social activity – is the second most important feature of the subject worthy of note. In my view, a thorough grasp of all the implications of this statement is absolutely essential if the time-pressed student is really to profit from study of the subject. The more I teach economics, the more I become concerned that the bulk of esoteric analysis that fills our textbooks is nowhere near as useful to the average student as this fundamental. It is so easy to spend your time struggling to make sense of complex theoretical arguments that you lose sight of what it is all for.

You may be surprised to learn that this can be as true for long-term practitioners of the subject as it is for newcomers. There is much criticism within the profession that academic economists are increasingly limiting their research to fields that may be susceptible to precise mathematical treatment, but which are of limited relevance to the 'big questions' at large. Because these questions are difficult to fathom, therefore, mainstream economics is being accused of the error outlined above: of burying itself in impressive computation and being unwilling or, worse, unable to see what is important on the pathway to knowledge.

There is a perverse comfort in this discovery. We all make mistakes. If you feel occasionally overwhelmed by the complexity of it all and nervous in claiming any special insights about society then you are not alone. But do not be put off. Keep on asking awkward questions. If reputable experts and the hefty, authoritative tomes they produce cannot answer you in a meaningful way then it is not necessarily you that is wrong. Maybe you are on to something.

This point is worth emphasising. I see economists engaged in investigating social phenomena, employing scientific methodology where they can as objectively as possible, but at the same time working within a specific social and historical context. Inevitably, this context influences the objectivity and scientific validity of the economist's product.

Every scientist possesses a certain world view and works with a given body of knowledge to back him/her up. We all attempt to contribute towards the advancement of knowledge but, consciously or otherwise, in so doing we may be promoting one particular perspective in place of another. In the evolution of science a number of schools of thought can be identified. Many may coexist together, though usually one 'paradigm' may predominate. If one such paradigm becomes a lasting, unquestioned research tradition then there is a danger of science stagnating. Knowledge advances best when new minds are continually challenging, re-interpreting the dominant tradition. Young students impatient with their teachers are to be welcomed!

The philosophy that underpins this text is a personal interpretation like any other. It should not go unchallenged. It is born of an emphasis on 'Positive Economics' – that is, we must attempt to scientifically test all claims to economic knowledge – but it also accepts that any assertion about society must be treated with caution, in the knowledge that all economists are subjective, value-ridden individuals, no matter how hard we might try to be unbiased.

There are problems in attempting to be 'scientific' about society. Any systematic, rigorous investigation of phenomena involves the tried and tested formula of scientific method. This methodological approach involves a strict and time-honoured procedure that must be satisfied if research findings at the end of it are to have any acceptance by the scientific community. But the searchlight of scientific method has its limitations: it can illuminate certain areas better than others. As a tool of investigation it is extremely useful, but the technical demands of this instrument of inquiry should not be the sole determinant of the goals of social investigation. It is a means to an end only. If there are important places where it sheds little light we must still continue to search, albeit rather tentatively. In the end, what the economist can unearth must be presented with all humility. Any pretensions to uncovering the truth will be set about with qualifications, since this is in the nature of social science.

Scientific method involves observation of phenomena; generalising of hypotheses; deduction of predictions and testing them for corroboration or falsification of theory. These are the essential steps involved in any scientific investigation from Galileo to Einstein; from Hippocrates to Sherlock Holmes. At all stages in this process, however, there are problems endemic to the social – as distinct from the natural – sciences.

Objective recording of data is an immense difficulty when people are studying people. What one observer perceives from a given social phenomenon another will not. The cultural values the observer brings to the scene are inextricably bound up with his/her allegedly objective report.

Take the example of a worker who considers that the wage rate paid for a job is insufficient compensation for the sacrifice involved. Is this a case of exploitation of the labour force? Other observers might say it is merely someone 'pricing themselves out of work'. If unemployment results here, is this 'voluntary' or 'involuntary'? It depends on your point of view. (What you perceive to be happening here has very important policy implications – see chapters 3 and 4.)

Everyone has prejudices. We cannot avoid them since we make

judgements every day based on our (inevitably limited) perception of others. It is essential for the student of social science to realise that it is thus impossible to be completely value-free, but if we can make just a little progress towards greater objectivity in our observations then this will be immensely more valuable to us than memorising whole bookshelves of algebraic theory.

In addition to the difficulty of defining and measuring certain phenomena in principle, this problem is compounded in practice by vagaries in the statistical record. Even supposing there was agreement between countries on what constitutes unemployment – or, say, how we might evaluate capital – the efficiency of data gathering can be questionable. In some places, just counting the population is difficult enough, let alone calculating what they do or what they produce.

What we observe to be happening in the world at large, therefore, is inevitably blinkered, right at the start. Our access to information is limited by scarce and/or unreliable data and even where our viewpoint is crystal clear our own perception is never uncluttered. What face do you first see in a crowd? Your own. All observation is to some degree subjective: you see what you best recognise.

Generating universal laws – the next stage in the scientific process – becomes more difficult the greater the complexity of the subject under the microscope. A fundamental difference between natural science and social science worth mentioning here is the distinction between what has been termed homogenous evidence and heterogenous evidence. In certain natural sciences you are dealing with pieces of data that are identical and behave the same way under similar circumstances (one hydrogen atom is the same as another) In social sciences the different bits of data (people) are not alike. As a result we can make extremely complex statements about the world in physics based on relatively few experiences. And we hold these views with something close to certainty: we know, for example, when Halley's Comet will return for thousands of years into the future, thanks to a very few observations. But we cannot make quite such confident claims about the world in biology (plants and animals constitute heterogenous data also) and even less so about humans. Who knows, for example, when unemployment in Europe will return to low, pre-1980 levels?

There are numerous general laws in physics, that most respectable, fore-castable of sciences. These are accepted by the scientific community and are of universal applicability throughout the cosmos. All such laws will tend to have a 'sell-by' date; that is, there comes a time as our knowledge improves when they are revised and a new scientific paradigm is formu-lated – Newtonian physics was superseded by Einstein, for example – but the point is that in the meantime, given our limited vision, our laws of light, gravity, etc., are upheld everywhere we look, without exception. They are general, universal axioms, infallible enough to build spaceships to the Moon and back. Natural sciences based on more complex building blocks (e.g. organic chemistry) will have substantially fewer such laws. In biology there is only one: the theory of evolution. But in social science there are none. In economics, which perhaps uses more scientific techniques of inquiry than the other humanities, there are many attempts at general laws, but all are only statistical tendencies where exceptions abound. General 'laws' in economics apply only if certain assumptions are maintained. (If workers ask for more wages, then assuming their motivation, efficiency and productivity in work does not change, businesses may employ fewer ...)

Deducing specific predictions from general laws in social science is not too easy either. Predictions may be precise, but they cannot be used to falsify or corroborate hypotheses with a great degree of certainty, since – unlike laboratory experiments – other factors in society can never be held constant. (Did the fall in UK and US inflation throughout the 1980s confirm or confound monetarist theory?)

This is a problem that laboratory science knows well enough (you may have done the experiment wrong!) but whereas the pure scientist can do it again (though at cost) and isolate the variables better next time, the social scientist has to take the world as he/she finds it, along with all its 'imperfections'. Unravelling what has been going on in society – whether particular changes have had more or less influence than others on subsequent events – is thus extremely difficult to determine when all sorts of things are happening all the time. Some scholars have asserted that since falsification/corroboration of general laws in economics is impossible to achieve, so the whole attempt to apply Popperian scientific methodology is pointless. This seems a bit extreme – we can rely on the scientific searchlight in some areas, if not all.

As a result of these difficulties, in comparison to the natural sciences, social scientists recognise the need for much larger and more representative samples, and much greater care in their interpretation, in order to make reasonable claims to knowledge. They are increasingly turning to more sophisticated computational techniques to assist them. Even then there is an inevitable lack of precision: as the price of oil rises, people will generally buy less of it – a 'law' in economics with a lot of statistical support – but how much they will actually buy next time is more difficult to say. Contrast this statement with what can be asserted if the *temperature* of oil rises: chemical engineers in oil refineries can predict to a calculable degree exactly what will happen to it.

A final point of caution: humankind has an insatiable curiosity and a capacity to theorise in the search for causes. If, for example, it is noted that on a number of occasions after a flash of lightning there follows a clap of thunder then not only can a general law be induced, but there is a natural impulse to ask: why?

Most people cannot accept not knowing why things happen and will rush into any causal explanation – from magic to the influence of gods, gurus and aliens – rather than be left with uncertainty. In the case of economics and social science, however, it is the purpose of this emphasis on the Theory of Knowledge to stop the drift into narrow-minded use and abuse of science, where nice theories impede rather than illuminate our vision. We should ask ourselves continually: 'Which is the most worthwhile area to investigate?'; 'How reasonable are my beliefs?'; and 'Am I certain that I'm not being selective in my choice of data?'

It is too easy to leap to erroneous conclusions when investigating urgent social problems. One of the world's most famous (fictional) social scientists, Sherlock Holmes, knew what he was up against: 'It is a capital mistake, Watson, to theorise before one has sufficient data' (from *Scandal in Bohemia*). It is advice we should all take note of: suspending judgement is better than slipping into prejudice.

KEY WORDS

Opportunity cost This is perhaps the most fundamental concept in economics. The true cost of doing anything is giving up the opportunity to do something else you would really like. This is as relevant to the student who chooses to bury him/herself in a textbook and tries to forget about the party that everyone else is going to, as it is to the speculator who invests a small fortune in one company's shares and hopes that the other one that looked attractive turns out to be as buoyant as a flat tyre. A choice has to be taken whenever scarce resources are employed – if time and money are no object then it does not matter what you do, but in the real world consumers, business executives and government officials are frequently confronted with difficult decisions as to what actions to take. The cost of opting for one course of action is losing the opportunity to follow another.

FURTHER READING

Bastian, Sue. 'What to do with logic – inductive inferences', in *International Quarterly*, Winter 1986/7.
Ormerod, Paul. *The Death of Economics*. Faber & Faber, 1994.

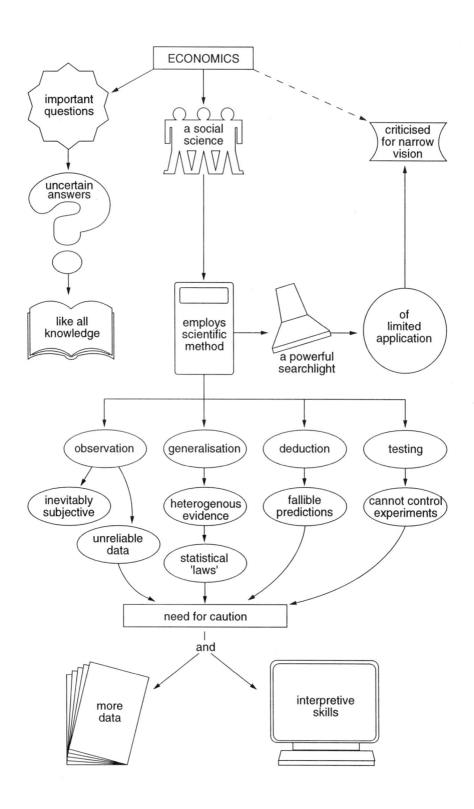

1 Command, market and mixed economies

Topics to be considered in this chapter

- The functions of all economic systems – what, how and for whom goods and services are produced
- Different mixes in building an economic system:
  i   centralised or dispersed decision making
  ii   communal or self-interest
  iii   planning or price mechanisms
  iv   public or private ownership
  v   monopoly or competition
- Problems encountered in command and market economies: government and market failure
- Getting the mix right

INTRODUCTION

Over the last seventy years or so, the world has witnessed a contest between two contrasting engines of economic development: one powerhouse has been led by central *command*; the other is ruled by *markets* – one has operated in Eastern Europe and the old Soviet Union; the other has been championed by the West.

You could say that this century has therefore hosted humankind's greatest-ever experiment in social, political and economic organisation. No one has been untouched by this experience, we have all been involved: either as active participants or as distant bystanders.

Now, according to many commentators, the great ideological battle between the two opposing economic systems has finally been settled – with victory allegedly going to the market model.

This chapter will consider this claim. Is the command system now to be consigned to the dustbin of history, or is there still life in the controversies that fostered this rivalry?

We begin by first examining what is meant by an economic system and then go on to consider the characteristics of (and criticisms against) the different forms of organisation.

ECONOMIC SYSTEMS

Economics studies the way societies organise their resources to satisfy their needs. Economic organisation in this context refers to the ownership and control of the means of production, how decisions of consumption and production are made and communicated to others and how efficiently economic changes are effected.

Fundamental economic decisions face all societies. Any community must decide *what* goods and services it should produce; *how* it should best employ its resources to secure these ends; and finally, for *whom* in society, and in what number, these benefits should be provided. We can therefore classify any given economic system by the way – either by accident or design – it resolves these issues.

Command and market economies approach these tasks in very different ways, but to begin by classifying the rich diversity of the world's differing forms of economic organisation into just two broad types is far too restrictive. There is a wealth of options for building a modern economy, and they can be assessed according to at least *five* dimensions. Command and market systems should be properly viewed as theoretical extremes, and all countries are in reality mixed systems, taking up positions somewhere along the spectrum of characteristics that follow.

The first dimension: the location of decision making

- Where are economic decisions made in society, and who by?
- Should the country produce more food or industrial produce? Guns or butter? Cars or trains? Comedy shows or computer programmes?
- What type of technology and labour force should be employed in these industries, and where in the country should such economic activity take place?
- Who in society should enjoy most access to the goods and services that are produced, and who is entitled to the least?

Decisions like these can be taken mostly by a community's leaders, at the centre; they may be taken by millions of others dispersed throughout society; or some decisions may be centralised, and others dispersed between a mixture of different economic actors with varying claims to importance.

The command economic system is characterised by *central control* – all major decisions regarding the community's organisation are made at the centre and communicated by command via a bureaucracy of subordinates.

What, how, and for whose benefit economic activities are conducted throughout society is thus decided by an authoritative administration, geographically located at a central government – though a political metaphor would be at the top of a pyramidal powerbase.

The leaders of a command system may inherit power, be elected, appointed, or seize it by force. They may be communist or fascist; a monarchy or republic. The political colour and constitutional validity of the organising authority is not at issue; the key aspect of this form of organisation is that the major economic decisions are taken by central command, and are not dispersed. Thus in the post-war Soviet Union it was decided by the country's leaders to accelerate the production of capital goods and energy supplies; to develop a network of new cities and industrial estates around for example Irkutsk in southern Siberia; and to guarantee wages and salaries in the region at 300 per cent above the Moscow average.

The image that illustrates where decision making rests in a pure market system with no government intervention is 'consumer sovereignty': where the consumer is king. All decisions regarding what activities should be practised in a free-market system are taken in accordance with individual demand. If consumers in aggregate want more of one product than another then their purchasing power will drive producers to comply. Nobel prize-winning economist Paul Samuelson likens the process to individuals casting dollar votes in an open contest (market) for the goods and services they prefer. Those commodities that receive the most 'votes' will inevitably be supplied.

How business is conducted, how society's resources are employed to produce what consumers want, is decided by independent managers throughout the economy who are free to choose production methods, and employ labour and capital as they so wish. They will make profits only insofar as how quickly they respond to consumer demand.

Decisions as to who benefits most in this economic system are spread widely and are made in accordance with those who have participated most productively in serving consumer needs. The popular football player may earn more than the doctor or social worker, but that is what people pay for. All decision making is thus decentralised: the authority to organise and control resources is dispersed throughout society. The consumer is the sovereign decision maker.

The second dimension: the economic philosophy

- What is the code of values that underpins social and economic organisation? What is it that drives individuals and institutions to perform their particular economic functions?
- Do people act to serve their own interests first above all others? Do the needs of society take precedent over the individual? Or perhaps a tribal or community-based ethic dominates all social interaction?

Such questions can be answered by studying the nature and conduct of the main producing and consuming agents in the economy.

For some countries there is a well-articulated ethic embodied in all main institutions, emphasising the prior needs of the state. Although most powerfully and consistently expressed in the communist doctrine, many countries of different philosophical persuasion have also exhorted the responsibilities of the people for the collective good as a means of consolidating and promoting nationhood. (Calls to patriotism are especially urgent, of course, during wartime.)

In the *communal ethic* of the command economy, resources are mobilised according to a coherent set of values, clearly set out with practical applications for subordinates to follow at all levels within the society. As an extreme example, the East German border guard was thus legally empowered to shoot anyone trying to flee from the country: there can be no clearer demonstration of the view that the state has supremacy over individual rights.

For many other communities, of course, collective values need not be brutally enforced. A communal ethic can be inspiring, not imprisoning. Whether it be a nation state, an army, a church or a business organisation, some unifying central code or philosophy or mission statement can be a highly effective means of organising, motivating, disciplining and giving direction to a society's resources. (Note that we are concerned here only with the effectiveness of communal doctrine as a means of economic organisation. No judgement is made on the power of such ethical codes in imparting value to peoples' lives.)

The contrasting ethic to the above is one that insists on the primacy of *self-interest*. Margaret Thatcher once claimed that 'there is no such thing as society', implying that the market society is best understood as an agglomeration of individuals. Often, the name of Adam Smith is reverently quoted in this regard, and the following passage is perhaps the most famous in all economics:

> Every individual endeavours to employ his capital so that its produce may be of greatest value. He generally neither intends to promote the public interest, nor knows how much he is promoting it. He intends only his own security, only his own gain. And he is in this led by an 'invisible hand' to promote an end which was no part of his intention. By pursuing his own interest he frequently promotes that of society more effectually than when he really intends to promote it.
>
> (Adam Smith, *The Wealth of Nations*, 1776)

Smith wrote this over 200 years ago as the professor of moral philosophy at Glasgow University, and was well aware of the ethical and institutional foundations upon which this assertion is based. The individual's right to property ownership, laws of contract and of fair and equal exchange requires rigorous protection. The state is the guardian of the individual, and the power of princes, politicians or monopolies to usurp these rights must be limited. Assured of protection, therefore, the consumer acts to increase wealth and welfare (what economists call 'utility'); the producer aims to maximise profits. The value system that pervades the free market is thus the pursuit of individual well-being.

The third dimension: the allocative mechanism

How are economic decisions signalled to all the relevant institutions throughout society? By what means are productive resources – skilled labour, capital equipment and enterprising management – all brought together in the desired locations and set to work in the most efficient way possible? How is it organised that the right quantities of agricultural output are produced on the farms, sent to the factories, processed into foods and then delivered to all the outlets in the country just at the correct time and place so that we can all enjoy fresh milk, bread and cereals for breakfast? We take this highly efficient arrangement for granted, yet any breakdown in what is actually a tremendously complex economic inter-action between millions of participants would mean that these perishable foodstuffs would go rotten before they got to us. The organising mecha-nism needed to allocate these resources, goods and services to all the various destinations in an economy will either be a system of planning, or prices.

Under a system of *planning*, all economic activity is subordinate to a strict, institutionalised logic. Anyone who has served in a large, hierarchical organisation (such as in the armed services) will know all about this, but as a means of administering a whole economy the old Soviet Union provides the example *par excellence*.

First, a systematic process is employed to formulate long-term goals for the entire community. This requires review of past performance, contemplating future ambitions and relating these to present resources. The highest decision-making authority in a country – in the ex-USSR, the Politburo – must be involved here. Once these national goals are agreed upon, they are handed down to the planning committee – the Gosplan – to be translated into specific targets for all sectors of the economy. Research is next undertaken into alternative strategies for achieving these targets. Having considered all the options, the decision is then made to implement the chosen strategy and to give the go-ahead to (typically) the next five year plan. Once underway, planners are responsible for monitoring progress throughout the economy, in order to feedback results ready for the next planning phase.

Administering the planning process is obviously a tremendously complex and important responsibility, and its success depends on high professional standards upheld by key officers – in the communist bloc, the *nomenklatura*. All institutions throughout the organisation are required to accept their 'planned' role and to be effective in executing it and to communicate delegated roles to subordinates. Individual goal-setting and independent action are constrained because no one low down the hierarchy has the ability to clearly see how their task fits into the grand scheme of things – such vision is necessarily only possible for those high up in the hierarchy who can see the bigger picture.

In a comprehensively planned organisation, the plan for any one sector is dependent upon or nested within the next highest order of planning, and in turn carries within it provision for lower-order plans. Thus in the Ukraine, within the agricultural sector, at the level of the individual collective farm in the Steppes, orders were given for the output of wheat to be attained, with the quantities of fertiliser designated, and the inputs of labour and farm machinery, fuel and incomes allowed. The margins of tolerance for the individual farm manager to stray from these targets were very limited since they would have been consistent with the plans given to all other agricultural and industrial producers within the economy.

A system of central command is naturally biased in favour of an allocative mechanism as described above, though not all command organisations will have experienced planning as extensive as that of the old Soviet Union. However, even there large sections of economic activity remained unplanned and employed rudimentary price systems (especially in consumer goods production); and, conversely, many market economies contain numerous institutions that function predominantly by planning.

The *price mechanism* is the dominant means of allocating resources in a market economy. It operates wherever buyers and sellers of commodities meet freely to conduct trade. The process of bargaining involves exploring weaknesses and strengths; gaining or conceding advantage; evolving deals that are acceptable to all parties – thereby demonstrating the flexible mechanism of prices.

All traders operate according to agreed rules and each individual market place is free to negotiate its own outcome. Prices thus reflect real (not prejudiced) forces operating in society and signal to all parties what activities are most (or least) in demand, most (or least) profitable.

If growing numbers of consumers decide that smoking cigarettes is bad for you and eating vegetarian foods is healthy, then they will reduce consumption of one and increase purchases of the other. Reduced demand for tobacco will cause market prices to fall and producers will start to lose profits. Conversely, farmers of soya beans, nuts and lentils will be enjoying rising demand and prices. Over the long term, if these market trends persist, then in the factories and fields, cigarette packers and tobacco pluckers will face falling demand, falling wages and fewer hours of work whilst wages and work conditions on farms producing organic foodstuffs via environmentally friendly methods will steadily improve. Workers will move; the allocation of resources will change; the pattern of production throughout the economy will adjust. All this is signalled by the movement of *prices*: in consumer-goods markets (for cigarettes and vegetables), in land and capital markets (rent, interest and profits), and in labour markets (wages).

In a perfect market system, therefore, all resources are priced in relation to their relative scarcity, are employed accordingly, and move their employment in response to price and profit signals from consumer markets. Social organisation is thus automatic, self-adjusting: Smith's *'invisible hand'*.

The fourth dimension: the ownership of resources

Ownership of productive assets imparts a vested interest in their use and in the distribution of the rewards that they earn. Should private individuals be free to own and employ all the means to produce wealth in an economy? If so, up to what (if any) limit? Or should this economic power be entrusted to the state?

Command systems that are communist, not fascist, in political make-up insist on *state ownership* of resources. The exact pattern differs according to the country concerned: in the old Soviet Union and in Communist China, for example, agricultural land was forcibly collectivised since the traditional, feudal/aristocratic pattern of former ownership was considered a direct impediment to economic development. In countries such as Poland and Hungary, however, the practice of collective farming was abandoned as unworkable.

With regard to industrial capital, in all of these economies it was state owned. Factory managers were appointed by the authorities and charged with running the enterprises consistent with planned instructions. Public ownership ensures that managers who control day-to-day operations have no entitlement to any profits made, beyond what is their due in salaries. There is no quarrel either as to the amount and nature of employment, nor to any changes in policy goals – state ownership of the means of production confers controlling influence to the leaders of the administration, not to individual factory heads. There can be no independent operators marching to a different tune. Full employment can be guaranteed; all production plans can be implemented; use of resources for any ends not sanctioned by the state is theoretically impossible.

In a pure market economy there is no state ownership of the means of production, all are subject to *private enterprise*. Individuals are free to own and employ whatever resources they can command. Decisions on how to produce what consumers demand are thus taken by independent entrepreneurs, who, if they calculate correctly, are then entitled to pocket any rewards left after paying off their costs. If incorrect, they are free to go bust.

Private ownership thus ensures that business practices are determined by those with a vested interest in successful outcomes. If entrepreneurs get it wrong, then – with no state support – they must move quickly to change their production plans. Going bust means they will have to sell out to someone else who will have different ideas on how best to employ their resources and how to spend any profits made.

Any dispute in the market place as to what, how or for whom the means of production should be employed is thus decided by the power of profits. Private property rights confer on the most successful the power to outbid others and thus to determine the direction and purpose of all economic activity. What style of football should the national team play? What repertoire will be featured in theatres, music halls and on the air-waves? Who will be employed doing what in the industrial heartlands? Those who have guessed the public mood correctly and most consistently in the past will have the deepest pockets and thus the economic power to make these decisions. The state will not.

The fifth dimension: the pattern of industry

What is the nature of interaction between institutions in the economy? Are they partners or rivals? Is it cooperation or competition? And is the pattern of production across the community characterised by a few giant monopolies or is it instead atomised into numerous smaller operatives?

Businesses can work in league with others; or independently and at odds with them. They can be large or small; many or few. The network of institutions within the economy may display a variety of such patterns.

An economy based on central command and the absence of any serious rival to state objectives will create *monopolies* in each and every sector of industrial activity. The production of steel, locomotives, energy and transport will all have to be coordinated to meet state requirements, for example – there is no economic sense in producing more locomotives than the country's transport network can handle. Efficient communication and cooperation between all producers is essential since all are performing complementary tasks. There is no economic rationale for competition in industry, given these circumstances. Indeed, it would militate against any sensible and efficient means of conducting business if different producers insisted on independence and tried to outdo, rather than assist, each other.

In command systems there is additionally and inevitably the incentive – in order to facilitate planning and to exploit cost-reducing economies of scale – to concentrate the resources of specific industries on one site, or at least on very few sites. State monopolies lead naturally to giantism in the heavy industries, therefore.

In contrast, the pure market economy cannot function efficiently without *competition*. Any coordination of decision making between different producers is not designed, not planned for, but is instead the evolutionary outcome of unregulated market forces.

Since there is no restriction on who can employ resources and make profits (or losses), all industry is characterised by the freedom of entry and exit of independent agents. Competition reigns: all are out to make money – ultimately at the expense of rivals. Such a situation ensures only the most efficient survive, and also that all consumers have alternative goods and services to choose between – all resources have alternative employments.

The need to succeed, and the fear of failure, make it imperative to improve resources all the time. Labour must continually upgrade its skills, capital must incorporate the very latest technology, land must be improved to increase its productivity and entrepreneurs must be ever more enterprising. Any mismatch between production and consumption decisions in the economy will be signalled through the markets by the relevant price changes, sparking off another round of adjustment between rivals.

Finally, the size of business units in a market economy will be determined by the most efficient size in the relevant industry (oil refineries will therefore be bigger than fashion-wear producers, for example), but the nature of unrestricted competition will tend to keep firms smaller and more fleeter of foot than would be the case if monopoly reigned.

THE FAILURES OF COMMAND SYSTEMS

So much for theory. The above identifies the various options available in designing an economic system; the ways that command and market societies organise their resources.

Whatever the choices a community makes, however, it is in the nature of economics that there are costs involved. The idealised accounts so far have glossed over the many problems involved in the way economic systems operate.

The failures inherent in command economic systems have thundered around the world – they have been significant enough to bring down the old Soviet Union and precipitate market reforms throughout all of the Iron Curtain countries of Eastern Europe – but market systems fail also, in more subtle and pervasive ways, and those who live by their dictates may often be too close to see the problems with any clarity.

We therefore need to turn our attention now to look at some of the weaknesses inherent in the systems described above.

It was mentioned earlier that all economic systems have to solve the fundamental problems of *what, how* and *for whom* in society production takes place. We can use this classification, therefore, in examining system failures.

The command model is based on the premise that the central authorities know what is best for their country. Planning is undertaken to mobilise all necessary resources, issuing clear commands to all sectors in order to bring about desired ends.

Where a country is underdeveloped, when there is little quarrel about what goods and services are needed for all, and where natural resources remain dormant awaiting exploitation, then command systems can be remarkably effective in securing economic growth. Corrupt and entrenched political institutions may be swept aside and living standards for all may be rapidly improved.

Problems arise, however, as economies develop and become more sophisticated. The premise that the centre knows best can be challenged. What consumers want beyond bare essentials is really only known to themselves, yet the entire rationale of planning is that orders are sent from the centre, above, rather than from individuals, below. As a result, *what* sort of goods are delivered when it is the administrators that place orders to industry, and not the consumers, can produce results that would be comical if they were not tragic.

As Alec Nove writes: 'One can issue an order – to produce 200,000 pairs of shoes – and this is identifiable and enforceable. To say "produce *good* shoes, that fit customers' feet" is a much vaguer, non-enforceable order' (*The Economics of Feasible Socialism*, Allen & Unwin, 1983). Since planning requires subordinates to meet specified targets from given inputs the typical result (given an order defined in numbers of shoes, above) would be for the factory to produce thousands of shoes fit only for dwarfs. (If a subsequent order is given to make bigger shoes, the factory will then dutifully produce thousands of pairs suitable for giants and policemen . . .)

So what do consumers get under central planning? A very limited range of poor quality goods and services. Products designed by a committee and supplied by a bureaucracy.

Martin Walker, USSR correspondent for the *Guardian* newspaper quoted in *The Economist*, describes the practice of 'storming' in a Lithuanian TV factory – the rush to meet planned production targets in the last few days before the deadline. Again, like all such activities under central planning, the incentive is to satisfy The Plan, not the customer:

> We never use a screwdriver in the last week. We hammer the screws in. We slam solder on the connections, cannibalise parts from other televisions if we have run out of the right ones, use glue or hammers to fix switches that were never meant for that model. And all the time the management is pressing us to work faster, to make the target so we all get our bonuses.

It was reported, meanwhile, that more than 2,000 times per year colour TV sets catch fire in Moscow alone. Together with them, the houses burn (*The Economist Survey of Perestroika*, 28 April 1990).

Nove concluded:

> Examples of wasteful or otherwise irrational practices designed to fulfil plans (not satisfy consumers) . . . could fill several bound volumes, all the examples being taken from Soviet publications. That so well-known

and well-studied a problem still resists solution is proof enough that it is genuinely difficult to solve.

Just as a command system therefore cannot avoid bureaucratic error in organising what commodities should be provided, so *how* production takes place is equally fraught with difficulties. Specifically, there is the problem of long communication chains and the potential for breakdown when decisions made by the centre are a great distance from the realities in the field.

A spectacular failure of Soviet centrally planned agricultural organisation was Khruschev's Virgin Lands programme. A five year expansion of wheat prairies in southwest Siberia and northern Kazakhstan – an area the size of Japan – was undertaken in the 1950s. The decision was taken in Moscow on the basis of inadequate information far removed from those working at grass roots level. This was in fact the natural consequence of years of neglect and low priority for farming: it was much less costly for subordinates to invent agricultural data rather than undertake the necessary research. Cultivation was thus pushed far into areas of very uncertain rainfall, severe wind erosion followed and with it the virtual collapse of the programme. With a tightly planned economy, major supply shortfalls impacted upon all industries and consumers. Shortages affected everyone and the political consequences for Kruschev were eventually terminal.

Many other examples of communication problems typical of command bureaucracies can be identified, some more significant than others. Chernobyl was an industrial tragedy of global dimensions. The nuclear reactor's meltdown in 1986 – which poisoned vast areas of the Ukraine and spread its pollution far across Europe and beyond – occurred at a time when the Soviet Union was beginning to implement *glasnost*: the freedom to express limited political criticism.

One month before the disaster, a letter appeared in a Kiev newspaper from Lyubov Kovalevska – a senior manager at Chernobyl. She wrote to complain about the sense of frustration experienced by workers on site at the amount of corruption, bureaucratic incompetence and consequent inadequate safety standards being practised in the construction of the nuclear facility. The Soviet ministries had created chaos by advancing completion of the project by one year, she said. Although plant workers were amongst the most skilled in the Soviet Union – many of them decorated for past achievements – the lack of building materials had made it impossible to meet the new construction deadlines at the required standards. For example, of 45,500 cubic metres of concrete purchased for the facility, 3,200 cubic metres never arrived and 'much of the rest' was substandard and unfit for its purpose.

At first, Kovalevska said, workers responded with enthusiasm to appeals to overcome the problems, but 'lack of organisation weakened not only discipline but also responsibility of each person for the overall result of the work'. As time went on, repeated appeals provoked indignation and eventually despair. One month later, the world had to pay the price for this 'lack of organisation'.

It is instructive in the above example that appeals were made to the communal ethic to overcome the organisational problems of planning. Workers were exhorted to place communal interests above their own.

Such an example is only one amongst many but it serves to remind us that the main reason for the creation of most command economies was, of course, to influence *for whom* in society economic rewards should be produced. Historically, the more important and influential command systems have been of communist persuasion, designed to improve the fortunes of agricultural peasants and the industrial working classes.

For that reason, prices where they operated in a command economy performed an entirely different function to those in a market system. Soviet prices, for example, were fixed by decree in accordance to planners' wishes, whereas market prices are determined by independent traders. What happens if market prices fall? Suppliers may have to cut their losses by offering less for sale. Not so under central planning – no one changes their economic behaviour unless commanded to do so. Prices for certain goods and services were therefore set deliberately low – in many cases below the costs of production (energy prices, for example) so that everyone could afford the essentials. But however socially desirable such practices may have been, such prices were unsustainable: they promoted dreadful waste.

After a visit to Kiev in 1991, the UK Chancellor of the Exchequer Norman Lamont told of how he had seen a Kazakh woman selling water melons on a street corner. She had flown thousands of miles to do so but only had to sell a few melons to recoup her fare since internal air transport was subsidised. The official value of water melons – under Soviet pricing – was therefore less than their real costs of production and distribution.

Similarly, in the late 1980s Poland had become an exporter of semi-tropical flowers, possible only because the fixed price for energy was a fraction of its true cost. Heating vast glasshouses to produce tropical plants was thus absurdly cheap and induced economic practices that had little to do with the original social intentions of inexpensive energy.

Instead of adding value through the production process, businesses that based their costs on such decreed prices, therefore, ended up by being *value-subtractors* – the value of their end-products was less than the costs of materials and energy that went into making them. In reality, they would have been better off selling the raw materials and not bothering to make anything at all. When such businesses entered into unprotected trade with the real world (such as the former East German manufacturer of optical instruments Carl Zeiss Jena) they went bust.

The end result of certain well-meaning policies to bring essential goods and services within the reach of even the poorest in society, therefore, was inefficiency, waste and economic ruin.

The final example of command government failure returns to an area referred to earlier – Soviet agriculture. When central authorities are convinced of the *righteousness* of their cause, then not all their policy commands are necessarily humanitarian.

Soviet collectivisation of agriculture was forced through by Stalin from 1928 to 1933. The process was essentially coercive and unaccompanied by material inducements, since any agricultural surplus was needed for investment in heavy industry. Millions of peasant smallholdings were thus collectivised into large-scale, state-managed commercial farms. There was no compensation. As a result, agricultural organisation under Stalinist authority was fraught with difficulty – with many peasants preferring to destroy their land and livestock rather than lose it all, and the government preferring to destroy such peasants. Untold millions of Soviet citizens perished – the very people it could be argued whose living standards should have benefited under central command.

Such events are a potent reminder of the offensive extremes that economic systems based on government commands can lead to. The problems of command systems, however, need not be laboured any further at this stage. For more details regarding the monumental changes now taking place in Eastern Europe see chapter 2.

MARKET FAILURE

It is important to contrast all of the above with the failings of market systems. Western critics of command regimes who can now triumphantly point to the evolutionary superiority of the market model need reminding that much is wrong with the system they champion. Indeed, it can be argued that a completely free (pure?) market economy would be relentlessly self-destructive.

As has already been noted, *what* goods and services a free market provides to consumers is determined by the pattern of their spending. There are two issues here: one of *normative economics* (i.e. the system might work, but do we like what it delivers?) and one of *positive economics* (the mechanism does not work; it does not deliver what is wanted).

Two of the more valuable items involved in international exchange are the illicit dealing in hard drugs and the (often undercover) trade in armaments (including nuclear weapons material). Millions and millions of dollars are spent each year on these commodities and – like it or not – the more money is forthcoming the more of the world's resources will be devoted to these industries. Can this really go unchallenged? The fact that governments seek (unsuccessfully) to control these trades is an indication of the unacceptability of free markets for such commodities. Note that not only can we oppose such dealing on moral grounds, but the very survival of society is threatened by unrestricted access to hard drugs and sophisticated weaponry.

With regard to communal interests, markets fail to provide essential *public* or *merit goods* like decent roads, defence and police forces, sufficient health and educational services. A mind-boggling variety of cars, guns, cigarettes, breakfast cereals and glossy magazines can be attractively promoted and sold across the counter to the willing customer, but the market has no means of reaching out and demanding payment from everyone who benefits from street-lighting, or national security, for example. There is an in-built bias to produce anything (no matter how trivial or harmful) for which demand can be stimulated and access restricted to individual fee-payers. Other goods and services which bring immense benefits to all the public and for which demand cannot be necessarily restricted only to those who pay for them will find few producers.

This leads us to consider more carefully *how* markets organise production, and particularly how well the mechanism of prices functions.

Do product prices reflect real consumer demand or is it sophisticated marketing that persuades us to pay monopoly mark-ups? Are consumers sovereign or is the multinational corporation king? Does the price mechanism signal what society wants to consume, or what multinationals want to produce? Vast business empires have been built up in the twentieth century to supply everything from oil and cars, to cereals and soap powder. With billions spent on product research and development, and megabucks splashed out on promotions and advertising, does the consumer really retain free choice? Economist J.K. Galbraith has emphasised the dominant influence of monopoly capital in the market place.

The provision of adequate medical services, housing, education, care for the aged and environmental beauty – all essential commodities – is never planned, packaged and promoted with the organised intelligence, efficiency and financial muscle that the giant corporations lavish on deodorants and diet coke.

To believe, therefore, that the control of immense economic power rests in the fickle and uncommitted hands of sovereign consumers is myopic folly. Through a gradual process of 'survival of the fittest', competition in industry has given rise to the growth of monopoly and *oligopoly* with the power to distort prices and incomes and secure the employment of resources (nationally and internationally) that best suit themselves.

Not only do market prices reflect some things they should not (monopoly power, above), but they also leave out other important elements that ought to be included.

For example, in a market system the low price of travelling by car compared to rail transport into a city should be a reflecion of the relative efficiency of the two services: if the cost to the private consumer of taking the car eventually increases (say due to rising fuel consumption, or time lost in traffic jams) then there will come a point when rail transport is preferred instead. But such calculation of private costs and benefits – which is at the heart of the free-market society – *takes no account of the costs imposed on society*. Cars kill and maim. They pour out pollution. They impose major transformations on urban landscapes. Lifestyles and social interaction are subtly but importantly affected.

The most efficient way to transport daily thousands of individuals from rural and suburban areas into city centres is *not* in separately cocooned and powered steel and metal death traps along massive land-gobbling superhighways. That is how consumers will choose to travel, however, so long as the price of car travel does not include the *social costs* of funeral and hospital bills, land purchase orders and environmental blight that such private decisions impose on others.

The price mechanism is thus not an automatic, objective, value-free device to organise an economy since the free market inevitably brings into the price calculus all sorts of hidden prejudices. The implications here are massively important. Not only will each and every price signal fail to some extent to reflect all the costs and benefits involved in its market determination, but by extension the sum total of these distorted market interactions will bring about an economy-wide outcome that must be far from optimum.

One result worth emphasising is the impoverishment of the environment. Priceless (literally!) natural assets such as clean air and seas are plundered without limit in unregulated markets and the long-term consequences for the planet are extremely worrying. (Of course, command economies run by governments that care little about the environment can cause the same, if not worse, problems. The point is, however, that free markets embody no mechanism that is responsive to all the needs of the planet. Informed regulation is therefore essential to ensure sustainable development. This important topic is analysed in more detail in chapter 13.)

Another far-reaching implication is that market systems are chronically unstable. Decentralised decision-making allows millions of consumers and producers the freedom to organise (distort) economic resources as they so wish, but the cumulative total of their market-revealed preferences may lead to a level of aggregate demand that is either too great or too little for society to sustain. Boom and slump, inflation or unemployment results, therefore. The cyclical pattern of economic disturbance to free-market societies is well-observed but still seemingly unavoidable – related perhaps to what the famous economist John Maynard Keynes called 'animal spirits': the herd instinct.

Enthusiasts for market economics have argued that the system is self-adjusting and that, rather than suffer the botched attempts of governments to improve matters, the free market should simply be left to find its own equilibrium. Unfortunately, swings in economic fortune like the Great Depression of the 1930s, the inflationary 1970s and the early 1990s world recession imposed penalties too great for most countries to ignore. *For whom* in society are market systems designed to serve? Only the lucky ones? Leaving the market to find its own solution is for many too passive and painful a policy recommendation.

And some market 'solutions' might simply fail. The classic remedy for unemployment, for example, is a cut in wages – people can thus price themselves back into jobs, it is argued. But low-paid jobs are perceived as low skilled/poor quality work and both buyers and sellers of this form of labour may not wish to trade in it. Unemployment will become entrenched. Additionally, as Keynes famously demonstrated, if wage cuts are imposed across all labour markets then the level of aggregate demand – and thus employment – will fall further. Governments should counter such market instability, not amplify it.

Lastly, market systems require labour and capital to be mobile – to move out of declining industries and areas and into growing ones. The very efficiency of this process, however, causes social distress, and in the extreme, cumulative economic divergence.

Resources flow from poorer regions into richer ones in pursuit of higher rewards. Society polarises and those that lose out find it ever harder to catch up and close the economic gap that separates them from success. The gulf between richer and poorer countries grows ever wider (see chapter 12, below).

At the same time, highly mobile societies lead to a decline in personal contacts and an erosion of social responsibility. Families break up; crime increases; concern for the disadvantaged fades. Physical barriers reinforce the social separation – richer people lock the doors of their cars and homes and employ security guards to protect their workplaces and shopping and leisure complexes. Market 'efficiency' is gained at the expense of equity; individual material success is pursued in preference to social cohesion and the welfare of the community.

Through an accumulation of influences, therefore, the dynamics of the modern, competitive, atomistic market place bring about a growing malaise in lifestyles. The pursuit of self-interest; the increasing economic liberation of both women and men; the market's need for geographical and occupational mobility and its lack of adequate valuation for a sense of community and of permanence all operate to assign a low price and priority to long-term social relationships. 'Short-termism' – the requirement to pay back investments quickly or face closure – is a profit horizon that rewards the break-up and sale of assets rather than putting in the time necessary to mend troubled relationships. This impairs not only the long-term health of businesses, it cripples also the development of communities, families and individual health. Statistics on crime and vandalism, divorce, suicide and mental disorder have all accelerated in the Western, market economies of North America and Europe. The numbers of divorces, single-parent families, old people living alone or apart from caring relatives continue to increase. A market system that slowly, relentlessly robs us of our humanity is not a system we can triumphantly celebrate. It can destroy the very fabric of society.

CONCLUSION: GETTING THE MIX RIGHT

Building an economic system is a practical problem not a theoretical exercise. No command system ever functioned without the presence of some markets; nor has any market economy ever operated without state intervention of some kind.

We have seen that normative and positive economic problems exist at either social extreme: in command and market economies, conditions are created that we find both distasteful and economically inefficient. Solving these problems, getting the mix right between how far markets should be left to themselves and how far central authorities should intervene, is the business of political economy – it is for each country to decide in accordance with its own political and economic institutions.

The end of the twentieth century has seen a marked shift in the world away from command systems and increasing resort to markets as a means of solving problems of economic organisation. This change has been most revolutionary in the case of the old Soviet Union and Eastern Europe (see following chapter), but it has also occurred on the mainland of China, which began to implement more market incentives in agriculture in the 1970s and has continued the spread of these reforms throughout the economy thereafter – and has been a feature of deregulating and privatising governments in Western Europe, North and South America, and Australasia. There are few countries around the world which have not felt the impact of this shift in economic philosophy.

The debate continues. How far should decisions on economic organisation be decentralised? Can public and merit goods and services such as the provision of law and order, or education, be safely delegated to private markets or quasi-markets? How far can state monopolies in the provision of these services be privatised, broken up and competition introduced? Are there gains in efficiency to be made – will everyone benefit from, say, cheaper and more efficient telephone services? Might not the sale of shares in newly privatised state giants lead to a concentration of wealth in the hands of a select elite and/or foreign entrepreneurs? These are some of the issues that are presently being debated in the countries of Eastern and Western Europe, amongst others, as we will see in the following pages.

There is no one mixed economy solution that is ideal for all communities, nor for one country for all time. The blend of central versus consumer sovereignty; state or self-interest; planning and prices; public or private enterprise; monopoly or competition must be kept continually under review by governments and individuals so as to maximise efficiency gains and guard against abuses. Changing internal or external circumstances bring unforeseen social costs or benefits, and so the mix must change again. No one economic system can stand still for long.

KEY WORDS

Command system An economic system where most decisions about what, how and for whom goods and services are produced are taken by a central authority. Planning, rather than prices, tends to be the organising mechanism in such communities. (Note that the *political* character of the central authority is indeterminate: it may be left or right wing; such governments may inherit power, seize it or be voted in. The key to economic organisation, however, is that most decisions are taken by command.)

Market system A market economy is one in which most goods and services are freely exchanged for one another and prices are determined by individual traders. People sell their labour to private industry and use their incomes so earned to purchase whatever goods and services they desire. The economic organisation of society is thus decentralised, invisible and automatic – the movement of prices indicates to producers and consumers where they can best employ their resources.

Merit goods are those which carry substantial external benefits, like education and health. Such services can be provided privately through the market place, but all of society gains if everyone has access to these at low cost. You benefit if you live in an educated community where all your neighbours are inoculated against disease – irrespective of their incomes.

Monopoly A monopoly is a large, single supplier that dominates an industry. Private monopolies can make huge profits by charging higher prices than a competitive firm would demand – for this reason they tend to be either outlawed in market societies or taken over by the state. Public monopolies are common, intending to provide public services (e.g. postal services, transport, etc.) at low cost. The lack of competition for such giants, however, whether privately or publicly owned, tends to breed inefficiency: there is no incentive to serve the public well since consumers have no other choice of producer to buy from.

Oligopoly This is an industry dominated by a few, large, economically powerful businesses. Monopoly – a single giant that has no rivals – is outlawed in many private market places since such operators inevitably charge exploitative prices with no fear of competition. Oligopolies are common, however, and where rivalry is confined to power plays between a select few big enterprises then marketing 'hype' becomes a sophisticated, multi-billion-dollar activity dedicated to manipulating consumer tastes.

Positive and normative economics A positive economics statement is one which is theoretically testable: it can be proven true or false. A normative statement involves a value judgement, the expression of a preference or opinion, and as such is not testable.

Public goods Some goods and services must be provided communally or not at all – like national defence. Consumers do not line up to pay for such services because if I enjoy freedom from foreign invasion so too does my neighbour. If I could buy such defence, therefore, my non-paying neighbour could not be excluded from enjoying it. No market system will supply such commodities if people will not pay the price. They have to be provided via public taxation.

QUESTIONS

1 What are the advantages of (a) state ownership; and (b) private ownership of productive resources? How far should privatisation be encouraged/restricted in your country?
2 Prices exist in both command and market systems, but they perform entirely different functions. Explain.
3 What are the principal normative and positive economic criticisms of command systems?
4 Market prices do not reflect the true economic costs of production. Why? What are the implications for market societies?
5 Contrast the suitability of planning and price mechanisms in organising the allocation of a nation's school students to university places.

FURTHER READING

Crouch, Colin and Marquand, David (eds). *Ethics and Markets*. Blackwell, 1993.
Nove, Alec. *The Economics of Feasible Socialism*. Allen & Unwin, 1983.
Schmookler, Andrew Bard. *The Illusion of Choice*. State University of New York Press, 1993.

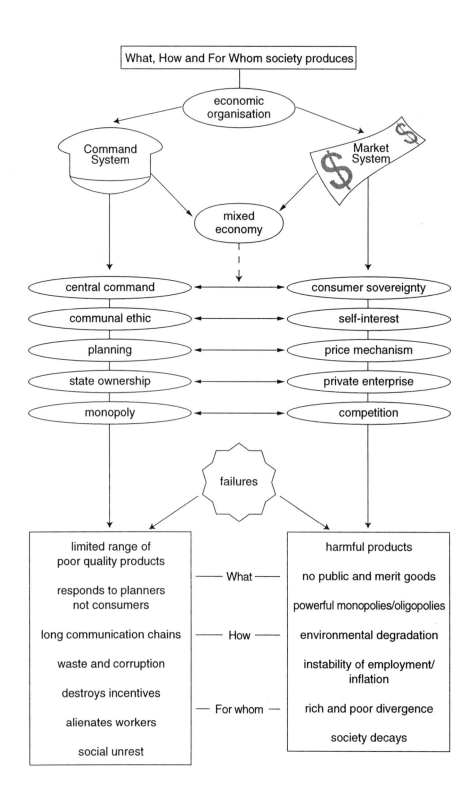

2 Eastern European economic transition

Topics to be considered in this chapter

- The inefficiencies of the Soviet command system
- The package of market reforms:
  - i privatisation
  - ii price liberalisation
  - iii new business start-ups
  - iv control of the money supply
- Quick or slow reform? Different Eastern European starting points
- Difficulties encountered in the transition to market economies

INTRODUCTION

The political, social and economic transformation at present taking place in the countries of Eastern Europe and the former Soviet Union is truly momentous. Armed and entrenched command economic systems that have taken scores of years to construct have been rapidly dismantled and the process of their conversion into market economies is – for most of them – well underway.

Why such enormous changes are happening; what is involved in this fundamental restructuring; and what progress has so far been achieved in the economies involved is the matter for consideration here.

The reasons behind the collapse of the former communist bloc countries are predominantly economic – triggering off the political and social revolutions in 1989 and thereafter that dramatically hit the headlines.

The key to all these events lies in the developments within the former Soviet Union. Once it became apparent that Soviet President Mikhail Gorbachev was preoccupied with his own country's difficulties and would not intervene in the social upheavals of Eastern Europe then the governments in each satellite country lost all effective power to continue. Thus the inexorable process of cumulative economic decline that had been underway for decades facilitated the sudden and sweeping chain reaction throughout the region. One regime after another was brought down in quick succession.

ECONOMIC DECLINE OF THE SOVIET UNION

The weaknesses of the Soviet economic engine had existed for years, indeed they were endemic, although the sheer size and power of the machine tended to blind the casual observer to the problems of its inefficiency and its failing capacity for growth.

The Soviet economic slowdown was plainly apparent in the 1970s, and despite world economic traumas such as the oil price shocks and the international debt crisis which tended to obscure the picture, certain observers were already predicting that difficulties would increase. *The Economist* in a typically partisan editorial in 1980 said that: 'Economic crisis is stalking not only Poland but the whole communist world. For the Soviet Union it could be terminal. There must be increasing hope that the Soviet system will not outlast this century' (*The Economist*, 1 January 1980, p. 14).

Evidence of this economic decline is given in table 2.1. (It should be noted that data on past Soviet performance are always quoted with reservation: official statistics require interpretation due to ideological differences in definition, quite apart from problems of political manipulation. Data available from Western sources may meanwhile not be fully complete. Whatever their source, however, in this case the overall trend is quite clear.)

Abel Aganbegyan, Chief Economic Advisor to M. Gorbachev and main architect of '*perestroika*', has stated that the data do not take into account hidden price rises and the falling quality of consumer goods and a more realistic picture is to assume that *no* GNP growth took place in the period 1980–5. Indeed 'unprecedented stagnation and crisis occurred during the period 1979–82 when production of 40 per cent of all industrial goods actually fell. Agriculture declined – throughout this period it failed to reach 1978 levels' (*The Challenge: Economics of Perestroika*, Hutchinson, 1988).

Table 2.1 Per cent growth rates, Soviet Union

	1950–60	1960–70	1970–5	1975–80	1980–5
GNP	5.7	5.2	3.7	2.6	2.0
GNP/head	3.9	3.9	2.7	1.8	1.1

Source: G. Ofer, 'Soviet economic growth', *Journal of Economic Literature*, December 1987.

REASONS FOR DECLINE

The paramount reason for such decline is the inefficiency of central planning as an allocative mechanism for advanced societies.

Firstly, there is an inherent bias towards producing quantity rather than quality. Planned targets to produce specific quantities are identifiable and enforceable. That such outputs be of good quality is a much vaguer, non-enforceable notion. Good quality cannot be adjudged by planners, administrators; it can only be determined by end-users, i.e. customers. It is for this reason, it was said, that you could only get shoes either for dwarfs or for hefty policemen – any suitable footwear had gone long before you got to the head of the queue. But 'how can this problem be overcome if plans are orders of superior authority (the central planners or ministries) and not those placed by users?' (Alec Nove, *The Economics of Feasible Socialism*, Allen & Unwin, 1983).

A look at the determinants of Soviet economic growth reinforces the impression of planning's inherent bias for quantity rather than quality and efficiency (see table 2.2). *Throughout its entire history* as a command economy, the Soviet Union has grown due to the increased employment of labour, capital and land inputs, whilst the productivity of these inputs has steadily declined. (This is diametrically opposed to the experience of all modern, market economies, which have grown predominantly due to advancing technological progress applied to fixed or slow-growing inputs.)

Such a growth model cannot be sustained, of course, not even in a country as huge and resource-rich as the former Soviet Union. There are limits to continually expanding employment, and in the 1970s, as is evidenced above, the Soviet Union ran up against them. With the developed world's highest rates of capital investment and participation rates of population in the labour force, there was now little potential left for increasing inputs. Without improvements in productivity, *diminishing returns* were inevitable.

But despite all the efforts to reverse this trend, Soviet productivity stubbornly declined. Indeed political insistence on catching up with the West served only to compound the inefficiency of the planning process. Too often unrealistic demands provoked confusion and chaos in production units (see the example of Chernobyl in chapter 1). According to Ofer, the 'strategy of haste' systematically constrained managers to meet current

Table 2.2 Per cent growth, Soviet inputs and productivity

	1928–40	*1950–60*	*1960–70*	*1970–5*	*1975–80*	*1980–5*
Combined factor inputs	4.0	4.0	3.7	3.7	3.0	2.5
Total factor productivity	1.7	1.6	1.5	0.0	−0.4	−0.5
		1.4*	0.9*	1.5*	−0.8*	−1.2*

Source: G. Ofer, 'Soviet economic growth'.
Note: * Alternative data compiled from CIA estimates.

planned targets at the expense of making more beneficial long-term investments. In the extreme, future projects were plundered in order to deliver existing orders (see Martin Walker's comment on TV production, chapter 1).

Hungarian economist Janos Kornai characterised the centrally planned countries as economies of shortage (J. Kornai, *The Economies of Shortage*, Amsterdam: North Holland, 1980), where there was high priority to invest in capital equipment in order to maintain growth and catch up the West, and inevitably lower priority attached to producing consumer goods. Allied to this there was an ideological insistence on a high defence posture and economic self-sufficiency (*autarky*).

Such a political/economic structure could not allow for failure to meet production targets in high priority sectors. Hence such production units operated with *soft budget constraints* (i.e. the government bailed them out if they squandered any inputs) and lower priority sectors had to go without. It should be apparent that *there is no incentive for an economy so organised to strive to be efficient.* Although there were steadily lengthening queues to obtain basic essentials, no mechanism existed to ensure producers met consumers' needs.

The number of Soviet and East European attempts to improve productivity after the death of Stalin were all limited by strict political control over how far such reforms should go. Kruschev tried to revitalise Soviet agriculture, and was evicted from office when he failed. Czecho-slovak market reforms in 1968 were too ambitious at the time for the Kremlin to stomach; creeping Hungarian reforms from 1968 to 1989 were more successful, but none really went far enough to prevent continuing economic deterioration.

Parallel with the growing incapacity of the command economies to supply their own needs was an increasing indebtedness to the West. When money was cheap after the first oil shock in the mid-seventies, communist governments – along with those in many other countries around the world – considered incurring debt was a sound policy. It was not so much the soaring interest rates of 1979–80 that prompted their eventual debt crisis, it was more the chronic incapacity of these autarkic, inward-looking countries to utilise their borrowed funds efficiently. In particular, the inability of the Soviet Union to help its satellite countries in Eastern Europe severely damaged its image as the strong, infallible leader of the region. On the contrary, falling deliveries of Soviet oil and other raw materials to its partners undermined any economic rationale for a *COMECON* pattern of trade and development and provoked more, not less, indebtedness to the West.

None of these developments escaped the notice of politicians, planners and bureaucrats of the countries involved, and every variety of economic reform consistent with Soviet dominated central authority was tried. But the message of these years is that partial economic liberalisation did not work. There is no 'third way' between a command system and a market economy. Despite all the efforts of Gorbachev's presidency to implement 'perestroika' and (in his own words) 'the union of centralism and independence of economic organisation', nothing could prevent the eventual collapse of the command economies in the massive upheavals of 1989–90. All the former Eastern bloc countries are now rapidly implementing policies to establish fully free-market systems within their territories. Eastern Europe is in transition.

THE REFORMS

The contrasting features of command and market systems give the key to the reforms required in the transformation from one form of economic organisation to the other. I have earlier characterised the two economic systems as opposing extremes in the following spectra:

Central control . . . . Consumer sovereignty
State doctrine . . . . Self-interest
Planning mechanism . . . . . . Price mechanism
State ownership . . . . Private enterprise
State monopoly . . . . Competition

The institutional changes required to move the various societies of Eastern Europe from the left side of this range towards the right are huge, costly and time-consuming, but there is general agreement on what needs to be done. Perhaps less well understood is that the necessary reforms are all interlinked: movement in one aspect is dependent on progress made in all others. This has strengthened the call for the 'big bang' method of introducing the following four measures simultaneously.

1 Privatisation of land and capital is the most difficult yet most fundamental and important reform required. Within the pattern of ownership of society's resources are embodied issues such as the relationship of the individual to the state; freedom to pursue private, rather than communal interests; rights to employ others; the establishment of contracts; systems of law; etc. *Privatisation* is central also to changing attitudes of the people from being passive dependents to becoming entrepreneurial participators of social evolution with vested interests in future outcomes.

The recent Chinese agricultural revolution has shown the great increases in productivity that are possible by giving the tillers of the soil the fruits of their own labour. Employing the same principle in industry means selling off the factories, setting up stock markets (to facilitate transfers of ownership), and allowing individual businessmen to decide for themselves which companies to form, which goods and services to supply and what resources to employ.

Only by allowing private capital ownership, with the right to retain profits, will investment in new technologies occur – ensuring that accumulated wealth is employed to society's benefit rather than being uselessly stockpiled, fleeing the country or funding corruption or extravagance.

2 Price reform is essential to open up markets in all consumer and producer goods. Eliminating all subsidies and controls may be painful but 'sensible market prices are vital for efficient resource allocation' (Jeffrey Sachs: Harvard professor and advisor to the Polish and Russian governments; quoted in *The Economist*, 13 January 1990).

For too long state enterprises in the command economies were nurtured on underpriced oil, raw materials and labour. The result was that vast segments of East European industry were *value subtractors* producing outputs with a net real value of less than their inputs, measured at world prices. (See earlier for examples of Polish tropical flowers and Kazakhstan melons.) Only a realistic and dynamic pricing system can overcome this.

This implies large price increases in precisely those goods that have been in shortage for decades, but this must occur if supplies are ever to increase. Farmers will only produce more wheat, and industrialists more textiles, if their selling prices and profits move up in response to demand.

Realistic prices imply a *convertible currency* at free-floating exchange rates, thus ensuring domestic goods are valued appropriately in world terms. Industries will export those goods in which they have a comparative advantage and import those which are too costly to produce at home. Inefficient firms unable to compete with foreign products will go bust, freeing up their resources to be more productively and profitably employed elsewhere.

3 Free entry of new businesses must be ensured by breaking up the old state monopolies and providing the legal and institutional framework for new start-ups, take-overs and the accumulation and investment of profits. Privatisation and free prices are not enough – that would only convert state monopolies into private ones which would then exploit their power. Only competition can guarantee that costs and prices will be kept down and businesses will be efficient.

Stock market prices will then correctly signal which businesses best cater for consumer demand and are deserving of more investment, and which businesses are less successful in following the market and less worthy of financial support. Capital will thus flow from declining to growing sectors – providing such mobility is facilitated and not obstructed by the state.

4 Tight control of the money supply is essential if any of the above measures are to work, but it is perhaps the most difficult short-run policy for pro-market governments to implement (especially since they are newly democratic and thus responsive to public pressure). If governments give in to public demands for wage increases; for unemployment benefits; for subsidies to huge, ailing state enterprises producing things that nobody wants to buy, then government deficits will get out of control, money supplies will increase and inflation will result. Resources will remain tied up in all the wrong employments; deadbeat firms will remain alive; productivity, public confidence and the real value of money will all be sacrificed. It is too easy for governments to create more paper money and distribute this to those sectors of the economy with the most political clout, but since real output is unaffected this can only be at the expense of others in the economy with little or no bargaining power.

IMPLEMENTATION: SHOCK THERAPY OR GRADUAL CHANGE?

In contrast to the market systems of the West, the East European ex-command economies have much in common with one another. Nonetheless, each country's situation is different, reflecting a unique set of political and economic realities. For some – e.g. Poland – sudden shock therapy was considered appropriate, all the required policy reforms thus being implemented in a 'big bang' on 1 January 1990. For others – e.g. Hungary – more gradual change has occurred. Hungary is the most market-oriented economy of them all and a mad dash to accelerate the process was judged unnecessary. Meanwhile Czechoslovakia, neither as crisis-ridden as Poland nor as liberalised as Hungary, chose an intermediate, 'minimum bang' approach.

The case for shock therapy in Poland was based on the advice that all the necessary reforms listed above must be introduced simultaneously since the success of any one requires success of them all. (Polish experts and advisors such as Jeffrey Sachs were convinced of this after the failure of earlier piecemeal reforms – e.g. economic liberalisation had proved incompatible with centralism: devolving management control without ownership meant industry bosses voted for pay increases and starved factories of new investment. This 'reform' did nothing, therefore, to prevent the ageing of East European capital.)

Releasing economies from shortage requires encouraging entrepreneurial activity, free prices and profits, requires competition and reliable money. Market reform is thus a seamless whole: economic efficiency is the product of competition; that demands privatisation and dismemberment, which in turn needs financial discipline. Prices must be free to reflect harsh economic realities, actual shortages and surpluses, not an autarkic, overprotected monopoly and inflation-distorted environment. That is, microeconomic efficiency is only possible with macroeconomic stability, free trade and convertible currencies. Everything is interconnected.

The speed of introducing reforms depends on the urgency of the situation. In Poland's case, serious shortages, hyperinflation, an unmanageable foreign debt and a rapidly deteriorating political crisis in 1989 all conspired to bring down the communist government. Any political reluctance to embrace the rush to a free-market system in those circumstances was condemned. The need to quickly bring under control hyperinflation that threatened to destroy social and economic order, the collapse of trade with other COMECON countries and the need to win Western financial support in renegotiating the outstanding debt all pointed to the appropriateness of a policy of radical surgery.

Thus a country's political and economic starting point is crucial in determining which process of implementation, fast or slow, is advisable. Poland had no choice but to try everything at once in order to prevent its economy from falling apart.

Hungary, in contrast, had been undergoing a creeping transformation for twenty years and could thus afford a more measured approach in the nineties. Developing commodity and labour markets were already functioning well before 1989 and, importantly, a small-scale private sector was flourishing throughout agriculture, industry and services. In consequence, Hungarian economist Andras Koves writes: 'economic agents (bureaucracy, managers, employees, consumers – the entire population)... had decades of experience with a more open and business-oriented system' (*Central and East European Economies in Transition*, Westview, 1992).

Of course, overwhelming state ownership of the means of production could not be seriously questioned throughout the Eastern bloc until after the political overthrow. Hungary, like the rest of its neighbours, still has a long way to go. Koves concludes: 'In spite of the relative advantages related to the long-standing economic reform, it would still be premature to assert that Hungarian gradualism is guaranteed to succeed.'

THE RECORD SO FAR

It was never going to be easy. All commentators predicted that the transition would involve hardship for every country involved since, however unsatisfactory, the command system *was* a system, and in the time between its collapse and the construction of the market alternative chaos threatens. Just how chaotic things can get is illustrated by the hyperinflation in the newly independent Ukraine. Its currency fell from 6,000 to the US dollar in mid-August 1993 to 19,000 to the dollar by the start of September. The Ukrainian prime minister warned that his country was 'on the brink of an economic disaster' (reported in *The Economist*, 4 September 1993).

What lessons can be learned from the experiences of Eastern Europe to date? In embarking on the journey from command structures of economic organisation towards market systems, what have been the difficulties and successes encountered?

Consistent policies

Firstly, economic regeneration is difficult, if not impossible, without political stability. The fragmentation of the former USSR, the bloody civil war in Yugoslavia and even the relatively amicable divorce of the Czech and Slovak republics all compound the difficulties. Commitment to the necessary reforms – consistently implemented through the lifetimes of transient governments – is essential if ongoing change of an entire economic system is to be achieved. Where there is a will, there is a way.

The willpower to ensure continuing reform must come from the bottom up – from the people who are suffering the costs involved – and should ideally be given voice, eloquently and tirelessly, by political leaders in a stable constitution.

The fact that market reforms remain on course throughout much of Eastern Europe in countries still fumbling with democracy and where living standards have slumped and unemployment has soared is a tremendous tribute to all concerned.

In Poland, for example, five different coalition governments have succeeded the collapse of communism. Political parties are still shaping and re-shaping themselves in response to rapidly changing events. The immediate economic legacy of the 'big bang' was a 12 per cent drop in national income (1990) and a remorseless rise in unemployment to over 16 per cent (1993). Weary voters are naturally attracted to new political alliances promising higher wages and protection from deprivation. Nonetheless the government they put into office in September 1993, although composed of more left-wingers and old communists than before, still persisted with a 1994 budget that promised no easy (and inflationary) solutions nor any return to a more centrist direction. With economic growth at last averaging 4 per cent in 1993 (the highest in Europe, though admittedly from a low base) recovery is hopefully in sight.

Financial discipline

As hinted above, the political temptation to protect wages and employment, and grant subsidies to the huge state enterprises, is one of the most pressing problems newly elected democratic governments have had to face. Succumbing to this, however, only postpones essential (though painful) restructuring of industry and condemns the country to financial irresponsibility and inflation. All countries have had this problem – some like Russia (now improving) and the Ukraine (worsening) have suffered more than others. Those politically more able to bite the bullet of wrenching change have come through the worst and can thus offer a more stable environment for future investment. (Poland was experiencing hyperinflation of around 80 per cent *per month* at the time of its 'big bang' but persisted with its medicine, and secured a consistent fall to an annual rate of 38 per cent by 1993 and is pursuing a target rate of single figure inflation.)

Governments in Eastern Europe (as distinct from those in the Commonwealth of Independent States) have generally tried hard to keep a grip on their budgets. The main cause of their difficulties has *not* been profligate spending on state industries but rather falling tax revenues – thanks to slumping incomes – together with increased demands for unemployment pay and social welfare spending. (This is a *budget-deficit* dilemma understood only too well by many recession-hit, Western nations.)

East European industry has therefore had to come to terms with the 'hard budget constraint' of governments with no cash. They have had to search for their own sources of finance in competition with governments seeking to borrow and balance their budgets.

In modern market economies, a banking and finance system exists to supply these rival demands for funds. A government with a budget deficit can borrow to keep up its spending commitments, though only at the expense of private-sector borrowers, thus forcing up rates of interest. A responsible central bank, separate from the government, ideally ensures that money supplies are not inflated to meet all the competing demands.

Exactly this sort of financial system is now developing in the economies of Poland, Hungary and the Czech republic. The discipline of economics, however, must come with it: when resources are in short supply, somebody has to pay the price. The free-market solution is that resources are rationed out in accordance with the ability to pay. Commercial banks and financial institutions will therefore prefer to lend to governments (which, in the extreme, can raise taxes to pay off debts in the future) than to fledgeling private businesses that may be at risk of going bust. Rates of interest currently being offered to Polish firms are 40 per cent or more (*The Economist*, 16 April 1994).

At these prices there are not many takers. The typical resort of entrepreneurs in countries with underdeveloped or missing markets is therefore to turn to the black economy; to avoid paying taxes; to find sources of finance and fixed capital wherever creative imagination leads. Inventive, grass-roots entrepreneurship in Eastern Europe's growing *informal sector* can be applauded as efficient where it economises on resources in response to social needs. Selfish profiteering, exploitation and crime, however, need to be contained.

Privatisation

The biggest continuing head-ache for all the old command economies is the break-up of monolithic state ownership and the generation of a dynamic private sector. The problems of privatisation have been more persistent than was originally envisaged:

- How much should state enterprises be sold for? Many heavy industries and weaponry establishments served COMECON markets that no longer exist. What is their value? In the absence of experienced stock markets, share prices are difficult to calculate. Should large enterprises be offered for sale whole or broken up and sold piecemeal?

- Who is eligible to buy shares? Might not foreign raiders or corrupt ex-communists with ill-gotten hoards buy up large chunks of industry at bargain-basement prices? Alternatively, if workers buy shares in their own factories which later go bust then they stand to lose not only their jobs but also all their savings.
- What are the rights of the original owners who were dispossessed by communist regimes? Should property rights be restored or compensated? The claims of old landowners and capitalists need to be addressed before new investment can be assured.
- How can the lack of consumer purchasing power, on the one hand, and the absence of a managerial elite, on the other, be overcome? It will take time for incomes to rise; for people to learn the ways of the market; for management skills and experience to grow.
- Widespread, uninformed ownership of shares means management may be outside of any effective control. Those in charge of a nation's entire economic resources are free to use them for their own ends, should they so wish. This is *the principal-agent problem*, found elsewhere in market economies. Agents frequently have different motives to principals and a mechanism to unite their interests can be lacking. In this case, elected managers (agents) have the capital and concerns of many small shareholders at their disposal, but the latter may have little power to exercise effective influence.

The complexity of these questions has inevitably slowed down progress, especially given the scale of the problem. It took Margaret Thatcher the whole of the 1980s to transfer up to twenty UK enterprises from public to private ownership. In Eastern Europe and the Commonwealth of Independent States there are thousands and thousands of such enterprises and it is not a matter of transferring them into an already functioning private market sector, it is matter of *creating* one.

It is instructive to compare the Czech and Polish schemes for privatisation. Both countries have been concerned to spread the ownership of newly created shares as widely and equitably as possible; to put in place managements that are efficient and accountable; and to privatise as much and as rapidly as is consistent with the above two aims. The two countries have differed with respect to the role envisaged for government in the privatisation process.

The Czech scheme was launched in October 1991 with vouchers issued to every adult in the country, entitling each to bid for shares in state firms offered for sale. Given widespread ignorance of the value and future business potential of these firms, numerous investment funds sprang up (just as in the West) offering to place people's money more knowledgeably.

These *financial intermediaries* can theoretically perform a vitally important function: on the one hand, they can build up the specialist expertise in appraising different companies that ordinary citizens do not have time to do when investing their funds, and, on the other hand, they can thus exercise more informed control over the activities of business managers. Such investment funds thus serve the two aims above of broadening the benefits of share ownership and simultaneously signalling to management how well they are doing in their jobs.

Under the Czech privatisation scheme these financial intermediaries were largely unregulated, and evolved from the free market. (Some were offering people a ten-fold return on their investment in just one year – which naturally attracted a lot of interest – but it is theoretically impossible to deliver this to everyone.) In addition to encouraging irresponsible financial activities, if such intermediaries are unregulated then the problem of supervising a country's management is not overcome, it is simply transferred away from emerging private industry to these new financial combines instead.

In Poland the growth of financial intermediaries has been slower and more closely controlled by the government. Experienced Polish and Western financial consultants are being screened by the government as the fund managers, and the assets of state firms being privatised are being distributed to these intermediaries (60 per cent), to employees of the enterprises concerned (10 per cent), and the remainder (30 per cent) being retained by the government's Treasury. Shares in the regulated investment funds only are for sale to the public.

The Polish government, both through its minority stake-holding in the enterprises themselves, and its watchful involvement of the financial intermediaries, therefore, exercises more control over the establishment of private businesses than is the case in the Czech republic. (Eventually this control, it is planned, will be sold off as the private sector becomes capable of supervising itself.) They have had fewer problems with their scheme as a result.

In the event, privatisation has taken place throughout Russia and Eastern Europe via a number of ways. In all cases, however, it has been the huge, dirty, out-dated, heavy industries of centrist control that have been the most difficult to dispose of. Nearly all still remain in state hands.

In contrast, service and retail businesses have quickly gone private. New owner-managers have not been slow in appearing, especially in Eastern Europe where memories of private capitalism still remain from before the period of Soviet domination.

Liquidation, worker/management buy-outs and joint ventures with foreigners have been faster and more successful when handled at the local level, freer from rules and regulations of government. In Poland over 1,500 successful privatisations were completed in the first two years from the 'big bang' and many more informal arrangements have inevitably gone unrecorded where the assets of bankrupt state companies have been pressed into service by opportunist local traders. This is privatisation from below, rather than top-down directed.

Germany, by comparison, has pursued the opposite path with the government agency Treuhandanstalt supervising the sale of former East German assets. Despite initial successes, and the massive advantage of its assimilation into Western Europe's wealthiest economy, issues of property rights and the valuation of East German capital have caused costly delays.

CONCLUSIONS

It is still far too early to give a full assessment of the progress and prospects of different Eastern European economies. Nonetheless, those countries that started earliest and have been boldest on the path to market reform have inevitably come the furthest. Political acceptability of the necessary changes has likewise been easiest in those Eastern European countries where central control was always resented as a recent imposition on previously successful and independent market societies.

Some reforms have gone better than others. Releasing prices from official controls and allowing them to to rise or fall as trade dictates is easier than remaining unmoved by the cries of suffering and refusing to print more money. Likewise, removing restraints on private entrepreneurs and allowing the rise of a private sector is easier than dismantling state enterprise or controlling the spread of crime and corruption.

Collapse of the autarkic COMECON bloc has removed the economic rationale for much of heavy industry. Those countries most dependent on that trade (e.g. Bulgaria) have suffered most. Those enterprises that can adapt their products fastest to Western markets have the brightest future. Sadly, too many East Europeans are still trudging off to work in the wrong direction, producing the wrong things in the wrong ways. As Sir John Harvey-Jones (ex-ICI chief) said on visiting a Polish glass factory: 'the first thing to do if you are stuck in a hole is to stop digging.' That advice needs more adherents.

The winners and losers under a market system are different to those in command economies. The miners, shipbuilders and steelworkers who enjoyed high status and pay under communism – and ironically were in the forefront of those pushing for reforms in Poland and Russia – are those the market has least need for. The future belongs to people with adaptive entrepreneurial skills, not heroic metal-bashers. Small traders, restauranteurs and informal, semi-legal businessmen have experienced a far faster appreciation of their earnings than state-sector stalwarts.

As stated earlier, sensible prices are vital. Setting the right price for a country's currency is particularly so: if it is overvalued then domestic industry will find it impossible to sell its products abroad. Imports of Western capital and consumer goods may be cheap (helping contain inflation) but the key constraint on restructuring a former command economy is finding markets for what can be produced. Selling rather low-quality products is difficult enough without overpricing them. East German industry's unique access to the immense European Community, for example, served only to drive much of it into bankruptcy since the Ostmark's union with the Deutschmark was at too high a price.

A realistic price for labour is important for exactly the same reason. In European terms, the old state industries are overstaffed and underskilled. Employment prospects are best, therefore, if local labour is cheaper than alternatives. Owing to wage demands secured after unification, East German workers now cost more than Portuguese and Irish labour but are far less productive. Small wonder they have attracted insufficient employment.

A willingness to adapt and adjust and not hang on dogmatically to central regulation has greatly aided the passage of privatisation and the emergence of vibrant new industry in places like Poland and even Russia. In the event, competition is more important than the structure of ownership – the state still retains possession of many of the shares of East European industry simply because their private disposal has not yet succeeded. Foreign direct investment has been particularly disappointing. The present pattern of ownership is thus chaotic and not at all what was planned, but many of the businesses so structured continue to operate competitively because they are responsive to the economic realities that surround them.

Finally, the right sort of Western help and support is essential. Managerial advice has frequently been too expensive, and insensitive to local practicalities. Direct investment in the East has been lacking. Restrictions on East European imports to the EC have been crippling and threaten the whole transition process. But tying Western aid and financial support to progress in restraining budgets and monetary growth has been productive. It has enabled shaky democratic governments to insist on painful but necessary financial discipline and to sell this to their constituents.

In the long run, however, with the difficulties of recession spreading throughout Europe and beyond, the more mature, wealthy market economies of the world can best help their newest, poorer neighbours by opening their doors and buying what they have to offer without restriction. As Lescek Balcerowicz, Poland's ex-finance minister and much-respected architect of its 'big bang' has complained: 'We need the EC to lower barriers now, not in four or five years' time.' (And he said that in 1991 . . .)

KEY WORDS

A **budget deficit** occurs when a government's spending exceeds its income, thus requiring it to borrow more. A budget *surplus* is the opposite.

COMECON stands for the Council of Mutual Economic Aid, set up in 1949, between Eastern European command economies and the Soviet Union with the aim of integrating planning and promoting mutual self-sufficiency. Cuba and Vietnam later joined. It became a means of tying-in dependence on the Soviet Union.

Convertible currency A currency freely exchangeable for any other, in markets unrestricted by government intervention. Most East European currencies were formerly subject to strict controls that kept their prices artificially high; implementing free convertibility meant their exchange rates plummeted.

The law of **diminishing returns** states that where at least one factor of production is in fixed supply, then increasing production must eventually occur at a steadily decreasing rate. That is, in any given factory or farm, each additional investment in capital and labour will secure additional outputs that progressively decline. This is so because factors of production are not perfect substitutes for each other. So long as *one* resource is fixed in supply, increased application of all others cannot continually compensate for its absence. More and more sophisticated capital equipment and technical knowledge can secure increasing output of oil and gas from a given production site, for example, but this increased production is subject to diminishing returns (see also chapter 9, p. 171).

Financial intermediaries are private, commercial banks and money lenders which act in the market place brokering deals between those who have surplus funds and those who have insufficient. That is, they attract funds from the millions of savers in a community and then loan these on to businesses which wish to invest. See chapter 7 for more detail.

Informal sector Employment in unrecorded, unregulated trade. It may be the inventive resort of indigenous entrepreneurs denied access to formal, legitimate industry, or – in the *black economy* – the deliberate attempt to avoid government regulation and taxation. (See also chapter 11.)

Perestroika Russian for re-structuring. This notion, and *Glasnost* – increasing press freedom – were key platforms promoted by Mikhail Gorbachev in reforming the Soviet economy during the 1980s. Perestroika was intended to mean devolving decision making to individual plant managers throughout the old USSR and thus to improve economic efficiency without overthrowing communist rule and state ownership of all resources. Trying to hold onto the tail of the free-market lion such that it could only go halfway out of its cage was doomed, however. Gorbachev got mauled; the lion got away.

The principal-agent problem Principals employ agents to act on their behalf and to secure them benefits; the problem is that, once empowered, if control mechanisms are not efficient, agents can be more interested in their own gain than that of their principals. Hence the growth of 'Fat Cats' in newly privatised businesses.

Privatisation A state-owned enterprise is privatised when it is offered for sale to private consumers/investors. The price of shares in such a privatised concern depends on how profitable the business is expected to be: a well-managed enterprise with modern capital equipment and a well-defined customer base is likely to have no problem in selling its shares at a relatively high price. Conversely, no one is likely to want shares in an outdated, inefficient dinosaur.

QUESTIONS

1 The fundamental reasons for the collapse of the old Soviet Union were economic. Discuss.
2 What package of of market reforms is necessary for Eastern Europe and what is the case for the 'big bang' method of introducing them all simultaneously?
3 Which market reforms have been most difficult to introduce in Eastern Europe, and why?
4 What are the financial difficulties involved in making the transition to a market economy? How can (a) a central bank, (b) private commercial banks/intermediaries, and (c) foreign banks help?
5 What policies could the developed, market economies of the world adopt to help the emerging economies in transition? Why should they?

FURTHER READING

Koves, Andras. *Central and East European Economies in Transition*. Westview Press, 1992.
Sachs, Jeffrey. 'Eastern Europe's economies', *The Economist*, 13 January 1990.

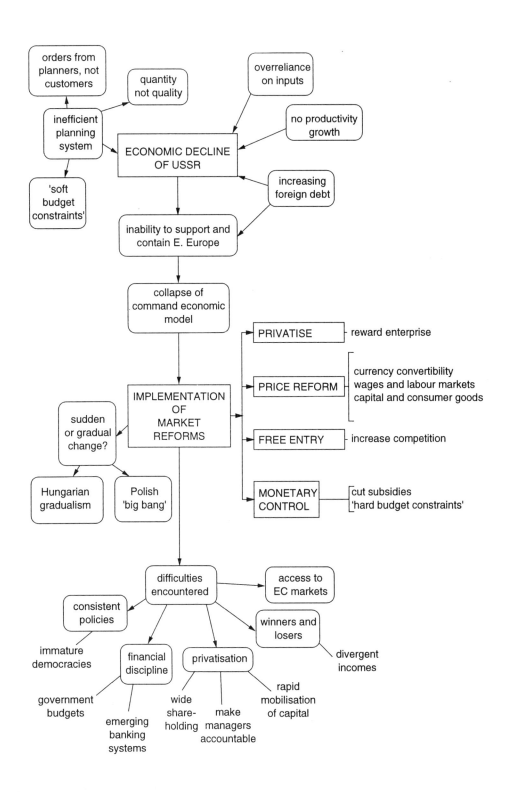

3 Microeconomics and macroeconomics

Topics to be considered in this chapter

- Microeconomics: the efficiency of markets
- Flexibility of prices vs. supplies
- Agricultural markets and labour markets
- Macroeconomics: the circular flow of national income
- The equilibrium level of incomes and spending
- The supply-side critique

INTRODUCTION

An understanding of prices is absolutely essential to an understanding of market societies. As was emphasised in chapter 1, the price mechanism is the key organising agency of the modern market economy – the invisible hand that directs the pattern of all consumption, production and distribution. It determines what is produced, which industries and economic practices will succeed or fail, and which resources will, or will not, be employed.

Prices can be considered at the level of the individual market place – the causes and effects of changes in the price of houses or health care, for example – or we can study the operation and influence of the price mechanism for the economy as a whole – the general level of incomes, inflation, employment, etc. The analysis of how individual markets work is *microeconomics*; the study of the economy as a whole – the behaviour of all individual markets aggregated together – is *macroeconomics*.

These two branches of theoretical economics have evolved because it has become apparent that economic policies and practices which are workable at the micro-level do not necessarily apply at the macro-level. This is not just a matter of dry, academic debate. When economists' policy recommendations are acted upon, the livelihood of millions is affected. This leads us to the *second* most famous quotation in economics, from John Maynard Keynes:

The ideas of economists and political philosophers, both when they are right and when they are wrong, are more powerful than is commonly understood. Indeed the world is ruled by little else. Practical men, who believe themselves to be quite exempt from any intellectual influences, are usually the slaves of some defunct economist. Madmen in authority, who hear voices in the air, are distilling their frenzy from some academic scribbler of a few years back. I am sure that the power of vested interests is vastly exaggerated compared with the gradual encroachment of ideas.

(J.M. Keynes, The General Theory of Employment,
Interest and Money, 1936)

Certainly these words are true of Keynes' own ideas which have revolutionised economics, government policies and people's lives. Keynes was the founder of modern macroeconomics and the book from which the above quotation is taken caused a fundamental re-think of classical economics. The distinct differences between micro- and macroeconomic theory and policy implications continue to excite controversy today and thus deserve to be more 'commonly understood'.

MICROECONOMICS

Classical economics, as derived from the earliest economists like Adam Smith and others, was and is concerned with the efficiency of individual markets – i.e. how to make the most efficient, economic use of given resources. This is microeconomics: the study of consumer and producer behaviour in the trade for specific goods or services.

In a free market for housing, for example, if consumer demand exceeds supply then prices will rise. Profit-seeking entrepreneurs thus have an incentive to produce more of this higher-priced commodity; they will hire construction workers, building materials and land away from less-profitable employments (farming?) and thus expand production of the homes that more and more people in the market increasingly want.

Prices are therefore vital signalling devices in market systems. They ration out scarce existing supplies between competing consumers and simultaneously induce businesses to mobilise resources, adjust production and thus eradicate any shortages and surpluses.

Let us look more closely at this interaction between prices, demand and supply.

There are many factors that influence consumer and producer decisions, and some markets react differently to others. Take the example of a local newspaper, on sale every day in a particular city. On the occasion of a major news story – perhaps the success of the local football team – there might be a rush in demand and the newspaper sells out, leaving many dissatisfied customers. How is the market likely to respond to this *disequilibrium* situation where demand exceeds supply at the ruling market price? In this example we can predict that on the following day, assuming continuing interest in the story, local shops and stallholders will order more newspapers to meet anticipated demand, and the printers will run off more copies. It is also possible that to avoid disappointment some consumers will leave the market – perhaps following the story on local TV and radio – rather than risk unfulfilled demand a second time.

In these circumstances, if suppliers have guessed correctly the quantity of newspapers will adjust to secure the necessary equilibrium between demand and supply. Sales increase; all consumers are satisfied; the newspaper price remains unchanged.

A different scenario may operate in the second-hand market for football tickets. On the day of a keenly contested match, those supporters who have been sharp enough to buy tickets early may find that there are many frustrated consumers desperate to pay inflated prices in order to secure entry to the vital football game. The ability of the local club to increase the supply of tickets is limited by the capacity of the ground so in this case the shortfall between supply and demand is closed by a movement in prices, quantity staying the same. Existing tickets are likely to change hands outside the ground, scarce supplies going to the highest bidders.

For many goods and services, a combination of both these movements will ensure demand equals supply: there will be some adjustment in prices and some change in quantities traded to bring about market equilibrium.

The key point necessary to emphasise here is that there are a number of different influences affecting demand and supply. Consumers' incomes change, their tastes and preferences vary, advertising has its impact – all these factors, as well as a change in prices, may influence demand for one product rather than another. In production, costs will alter, technological breakthroughs occur, random shocks (from earthquakes to exchange rates) have their effect. These issues, as well as the prospective price the entrepreneur is seeking, will influence the quantity of the product eventually supplied.

Some of these factors are more variable than others, and the 'art' in the science of economics is to identify – in the case being studied – which is the key variable, and which factors in comparison are relatively unchanging. A theory of demand, supply and price can thus be constructed and, given factor x changes and y remains constant, we can thus predict the market outcome.

Whether, of course, economists' predictions are fulfilled depends on whether or not they guessed right on the variables that changed. If x was constant and y changed – or, worse, x and y stayed the same and z varied – then their theories need revising. Here you can begin to see the source of controversy in the subject.

Some examples will make these issues clearer.

Agricultural markets are typically unstable. Supplies of coffee have been decimated by frost; fine weather can produce unexpectedly good wheat harvests; hailstorms can ruin a wine vintage. Even normally stable demand for basic commodities like beef or eggs can be drastically affected by health scares such as salmonella poisoning or 'mad cow' disease.

When random shocks frequently disturb commodity markets and supplies cannot change rapidly (it takes another year to the next harvest) the prices alone must adjust to the new circumstances. As a result, the prices of farm produce in unregulated markets are typically subject to wild swings from one year to another. Farm incomes are similarly affected since the one impacts on the other.

For many countries, such instability is not acceptable in so important an industry as food production. Variability and unpredictability of prices and incomes is a considerable disincentive to agricultural investment and future food supplies. For this reason many governments all around the world intervene to support their farming sectors.

One type of agricultural intervention is to guarantee minimum *price floors* to farmers, as is practised, for example, for cereal markets within the European Community's Common Agricultural Policy (the CAP).

In theory, the best remedy for extreme short-term price variability is to guarantee a median price to farmers that evens out the fluctuations between good years and bad. Surplus supplies can be stockpiled in years of good harvests and sold back into the market when there is a shortfall. Looking back over past years it should be easy enough to pick out the long-term trend in farm outputs, prices and incomes. All that is therefore necessary is to reassure farmers that these prices will be guaranteed into the future. In years where market prices dive below the relevant support price the CAP promises to pay the difference. In years where prices move above this floor the CAP will keep the mark-up. The beauty of this proposal is that if the median price is correctly calculated the scheme pays for itself: support payments made one year are balanced by earnings in another.

The CAP in practice has not found things so easy. In volatile commodity markets, guaranteeing farm price supports creates a certainty where before there was none. This shifts perception and thus behaviour.

With a guaranteed floor, farmers know that *whatever they produce they will now be able to sell at a constant price* – if not to the market then into a stockpile. Over time, therefore, they will plough up hedgerows, press into service all their marginal land, pile on fertilisers, pesticides and whatever technology is available to increase yields and thereby maximise their incomes. Whatever price level the CAP picks as a middle value between expected market highs and lows they will soon find inappropriate – it will induce quantities supplied far greater than originally estimated. As a result the CAP has to continually come up with other interventions to correct the tendency for overproduction – taking 'set aside' land out of production, enforcing quotas on farm outputs, re-fixing prices at lower levels, etc.

Whereas before any imbalance between demand and supply was mediated by strong price movements, now price becomes unchanging and supplies inexorably grow to outstrip demand. No automatic mechanism exists to bring about equilibrium.

Critics argue that overproduction – the alleged butter mountains and wine lakes – will be a continuing feature of the CAP until the market is free of intervention and price flexibility is restored. Others say that this does not solve anything and simply returns us to the original problem of instability.

The notion of free markets has a particularly strong hold on classical economics. Price flexibility is considered essential to efficiency and the evolution of an equilibrium price that equates demand and supply and thus 'clears the market' is a theoretical process that has a powerful influence on the mind-set of microeconomics.

It should be noted, however, that to advocate price flexibility in examples like the above is in fact to declare the value judgement that short-term *allocative efficiency* in clearing markets is more worthwhile than other alternative objectives, such as long-term agricultural stability in this case. This important point, that economic policy recommendations embody judgements as to which objectives are more valuable than others, is worth bearing in mind whenever you are trying to disentangle controversies in economics.

Consider the application of microeconomic theory to labour markets: this can provide us with one explanation for *unemployment*. If there are too many people without jobs it is because supply of labour is greater than demand. To clear this particular market place, the theory states that wages (the price of labour) must fall. Employers would then find hiring workers more attractive; similarly fewer workers would offer their labour to the market. Registered unemployment would decrease.

The notion that people price themselves out of work and that wages must be free to fall is an important tenet of classical (pre-1930s) and modern neoclassical economics. In Britain in the 1920s this policy was enacted – prompting the General Strike in 1926 when coalminers refused to accept this alleged solution to their country's economic ills. Widespread wage cuts were resorted to also in the USA in the attempt to reduce unemployment in the Great Depression in the 1930s, and history repeated itself again recently in the late 1980s/early 1990s recession when certain economists argued for 'flexible labour markets' and politicians urged workers to price themselves back into jobs. The UK Conservative government's refusal to adopt the 'social chapter' (which includes guaranteed minimum wages and social benefits) in the European Community's Maastricht agreement was based on this principle. The UK government's stance was not shared, it must be said, by all other European parties to this accord.

Should wages be flexible (downwards)? Is this an acceptable solution to unemployment? Or, if the supply of labour exceeds demand perhaps some variable other than its price/wage should adjust to secure equilibrium?

In line with the first strategy, during the 1980s UK premier Margaret Thatcher accused trade unions of causing inflexible labour markets and wage stickiness and enacted policies to curb their powers (see next chapter for further details).

The alternative strategy is to accept that low pay/low skill jobs attract few dealers in modern, Western economies and rather than encourage wages to move, training and productivity deals should be implemented to enable workers to upgrade skills and become mobile between jobs. The more labour supply becomes flexible the less wages need to be (in which case minimum wage laws *can* become tenable).

This example therefore illustrates the point that market equilibrium can be closed either by price movements or by adjustment in the quantities traded. Unemployment may perhaps be more quickly reduced if you can persuade businesses to take on more people to work for less pay, but long-term labour market equilibrium is perhaps better secured if investment in *human capital* occurs. Job stability is more assured for high-skilled rather than low-skilled workers.

Meanwhile, back in the 1930s Great Depression, governments in Europe and North America followed the classical economic prescription of wage cuts to stimulate more industrial demand for labour. In this case, however, instead of reducing unemployment, this policy only served to make matters worse – to the consternation of governments and the bafflement of their economic advisors. Unemployment in supposedly modern, civilised economies rose to historically unprecedented levels of up to a quarter of all workers and showed no apparent tendency to fall. Why? What had gone wrong?

John Maynard Keynes had to formulate a new general theory of economics to answer this question. In doing so he looked beyond classical microeconomics (the efficiency of one market place as compared to another) and opened up an entirely new field of enquiry: macroeconomics – concerned with the general level of incomes, expenditure and employment in an economy as a whole. It is to this area of economics that we now turn.

MACROECONOMICS

There are many criticisms of market theory (see the previous chapter on command and market systems) but the one we most need to focus on here is that of *the fallacy of composition* – that is, the assumption that what works for the community in an individual market place will work for all market places throughout an economy added together.

Specifically, all the millions of independent decisions by consumers in markets up and down the country may add up to a general level of national demand for resources that is insufficient (or alternatively, too great) for the economy as a whole to sustain. Insufficient aggregate demand will mean unemployment and recession; too much demand means inflation.

Keynes argued that cutting wages, in the hope of pricing people back into work if implemented on a large scale, only serves to drive down the general level of incomes and consumption, thereby reducing employment prospects still further. Which businesses will take on more workers and produce more goods and services if incomes and spending throughout the economy are falling? Aggregate demand in the 1930s was insufficient to keep the bulk of the labour force in employment, and Keynes argued for expansionary government policies (the very opposite of wage cuts) in order to remedy the situation. Many Keynesian economists all round the world argue precisely the same today.

Let us look at Keynesian macroeconomics in more detail. If we ignore the influence of governments for the time being, we can divide an economy into two sectors: producers and consumers. For the sake of simplicity we can say that all production is located in business firms and all consumption occurs in households (see figure 3.1). There is thus a *circular flow* of money and incomes between households and firms within the economy. Incomes are earned at work and spent at home on those consumer goods and services produced by business.

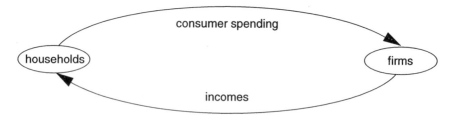

Figure 3.1

All income in a market economy is derived from the production process. It may be earned in the form of wages or salaries for direct work, or it can be earnings from the ownership of capital or land. Either way, these resources of labour, enterprise, capital and land can only generate earnings if they are employed in production. And eventually all these incomes, from whichever source, will find their way into someone's household where they will be spent or not as the case may be.

Looking at the household sector for the moment, we can say that any income received that is not directly spent on consumer goods and services is 'saved', that is, it is not passed on through the market place to producers. It therefore leaks out of the circular flow (see figure 3.2).

If we consider now all expenditure in the economy, we find that it is made up of spending on consumer goods, plus some fraction spent by firms on business investment – that is, building capital goods to provide for future production. Either way, all spending goes through firms and contributes to the income they generate (see figure 3.3).

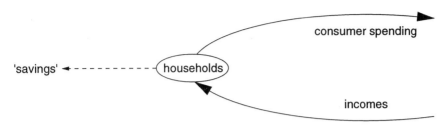

Figure 3.2

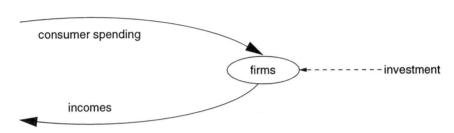

Figure 3.3

We should add the qualification at this stage that households buy many imported goods and services. Thus some consumer spending will always leak out of the circular flow in one country and enter that of another. By the same argument, every trading country will receive some foreign spending on those exports it sells abroad.

Putting all these elements together, we can thus see the full picture for the whole economy (see figure 3.4).

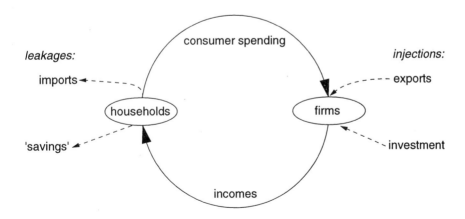

Figure 3.4 The circular flow of incomes and expenditure

According to this circular flow model, the economy is in equilibrium if net additions to money circulation equal net leakages and thus aggregate income equals aggregate expenditure. So long as the injections of export revenues and investment equal the outflows of import spending and savings then the amount of money flowing round the system must remain constant.

What happens if this equilibrium is disturbed?

If, for some reason, there is a general reduction in wages then clearly incomes would fall, households would be able to spend less and there would be a fall in the circular flow of incomes, consumption and therefore employment.

Key variables here are the propensities of households to save, spend, and spend on imports. The greater the fraction of households' income that is spent on domestic goods and services, the greater the impact any change of income will have on firms' revenues and production plans. An economy-wide wage cut will thus be rapidly transmitted through to increased unemployment. Conversely, any increase in incomes will quickly generate increased production and the creation of new jobs.

Because there is a circular flow involved here, any small change to the system has a cumulative, *multiplier* effect. Suppose, for example, wages are cut first in the construction workers industry. Falling incomes will not only impact on those families directly involved, but because their spending represents someone else's income then the recessionary impact spreads further. Local shops, transport firms and other related services will lose custom, and they in turn will pass on less spending and hence revenues to businesses dealing with them. Incomes and, therefore, expenditure fall round all the economy. As the recessionary outlook begins to take hold, the spiral of decline gathers pace. Is there no bottom to the depression?

This was the fear expressed in the 1930s. Indeed, thanks to the fact that one country's imports represent another country's exports, falling incomes and spending in the USA rapidly impacted on all other trading nations. The Great Depression was transmitted world-wide.

As can be seen in the macroeconomic model above, incomes and spending will fall and keep on falling so long as leakages from the circular flow exceed injections. Stability is only attained when outflows equal inflows, and Keynes' great insight was that there was no inherent necessity for such an equilibrium to exist at full employment within an economy, it could just as easily obtain at lower levels of economic activity – an unemployment equilibrium.

So countries could get stuck with a quarter of their workforce unemployed, and no private businesses still operating would see any reason to expand.

If the private sector sees no future in investment, if no consumers at home or abroad have money to increase their spending, how is the gloom to end?

The answer according to Keynes was that governments could bring about an autonomous increase in injections. The multiplier process outlined above could thus be made to work in a positive fashion: if governments place orders for building, say, more roads and houses (and, in the 1930s, military spending) then 'first round' employment and incomes will rise. Subject to some fraction not being spent, the rest of consumers' incomes will be passed on as 'second round' expenditure, incomes and employment, which in turn stokes up 'third round' and further recovery.

The economy will grow and grow until the cumulative total of leakages just rises to equal the size of the government-induced injections and thus the circular flow re-balances itself: at a higher, aggregate total of national income.

As noted before, it should be seen that the speed and extent of the expansion (or contraction) of the economy depends on people's propensity to spend any slight increase in their incomes. That is, the greater their *marginal propensity to consume*, the greater will be the multiplier effect.

In the thirties, the pressing economic problem was to devise a new form of analysis and new policy prescriptions for a world wallowing in a deep depression. Note that Keynesian macroeconomics was concerned solely with the general levels of income, output and employment of an economy. Microeconomic discussion about whether or not labour should be deployed here or there, released from industry A in order to transfer to industry B, was outside its concern. Keynesians might well have argued that such debate is irrelevant when millions are out of work and all industry is below capacity.

Such debate is not irrelevant in the 1990s, however. Neoclassical, *'supply-side'* economists have said that too many resources in Europe and North America are tied up in inefficient, declining industries. Unemployment *ought* to rise in such sectors, freeing up workers to move to newer, growth areas. Current unemployment is thus alleged to be a measure necessary to reallocate resources within the economy. Wage rates should fall in mining, steel, etc., tempting workers to leave these un-competitive, low-skill industries and move into better high-wage, high-skill employment. The problem, therefore, is the classic, microeconomic one of allocative inefficiency. Any government policy to stimulate aggregate demand will only delay the necessary re-deployment of resources within the economy.

Modern Keynesian economists argue, however, that the current (particularly European) unemployment level is excessive and partly due to government policies of restricting money supplies and aggregate demand. If spending in the economy as a whole is made to rise, employment and output in all industry would rise. If private sector demand is depressed then government has the responsibility to increase spending and thus create an upturn in the economy. More demand will cause more entrepreneurs to hire more labour and supply more goods.

'No!' cry the supply-siders. Increased spending will not generate more production, but only trigger off more inflation; it cannot create more jobs if unemployed workers have been thrown out of inefficient businesses and are predominantly equipped with the wrong skills (or are unskilled) to cater for consumer demand. It is not the aggregate level of spending that is wrong in the economy, they argue, but the balance of efficient versus inefficient industry that is at fault.

CONCLUSION

This modern controversy has, in fact, moved macroeconomics forward, past original Keynesian concern with manipulating levels of aggregate demand, to focus policy makers' attention also on the overall capacity (or incapacity!) of the economy to produce: i.e. the aggregate level of supply.

Such economic thinking has been the reaction to the dominant Western economic problem of the 1970s and 1980s – inflation and slow growth. The notion that increased aggregate demand would pull an economy upward into growth has been shown to be inflationary where economies have experienced bottle-necks in their productive capacity. Where vital labour skills and applied technology have been missing in industry then short-term boosts in consumer spending have not been met with increases in production – but rather the shortfall in supplies has been closed by an increase in general price levels (inflation) and buying more imports (i.e. balance of payments problems).

So we need to get the balance right between aggregate expenditure and aggregate supply. The end result today is that we recognise different types of unemployment and it is important to diagnose each problem separately and apply the appropriate remedial policy according to the situation. Keynesian 'demand-deficient' or *'cyclical' unemployment* requires an injection of increased spending. *'Structural' unemployment* where there is a mis-match between available skills and job opportunities requires education and re-training of the workforce. (*Which* type of training, and *how* it is implemented are important microeconomic questions that depend on the economy in question.) Apply the wrong medicine and, either way above, the result will be continuing unemployment, trade deficits, no or slow growth and a rise in the general level of prices.

Western economies are now emerging from the 1990s recession but they are still searching for the Holy Grail of sustainable, non-inflationary growth. Questions that might be asked to help to resolve some of these issues include:

- Have the more efficient, high-tech. businesses in the economy been laying off workers? If so there may well be a deficiency in aggregate demand.

- As the recovery takes place, will there be increased demand for goods and services that the economy has no spare capacity to produce? If so this may prompt an increase in inflation and a rise in imports – symptoms of a supply-side, microeconomic imbalance.
- The controversy now is not theoretical but empirical – what does the evidence show? This is a matter for each society to settle for itself.

KEY WORDS

Allocative efficiency Economics is classically concerned with the efficient allocation of resources. A change in consumer demand away from foods stuffed with additives, colouring and flavouring in favour of environmentally friendly health foods will leave shops, factories and farms with unwanted stocks of some goods and shortages of others. Some productive resources will be made redundant, others will now be in short supply. Similarly, a breakthrough in technology – like in the exploitation and transport of natural gas – can make some productive processes much cheaper, others more wasteful than before. The speed and efficiency with which producers can adjust to changing conditions, the less the amount of waste generated, the more efficient the allocation of society's resources.

Disequilibrium This is where the forces in the market place are too weak-acting to overcome obstacles and to secure balance or equilibrium.

The fallacy of composition What works for one individual may not work for all individuals if they act together. A man can miss the traffic jams and get home quickly if he leaves the office half an hour early, but this policy will not work if everyone thinks and acts the same. Similarly, if one person demands and wins a large pay increase, then good for him/her; but if all workers succeed in gaining higher wages then industrial costs rise, fuelling inflation and the real value of the wage increase thus falls to zero. Everyone loses.

Human capital Capital, in economics, is a resource capable of producing goods and services. Human capital is thus gained if people's health, education and vocational training improves such that they become more productive in employment.

Macroeconomics The analysis of levels of aggregate demand and supply on a national scale. Rates of inflation, unemployment and economic growth are considered, as are government policies to influence these variables.

The marginal propensity to consume (mpc) How much a community will spend, rather than save, from a given increase in its income. If you were given $10 and spent $7 then your mpc would equal 70 per cent.

Microeconomics The study of how resources are employed and goods and services are produced and consumed in an individual market place. The supply, demand and determination of price of one product compared to another is analysed, as is how efficiently, economically, changes from one market are communicated to another.

The multiplier A Keynesian concept which refers to how much national income is affected by a relatively small change in spending injected into the economy. Any one monetary injection may flow round and round the economy a number of times. For example, if domestic investment rises by x million and, as a result, national incomes rise by $5x$ million the *investment multiplier* is 5. Similarly, if there is a rise in y million in export earnings and incomes rise by $3y$ million, then the *foreign trade multiplier* equals 3.

Supply-side Economic theory which emphasises the importance of policies to free up markets from government regulation, thus allegedly stimulating supply.

Unemployment This can be defined as the amount of people who are actively seeking work but cannot find it. Who is 'active' or not is a matter of contention which leads to changing official statistics and arguments between theoretical economists.

QUESTIONS

1 Examine how prices and the employment of resources would move if there was a sustained increase in the demand for natural gas in the place of coal. What are the implications if either (a) prices or (b) resources do *not* move?
2 What causes price variability in agricultural markets? Should such variability be prevented? Why or why not?
3 Under what circumstances will a cut in wages (a) reduce or (b) increase unemployment?
4 Under what circumstances will an increase in the aggregate level of spending in an economy lead to (a) increasing employment and incomes or (b) inflation?
5 Microeconomics is concerned with efficiency and macroeconomics is about aggregates. Explain and discuss.

FURTHER READING

Almost any introductory text on economics will enlarge upon the theories of price determination and on the macroeconomics of aggregate demand and supply. Particularly recommended is:
Parkin, M. *Economics*. Addison Wesley, 1990.

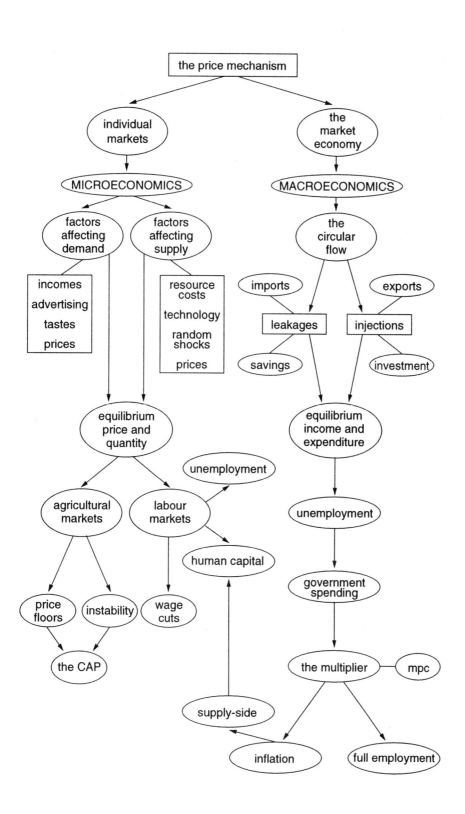

4 Unemployment and inflation

Topics to be considered in this chapter

- Creative destruction
- Keynesian demand-management policies
- The Phillips curve
- Supply-side policies
- The UK Thatcher government programme
- The inflation/unemployment record in selected countries

INTRODUCTION

Unemployment is not a natural phenomenon. No creatures in the wild are unemployed – you do not see any birds or animals lying idle. Nor are people in tribal or agricultural societies ever unemployed. In the Middle Ages mass unemployment was unheard of. There was simply too much to do: crops to be harvested; cloth to be woven; stone to be quarried, shaped and placed in construction. Today, in poorer parts of the world, in those remote corners untouched by so-called modern civilisation, you will not find anyone unemployed either. No. Unemployment is solely the creation of modern, industrial society. It is not natural. It is not even man-made. Unemployment is rich-man-made.

The world's first industrial revolution took place in Great Britain. People moved from the land into the growing industrial centres. New products, new processes, new sources of power were created and with them revolutionary changes imposed on society. Factories were built requiring modern workforces. Cities grew. Transport and trade links were forged that brought in sources of supply and facilitated the distribution of final products. And the enormous increases in wealth that were accumulated fed increasing populations, trade and investments of global proportions.

From British shores modern industrialisation and urbanisation spread quickly across Europe and thence further overseas. International trade blossomed as change spawned further change, bringing more and more people into the money economy.

The growing sophistication and integration of world trade brought with it growing specialisation, interdependency and thereby *fragility*.

The very success of trade means individuals specialise in those employments that can earn them most money. Sophisticated products such as a modern motor car are the outcome of millions of specialised tasks and production decisions spread across many different factories, regions, even countries. Every person's job is dependent on someone else's, and all are dependent on the final consumer demanding the finished product.

CREATIVE DESTRUCTION

What happens when new products appear on the market place; when consumer tastes change?

Austrian economist Joseph Schumpeter described modern economic and social evolution as a process of *creative destruction* – new products and processes are created at the expense of old ones. New jobs destroy traditional ones.

But one of the features of modern economic society is that the destruction of the old is frequently far removed from the creation of the new. In medieval, village society, for example, specialisation had not progressed to the extreme where single skills were concentrated in whole regions; where buyers in one place did not know the producers in another; where one could not see the consequences of one's decisions of what, and what not, to buy. But in modern trade, economic interdependency links distant communities in ways impossible to see, and of course what the eye does not see, the heart does not grieve over.

Cynics might argue that this was particularly true in the days of the first industrial revolution when the traditional societies destroyed were full of brown-skinned people in far-off lands. What do cotton mill owners and workers in the north of England – and consumers of their products – care about the destruction of traditional Indian industry?

Such beggar-my-neighbour attitudes caught up with the Western world in the thirties' Great Depression. The economic fortunes and destiny of modern trading nations are inevitably interlinked. The attempt by some countries and communities to increase their wealth at the expense of others (in tariff and trade wars) meant that world trade and thereby incomes quickly collapsed. From there, the Second World War served forcibly to underline the destructive dead-end of blinkered nationalism.

In 1945, the Western nations sought to create a better post-war world. And following the work of John Maynard Keynes, government economic management was thought to be the key to minimising unemployment. If modern market economies are inherently unstable and liable to cause booms and slumps then governments have the duty and ability to intervene and smooth out the path to growth via macroeconomic, *contra-cyclical* fiscal and monetary policies.

It seemed to work at first. But since the 1970s creeping and then galloping *inflation* has appeared as the price to pay.

UNEMPLOYMENT VERSUS INFLATION?

Modern Western nations have recently been unable to escape from a rising cycle of unemployment. Success at restraining joblessness has only been at the expense of releasing increased inflation; and vice versa. Whereas in the 1960s inflation was kept down at the cost of less than 4 per cent unemployment, today in the 1990s inflation has only just abated in Europe with over 10 per cent of the labour force out of work. Present governments are inhibited in their dash for growth and more jobs by the fear of notching up another ratchet in inflation.

Unemployment today affects an increasingly wide range of industries and individuals. Around 19 million are registered as looking for work in Europe and we can assume many more are unregistered. Although traditionally the older mining and manufacturing industries have suffered most, that is no longer the case – the growth in joblessness in the 1990s has been fastest in professional, white-collar services.

The worst currently affected are the young, unskilled, the ethnic minorities, men more than women, and those working in manufacturing and construction. But the early 1990s recession has hit all job categories in all regions, and the long-term unemployed are a growing percentage.

Certain microeconomic explanations for unemployment are under attack: powerful trade unions, overgenerous unemployment benefits, inefficient, uncompetitive industry, immobile labour. Some countries have been more effective in hitting these targets than others.

So long as the pattern of world demand continues to change, however, then the market economy's production of goods and services must keep pace with it. Any cyclical slump in world trade will affect all countries, but those structurally rigid, least-flexible economies will suffer most of all. Japan can hold inflation steady with less than 3 per cent unemployed. Not so in Europe and North America.

A number of issues are raised here. Just what exactly *is* the relationship between unemployment and inflation? Does the one affect the other? If so, is this relationship stable over time, and how does it differ between countries? We need to examine the arguments and the evidence involved.

It has been asserted above that both macro- and microeconomic influences are relevant: the general level of activity within an economy and the flexibility of labour markets both impact on unemployment and carry implications for inflation. But whereas some economic theorists argue that these two phenomena are alternatives, that there is a *trade-off* between unemployment and inflation, others say that no such relationship exists, or – if anything – there is a positive correlation at work.

Keynesian theory puts the case that these two economic evils are opposites – policies to reduce inflation will exaggerate the rate of unemployment. Supply-side theorists – in the ascendant after the oil price shocks to the world economy during the 1970s – have argued that there is *no* long-term conflict between unemployment and inflation. Countries can have less of both if they free up market rigidities and thereby release the forces for economic growth. It is time to turn to an examination of these rival claims.

The Keynesian orthodoxy Keynesian economists held centre-stage throughout the post-war years up until the end of the 1960s. Government policies, informed by Keynesian emphasis of aggregate *demand management*, were successful in keeping unemployment down to unprecedentedly low levels, albeit at the (relatively minor) cost of creeping inflation (see figure 4.1).

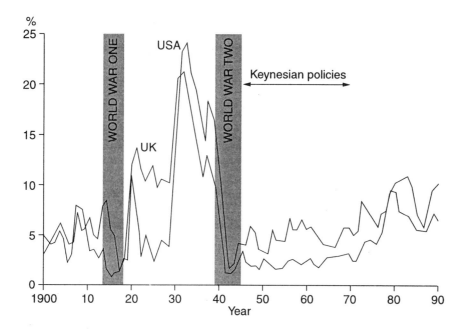

Figure 4.1
Source: Datastream.

Textbook Keynesian macroeconomics held that a country is in stable equilibrium where the level of *aggregate demand* flowing round the economy (that is, the combined total of spending decisions of all households, firms and public authorities) just equals *aggregate supply* (total output of all producers). Since the former tends to be more unstable than the latter (Keynes particularly emphasised the volatility of firms' investment plans) then governments must accept the responsibility of spending more in times when private consumers were uncertain and witholding expenditure, and spending less/taxing more when confidence was high and aggregate demand in danger of running out of control. Despite the market economy's tendency for cyclical booms and slumps, therefore, government contra-cyclical demand-management policies could keep the system in stable equilibrium.

Note that unemployment and inflation were characterised as opposites. If aggregate demand exceeded supply then this excess pressure would force up the level of prices: inflation would occur. If aggregate demand was less than supply then unemployment would result. The presence of either symptom in the post-war period was put down to difficulties of 'fine-tuning' the required demand-management policies.

All the evidence of these years reinforced the ascendancy of Keynesian thinking. In contrast to the economic instability of the interwar period when governments were generally non-interventionist, active post-1945 demand-management policies coincided with steady growth and full employment in the Western world. When A.W. Phillips published his famous findings on unemployment and inflation in 1958, the victory of Keynesian theory over classical views on unemployment was complete.

Professor Phillips was concerned about the link between the rate of change in money wages and unemployment. Working at the London School of Economics, he correlated UK inflation and unemployment performance for almost a hundred years from 1862 to 1958 and found that the relationship between the two was remarkably stable. The *Phillips curve* (see figure 4.2), illustrated below, shows a clear trade-off between unemployment and inflation with the unavoidable policy implication that, in the short run, if a country opts to reduce one it must exacerbate the other – exactly in accordance with orthodox Keynesianism.

The Keynesian 'revolution' of the 1930s had thus become the mainstream orthodoxy of the 1950s and 1960s. As always in economics, there was a continuing academic debate between adherents and critics of these views but this had little impact on the practical policy makers. Keynesian demand management was predominant in Western governments.

The onset of the 1970s, however, blew all these certainties out of the window. This was the decade when everything seemed to go wrong for most developed and many underdeveloped countries of the world. Unemployment and inflation accelerated together, trade balances went into the red, economic growth slowed down and – for some – went into reverse. No amount of manipulative 'fine-tuning' could fix things. Major structural changes in the world economy were at work and Keynesian orthodox economics which had failed to foresee this and seemingly contained no policy prescription for it was thus discredited.

In evolution, the death of the dinosaurs – due it seems to some external earth-shattering impact for which they were not designed to cope – left the field wide open for other, until then relatively insignificant, mammalian creatures to populate.

So it was that 'supply-siders' – evolutionary heirs to the earlier strain of

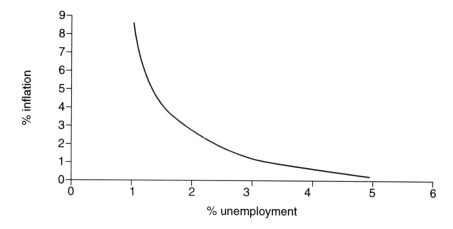

This data supports the Keynesian hypothesis that unemployment and inflation are inversely related in general – as inflation falls, unemployment rises, and vice versa.

Figure 4.2 UK Phillips curve data, 1862–1958

classical economics but until the 1970s generally populating the fringes of academic debate – were suddenly able to inhabit the centre ground left vacant by floundering Keynesians.

Supply-side economics Two developments are generally held responsible for switching the attention of economic commentators to the importance of aggregate supply in the equation quoted earlier in this chapter. The first of these developments, all would agree, was sudden and thunderingly obvious – the massive oil price shocks of the seventies which greatly increased energy costs and enforced large transfers of world incomes from Western consuming nations to exporting (particularly Middle Eastern) nations. The second (and more disputable) development was cumulative and imperceptible until too late – the gradual sclerosis of certain micro-economic organs of mature market systems.

The supply-side critique of Keynesianism focused on *government failure* in a mixed economy – specifically, that well-intentioned interventionism impaired the efficient functioning of (especially labour) markets, frustrated economic growth prospects, led to government budgets getting out of control and increased a country's inflationary tendencies.

The capacity of the supply side of the economy to respond to rapidly evolving consumer demand is considered essential to the long-term health of an economy. Governments and public-sector institutions are blundering dinosaurs compared to the fleet-footed market mammals of private enterprise. Economies dominated by the former need to be de-regulated and re-populated by the latter, it is argued.

This requires the unrestricted mobility of labour, capital and enterprise to flow to those employments in an economy that are most popular, productive and profitable, and away from those sectors that suffer declining demand.

Policies to promote such mobility of resources imply *deregulation* of markets (i.e. removing government controls); adjusting tax and benefits systems; *privatisation* of public enterprise; and the breaking up of private monopolistic and restrictive practices.

By such measures, supply-siders assert, increasing productivity and long-term economic growth can be secured. Unemployment will fall and – since aggregate supply can thus keep up with growing aggregate demand – inflation need not occur.

This supply-side economic philosophy is basically a reassertion of the fertility and efficiency of free markets – a breeding ground of growth allegedly denied sustenance by governments concerned to promote 'welfare capitalism'. That is, critics of liberal Keynesian political economy asserted that by trying to spread the benefits of post-war capitalism more equitably in society, rather than concentrating rewards on the primary wealth-creators, lumbering governments had trampled on the main source of economic growth. It was time to make room for the overtaxed, underfed but still success-hungry enterprise culture. As such, therefore, the *key* distinction between Keynesian and supply-side economics is not so much about policies but about objectives.

This philosophy was most famously associated with two politicians separated by the Atlantic Ocean: Margaret Thatcher in the UK and Ronald Reagan in the USA. Of these two, the one who was least constrained by any political opposition and was thus most effective in pushing through radical supply-side policies was Britain's Margaret Thatcher. The 1980s was very much the Thatcher decade and those years provide an excellent case-study of the supply-side experiment in action.

There was a third politician associated during the 1970s and 1980s with this right-wing economic philosophy – President Aguste Pinochet of Chile. The move from state-regulated protectionism and welfare provision to radical, free-market monetarism was even more extreme in the Chilean case. This shift in national direction, however, was not an economic experiment undertaken with much political support – it involved the bloody overthrow of an elected Marxist government by a military dictatorship. It also facilitated the dominance of the economy by relatively few, wealthy, entrepreneurial groups which distorted financial and commercial markets, led to a monetary crisis (in 1982), soaring international indebtedness and government reintervention and rescue. As such, the Chilean experience illustrates some of the problems of right-wing economics applied in a unique, small, developing-country context and it may not be a relevant supply-side model for all; though undoubtedly a number of free-market reforms – such as extensive privatisation and diversification of the economy – have contributed to this country's steady growth since the mid-1980s.

THATCHERITE SUPPLY-SIDE POLICIES

The story begins prior to the eighties with the world's first oil price shock at the time of the Middle East 'October War' in 1973. Oil prices increased 400 per cent between September 1973 and January 1974.

As all the world's energy costs rose, many industries cut back on employment in order to survive. In global terms, OPEC incomes were growing at the expense of consumer countries and no amount of Keynesian demand management could hide the fact that Western standards of living had to fall in relative terms.

The political and economic fallout in democratic countries was inevitable. Governments were forced out of office, and out with them also went their liberal, Keynesian economic policies. The age of Thatcherism and Reaganism was upon us. Supply-side economics was introduced in the West just as the second world oil price shock (of 1979) took effect.

Thanks to the Iranian revolution and the removal of their oil from world markets, the cost of energy jumped again sending another inflationary impulse around the globe.

Inflation, according to supply-siders, is public enemy number one. Unemployment in declining sectors is unavoidable and indeed to be accepted rather than prevented if resources are to transfer their allegiance. Inflation, however, distorts relative prices and incomes, affects everyone in an economy and particularly prejudices business confidence in the future. As such, it inhibits investment and thereby economic growth.

The economic priorities and policies of US and UK governments were quite clear, therefore: inflation was a more important concern than unemployment. And in the case of Mrs Thatcher at least, her authority to implement the new right-wing economic doctrine was unchallenged.

In May 1979, the Conservative (Tory) party came into office in the UK, trumpeting the virtues of supply-side policies and it immediately set about implementing them.

Deregulation began in *financial and capital markets* with the abolition of foreign exchange controls (October 1979), and the removal of a variety of restrictions on credit (May 1979, June 1980, August 1981). The division between banks and building societies disappeared (October 1983) and along with it went out any rationing of long loans and mortgages.

The notion here was to improve the competitiveness and efficiency of money markets. It should be emphasised that – following the writings of the influential Chicago economist Milton Friedman – government control of the overall money supply was considered essential, although its allocation between competing users was thought rightly a matter for the markets to decide.

This is easier to pronounce in theory, however, than it is to put into practice. Modern money is a very slippery concept (see chapter 7, below) and freeing up competitive forces both within the UK domestic banking sector and on the foreign exchange markets meant that it was impossible in the early eighties for the government to contain money supplies within the declared target range. (For this reason, by the late eighties the government had abandoned any attempt at monetary targeting.)

With the reforms introduced, there were no direct controls on funds entering or leaving the country; on the rapid expansion of UK banking activities and on the multiple creation of credit. Nigel Lawson (Chancellor of the Exchequer at the time) has written that 'the only checks on excess were the price of credit (i.e. the rate of interest) which the government could control and prudence (on the part of bankers and financiers), which it could not' (*Financial Times*, 27 January 1992).

Since deregulation and the growth of the financial services sector was to be encouraged, yet the amount of inflation was not, then rates of interest had to rise. There was no other way – as the quantity of money could not be influenced, its price had to be.

The consequence was that in the early 1980s, with high interest rates and energy costs, British industry suffered a severe slump (see data below). Many manufacturing businesses closed, causing much unemployment, though this was explained away by supply-side advocates as the justifiable extinction of inefficient industrial dinosaurs. (Note that this high interest rate policy of Thatcher/Reaganite supply-siders had international repercussions that spread far beyond the slump in domestic industries alone [see chapter 10 on international debt, below].)

Deregulation of *labour markets* meant, for the Tories, destroying trade union power to affect wages and inhibit labour mobility. Legislation to curb the unions was enacted in the 1980 and 1982 Employment Acts and in the 1984 Trade Union Act. These outlawed 'secondary picketing' (i.e. workers going on strike to support others' grievances), enforced pre-strike ballots and limited union 'closed shops' (i.e. the demand that all employees at the same workplace join the same union). That trade union membership and influence declined in Britain over these years is undeniable. Whether this was the result of government action or simply the reaction to growing unemployment and despondency is debatable.

In addition to enfeebling the unions, there was a call to restructure welfare provision to labour in order to reduce the financial incentive for (particularly young people) drawing unemployment benefit rather than seeking work. School leavers' entitlement to register for dole money was withdrawn and 'make work' Youth Opportunity Programmes and Youth Training Schemes were introduced (1983, 1988).

Perhaps the most important policy with regard to labour markets was the government's acceptance of high levels of unemployment. Supply-siders argued that Britain's jobless rate was 'voluntary' in the sense that more and more people were allegedly preferring not to work, rather than accepting whatever they could find at the going wage. That is, the level of *'natural'* *unemployment* necessary to persuade people to become occupationally mobile had increased. The government's willingness to accept jobless people's pain was necessary, therefore, to force changes through.

Privatisation of Britain's public enterprises was embarked upon to 'roll back the frontiers of the state' and to unleash the supposed forces of the free market throughout the economy. Three purposes were allegedly served by this policy: to increase economic efficiency; to reduce dependency on government finances; and to increase the spread of share ownership (people's capitalism). Other critics (notably former Tory prime minister Sir Harold Macmillan) simply called this a policy of 'selling off the family silver'.

From British Aerospace to Rover Cars, British Gas to local water authorities, scores of state-owned corporations and public utilities were sold off, raising around £30,000 billion between 1979 and 1990.

One continuing concern of the privatisation programme to date has been the conversion of state monopolies into private ones. Supply-side reform is best served by increased market competition. Economists have argued that selling off giants like British Telecom without breaking them up has been premature. Despite the difficulties of dismantling certain natural monopolies (those public utilities that *cannot* operate efficiently on a small scale, e.g. in the distribution of gas, electricity, water, telecoms, etc.) more could have been done to promote dismemberment into competing units.

In the education and health sectors, where full-scale privatisation was not possible, '*quasi-markets*' were promoted: that is, changes were introduced to devolve financial management down to the level of each school and hospital; to encourage 'opting out' of local authority control; and to introduce as far as possible the practice of competition between 'consumers' and 'suppliers'. Consumers in this context were school students or hospital patients. For every student/patient on a school's/hospital's list the government allocated state funds. If such consumers transferred their 'custom' from one school/hospital to another, state funds would transfer accordingly. The notion of free education and health care for all was supposedly not under attack, but competitive, efficient supply was supposedly enhanced. It is questionable, however, how far profit-seeking market ideology is applicable in the provision of social services. How far, for example, does society gain when schools and hospitals compete for the custom of certain students/patients and offload others that they do not want?

Tax reform, in addition to all of the above, was part of the doctrine to promote the spirit of free enterprise. Tax cuts give people more freedom to choose what they wish to do with their money, it was argued, *and* they give greater marginal incentives to work. ('Why work an extra hour's overtime if it only puts you into a higher tax bracket?') The basic rate of income tax was brought down over the 1980s from 33 per cent to 25 per cent and the top rate came down from 83 per cent to 40 per cent. Corporation tax on business profits was similarly reduced from over 50 per cent to less than 40 per cent. (In compensation, VAT rates were raised in stages from 8 per cent up to 15 per cent and the infamous Poll Tax was introduced.) The supposed beneficial impact on incentives, enterprise and thereby economic growth of these tax changes was considered paramount. A steeply *progressive tax* system was thus weakened and made more regressive. The distributional effect of widening the gap between rich and poor was considered a price worth paying.

The impact of all these changes on the British economy has been profound, reaches far beyond the focus of economics alone – as comments above imply – and it is still underway. Our primary concern here, however, is to examine the impact on UK unemployment, inflation and economic growth during the eighties (see figures 4.3 and 4.4). Within this frame of reference in particular, has supply-side economics been vindicated, or does the Keynesian theory that it supplanted still have relevance for the nineties?

The evidence revealed in Figure 4.3 is mixed. Inflation in the UK over the period has fluctuated above the European average, rising again in excess of 10 per cent by the beginning of the 1990s, though it has since fallen. The most significant sustained change has been the establishment of high unemployment levels compared to earlier decades: the lowest attainable jobless rate in the 1980s was higher than any unemployment peak since the war.

The supply-side contention that growth can be attained with falling inflation and unemployment has *not* been achieved over any long period (though it may be possible in the short term whilst recovering from recession: unutilised resources are simply re-employed, thus contributing to growth at little extra cost).

Figure 4.3 still shows a Phillipsian trade-off, albeit at a higher level than before (the curve has shifted out?). The major difference now is that the present government seems to prefer high unemployment to high inflation.

It must be said that this evidence of the eighties is not very complimentary for supply-side enthusiasts.

Deregulating UK financial markets together with large tax cuts led to the speculative boom at the end of the 1980s decade. The supposed supply-side effect of tax cuts freeing up enterprise was less obvious than the (Keynesian) impact on inflating consumer demand. The rapid rise in house prices (especially in crowded southeast England) contributed to increased immobility of labour (how could unemployed northerners move south in search of jobs?) and at the same time drove capital and enterprise into unproductive property speculation. The resulting return to inflation had to be brought to an end by hoisting up interest rates, thus provoking a recession.

Thatcherite attempts at freeing-up labour, capital and enterprise markets and 'taking the government off the backs of the people', therefore, cannot so far be enthusiastically applauded for promoting long-term, 'sustainable' growth in the UK. The recent recovery from the 1990s recession is no great achievement if the recession was induced by such policies in the first place.

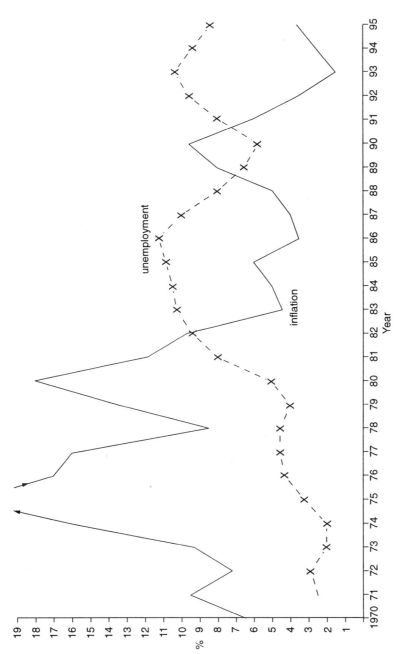

Figure 4.3 UK inflation and unemployment: time series, 1970–95
Source: Datastream.

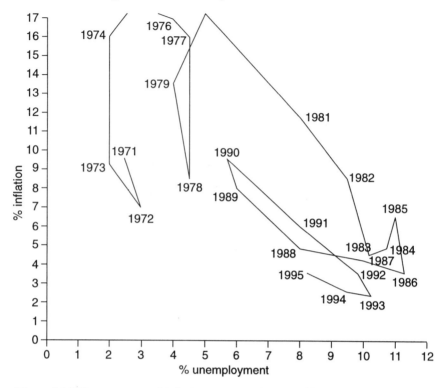

Figure 4.4 UK percentage of inflation to unemployment 1971–1995, year to year movement. Compare to figure 4.2. Has the Phillips curve shifted out?

How do other countries' experiences of inflation and unemployment during the 1980s compare with that of the UK's (see figures 4.5 to 4.11)? Although few other nations implemented radical right-wing economic policies as consistently as Margaret Thatcher's government, nonetheless supply-side philosophy won general acclaim from most commentators in most countries during this period. Have other developed economies therefore succeeded in bringing down inflation and unemployment together, as was allegedly possible?

There are, of course, a vast number of variables that are at play here in determining the economic fortunes of the countries surveyed above. The pattern which emerges in comparing the UK, the USA, France and Germany, however, is remarkable for its similarity. Inflation and un-employment swing up and down in opposition to each other almost without exception. The Phillips-type pattern of a short-term trade-off between the two seems remarkably well illustrated in all cases. The precise relationship between inflation and unemployment may not be as stable over time as it was in Phillips' day, but nonetheless these two economic objectives *do* appear to be alternatives – at least in the evidence featured to date.

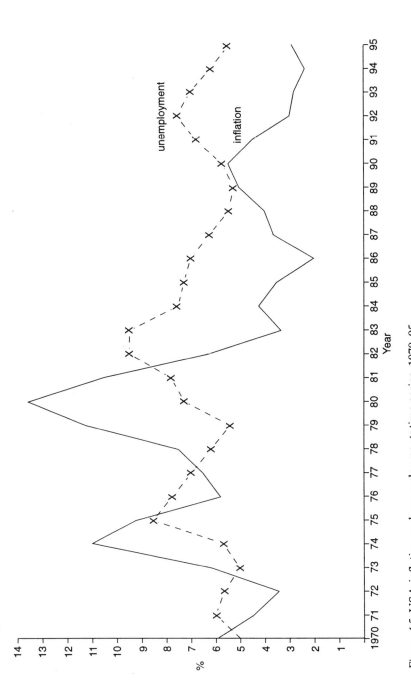

Figure 4.5 USA inflation and unemployment: time series, 1970–95
Source: Datastream.

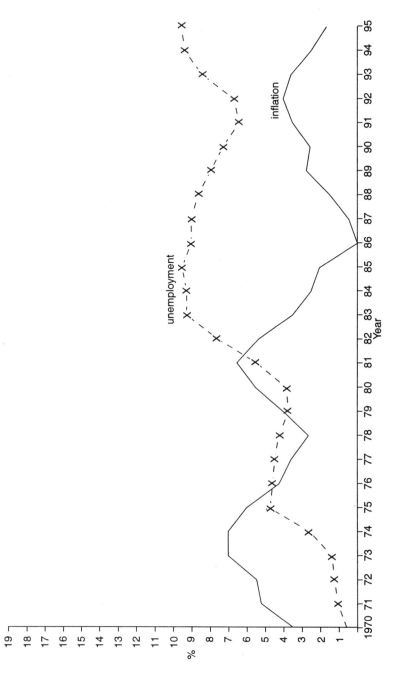

Figure 4.6 West Germany inflation and unemployment: time series, 1970–95
Source: Datastream.

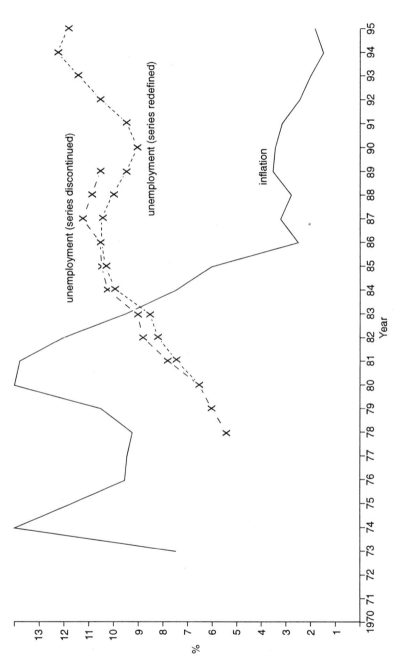

Figure 4.7 France inflation and unemployment: time series, 1970–95
Source: Datastream

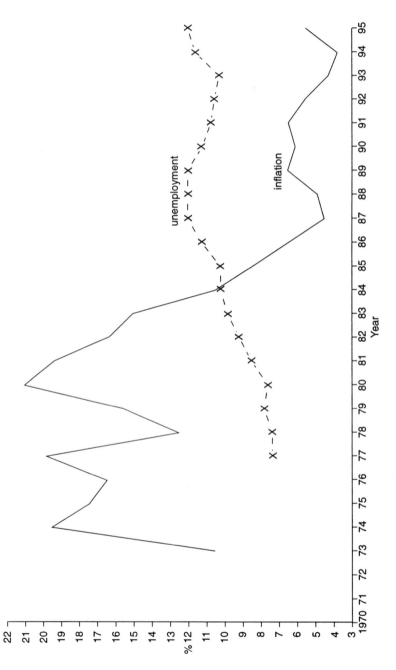

Figure 4.8 Italy inflation and unemployment: time series, 1970–95
Source: Datastream.

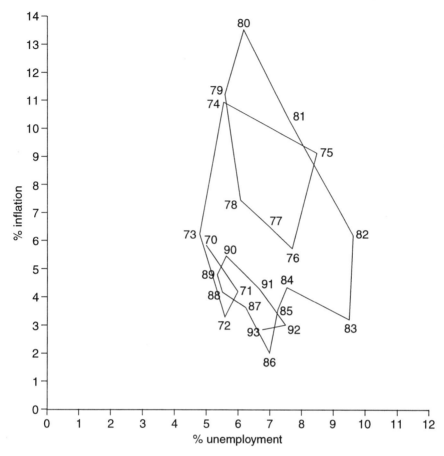

Figure 4.9 USA percentage of inflation to unemployment 1970s to 1990s, year-to-year movement

US economist Alan Blinder uses a very helpful analogy to illustrate how managing a national economy in the stable world environment of the 1950s and 1960s compares to the crisis-ridden 1970s and thereafter. It is like driving a car – there is always a short-term trade-off between speed and safety. The faster you go, the more dangerous it is: speed and safety are alternatives. Now consider what it is like driving in clear weather on a good road, compared with driving in blizzard conditions in unknown country. The same trade-off still exists, but now the relationship shifts to a completely different level. Hazardous external conditions have transformed the way these two alternatives operate on your driving.

Look at the inflation/unemployment trade-off in the early 1970s; compare the data for the late 1970s/early 1980s; and consider again the late 1980s/ early 1990s. External conditions seem to indicate different levels of trade-off, different Phillips curves, for each of these periods. Compared to

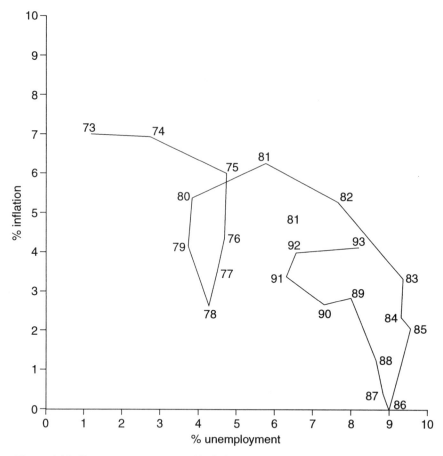

Figure 4.10 Germany percentage of inflation to unemployment 1970s to 1990s, year-to-year movement

the 1950s and 1960s when a stable international environment existed with fixed exchange rates, the oil shocks and financial instability of the early 1970s and early 1980s hit the major trading nations like a storm. The effect of taking aboard a fanatic supply-side driver in the 1980s has not helped either – if anything it has only meant hammering one side of the road rather than the other. Management of national economies in unstable times – keeping the car on the road – needs sensitive handling, with regard to a number of policy instruments, and it is not helped by dogmatic reliance on the free-market accelerator only, with a blinkered disregard for bystanders.

The conclusion offered here, therefore, is that the Keynesian inflation/unemployment trade-off has not been discredited. On the contrary, supply-side economics still has something to prove. Modern critics argue that the major legacy of the radical 1980s experiment has been nothing other than to reintroduce the economics of boom and bust – to re-expose the

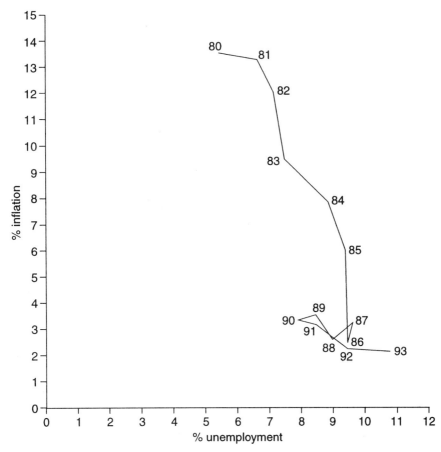

Figure 4.11 France percentage of inflation to unemployment 1970s to 1990s, year-to-year movement

instability of unregulated market economies which Keynes warned about in the 1930s. For a variety of political reasons, the policies of the late 1980s and early 1990s involved maintaining high interest rates around the world – penalising industry, house owners and anyone who borrowed on cheap credit. Locked into a supply-side fear of inflation and unable to risk any employment-creating expansion, world governments resorted to an old-fashioned slump: reining back aggregate demand and allowing rising unemployment to squeeze inflation out of the system. Agreement between finance ministers of developed countries, opinion makers and officials of the IMF has been total. According to the theories, priorities and politicians of the day, unemployment was the 'price worth paying to secure low inflation' (Norman Lamont, UK Chancellor of the Exchequer, in a statement to the House of Commons in 1991). Many ordinary people remain to be convinced, however.

CONCLUSION

It has been argued that unemployment is the creation of modern, Western society. Its causes are manyfold: there are both macro- and microeconomic factors at work. It has been mentioned that sophisticated, integrated economies must continually evolve if sufficient new jobs are to be created to replace the old. Macroeconomic, contra-cyclical policies to maintain a consistent, high level of aggregate demand are important as are micro-economic job information services, re-training packages and the re-targeting of government hand-outs to subsidise labour mobility and redeployment rather than redundancy and welfare dependency. Because there are social and private costs and benefits involved, governments, employers and employees *all* need to be involved in sharing the responsibility for new training and employment programmes.

In particular, unemployment concerns the nature of the relationship of the individual with the state. The individual cannot say: society owes me a living; nor can society insist that unemployment is always and every-where the fault of the individual. Coal miners cannot be blamed for the development of undersea oil and gas.

In the 1980s, British politicians such as Norman Tebbitt could say: 'Get on your bike' (and look for work) and Norman Lamont add: 'Unemployment is a price worth paying' – but this places too much onus on the individual. The structural changes now required of mature economies are great. Politicians remote from unemployment maybe cannot see or feel suffi-ciently its ill effects. Arguing that market forces alone will solve the problem with minimal government 'interference' is a declaration of faith unlikely to be shared by those whose jobs are no longer in demand.

This is not to deny that inflation is an important consideration also. Rising prices will reduce the standard of living of all those whose incomes cannot similarly increase. As well as effecting a change in the relative distribution of incomes, the functioning of the price mechanism for all goods and services within the economy becomes impaired. Efficient organisation of the entire economy suffers. Inflation, once uncontrollable, can just as surely lead to social and economic misery as increasing unemployment.

The solution of difficult social problems requires a flexibility of approach from us all: individuals must seek perpetually to upgrade their skills; society must subsidise their efforts.

Unemployment represents a colossal waste of resources. It is inefficient, uneconomic to have human potential lying idle; deteriorating over time. But this is an issue of normative as well as positive economics: unemploy-ment is the creation of the modern market economy and therefore society needs a moral vision that is as geographically far-reaching as the spread of its trade.

Traditional communities – wherever they live and work in the world – will continue to be overtaken by revolutions in the global market place.

Unemployment matters wherever it occurs, and individuals, employers and governments must all assume responsibility for making efforts to overcome it.

KEY WORDS

Deregulation This usually refers to the removing of government regulations, restrictions and rules on the provision and sale of goods and services.

Inflation The percentage rise in the general level of prices of a country over a year, measured by reference to an officially recognised price index.

Progressive tax This is a tax which takes a rising fraction of people's income as their incomes increase: for example, an income tax which takes nothing from a poor person; taxes 25 per cent of those earning above $20,000 p.a.; 30 per cent of those earning above $40,000; etc. Such a tax contrasts with a *proportional tax* – which charges the *same percentage* on incomes on all people, whatever their earnings – and a *regressive tax* which takes a higher percentage of a poor person's income than a rich person's. (A *poll tax* which charges the same *amount* – say $100 – on all people irrespective of their incomes is an example of a regressive tax.)

QUESTIONS

1 'Any cyclical slump in world trade will affect all countries, but those structurally rigid, least-flexible countries will suffer most of all.' Explain and discuss.
2 What is meant by Keynesian, 'counter-cyclical' government policies? How could such policies be used to reduce (a) unemployment; (b) inflation?
3 What are the objectives of 'supply-side' economics? What are the policies involved? Are there any costs in implementing them?
4 What causes inflation? Distinguish between Keynesian and supply-side views.
5 'The Phillips curve trade-off between unemployment and inflation still holds, only it has shifted out.' Is this true? If so, why?

FURTHER READING

Blinder, Alan S. *Hard Heads, Soft Hearts*. Addison Wesley, 1987.

Johnson, Christopher. *The Economy under Mrs Thatcher, 1979–1990*. Penguin, 1991.

Nell, Edward J. (ed.). *Free Market Conservatism*. Allen & Unwin, 1984.

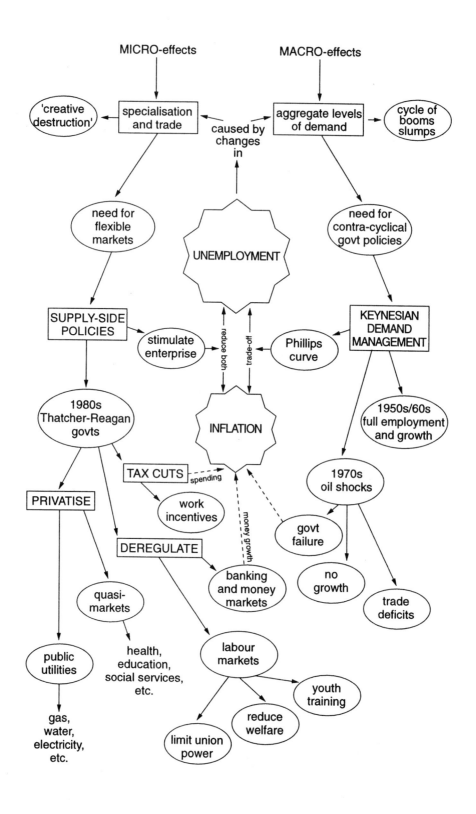

5 Free trade, regional agreements and strategic policies

Topics to be considered in this chapter

- Protectionism
- Trade agreements – a range from independence to economic and political union
- The theory of comparative advantage
- NAFTA and the challenge for Mexico
- Strategic trade policies
- Japanese economic development

INTRODUCTION

Free trade in world markets randomly visits misery on groups of workers and business people whose products seem suddenly to go out of favour. Most countries can find examples of established industries that – thanks to changing technology and the costs of production, or some fickleness in consumer demand – have lost their markets to new competitors.

- Naturally occurring nitrates in the Atacama desert were the main export and source of income for Chile at the beginning of the twentieth century until Germany developed synthetic substitutes.
- The sudden oil price rises of the 1970s meant that large, gas-guzzling American automobiles could not compete with the increasingly efficient products of European and Japanese car industries which were far quicker to react to the new market realities.
- Matsushita and Sony, two of Japan's and the world's largest consumer electronics giants, closed down plants and reduced their staff at home in the early 1990s due to falling demand and a flood of low-priced imports from Asian rivals.

The process of creative destruction that causes distress to some brings opportunity to others, of course, but the differential impact on costs and benefits means that the misery can be painfully concentrated in certain regions and countries at certain times. The benefits may seem too often to be more accessible to other people, other places. During periods of instability and wrenching change the political impetus for protectionist policies – to cushion certain communities and industrial sectors from the harsh realities of international competition – may thus prove unstoppable. It often plays on the short-sighted sentiment that a country's wealth and welfare is best ensured by denying foreign advantage.

TRADE PROTECTION

Mercantilism has a long and sorry history. It advocates securing trade gains at the expense of other countries; erecting barriers against imports whilst aggressively promoting exports. At the extreme, it drove eighteenth- and nineteenth-century European empire-building and colonialism – the rush to carve up resource-rich and militarily less-powerful American, African and Asian lands before rivals could do likewise. In the 1930s, mercantilist 'beggar-my-neighbour' policies were pursued in the attempt to escape the Great Depression. The same protectionist, nationalist sentiments emerged across the world during the stagnating 1970s and the recessionary late 1980s.

Such thinking never goes away. As implied above, it is simply more apparent at some times and places than others. When the world economy is booming it becomes less relevant since all are becoming richer; when world economic growth slows, becomes stagnant or shrinks, however, then one country's economic fortune can be at the expense of another's. The protectionist barriers go up.

At such times it requires considerable diplomatic effort to prevent trade restrictions from spreading. A general collapse in world trade, everyone agrees, is bad for all, but what does it matter if *my* country alone subsidises its exports and protects its vital industries? Such is the argument of the *free rider* – who benefits most if everyone *else* agrees to the rules.

The *General Agreement on Tariffs and Trade* (GATT) was set up in 1948 as part of the attempt to rebuild a positive world order after the disasters of two world wars and an intervening depression. Despite all the difficulties, it has been outstandingly successful and it has now grown to become the *World Trade Organisation* (as of 1 January 1995). Originally, 23 countries participated in the first GATT round of discussions in Geneva. At the close of the Uruguay round, which started in Punta del Este in 1986 and was finally finished in Marrakesh, Morocco, in December 1993, 116 countries signed in agreement. In the meantime the average tariff on world trade has come down from around 40 per cent to less than 4 per cent; the global economy has more than doubled in size and international trade grew by over 500 per cent up to the mid-1970s. Although the pace has slowed in an unstable world since, the World Bank still estimates an average 1980–90 growth rate in merchandise trade of over 4 per cent per year.

Negotiating world-wide reductions in trade barriers, although worth-while, is extremely slow going. The binding principle that drove GATT and now the WTO is the commitment to end discrimination in trade and to generalise 'most-favoured nation' status to all. Thus any advantage granted to one trading partner must be extended to every signatory. This is time consuming to arrange. The issue that inevitably slows progress the most is the distribution of gains involved in any new round of cuts. Why should one nation agree to reducing *tariffs* and *quotas* if these seem to give greater competitive advantage to another? Poorer countries dependent on the export of a precious few products are wary of the exploitative power of rich nations with highly developed industrial bases; old rivalries amongst mature economies are easily awoken; agreement has been impeded on the Uruguay round since *newly industrialising countries* accuse richer nations of using environmental standards as a new form of protectionism.

The fewer the parties involved in any negotiations, and the more they have in common, the easier it is to secure agreement. It is for this reason that regional trade blocs have grown rapidly, against the background of a GATT-inspired, general expansion of international trade. So long as the regional deals involved do not lead to a raising of barriers to outsiders then, somewhat pragmatically, GATT rules do not prohibit such arrangements. Realistically, the post-war movement towards European Union (EU) in particular – although highly discriminatory with respect to farm trade – has been unstoppable. The very success of the EU has been an added reason for the growth of other regional associations, both in the desire to emulate its success and in the fear of losing out in a world increasingly subdivided into power blocs.

TRADE AGREEMENTS

It would be helpful at this stage to define the different types of trading agreements between nations before going on to discuss in further detail some of the issues involved. There are various levels of relationship possible – from negotiating a limited reciprocal reduction of tariffs on certain goods only, all the way through to the full integration of entire economies. The spectrum of choices involved appears below in order of increasing complexity.

1 Independence A country may opt not to join any regional trade grouping but choose to arrange its own policies on a bilateral, country-by-country basis. This way it is not constrained by any rules set up by prior agreement with others. Minimum levels of commitment, sovereignty loss and gains from trade are involved.

2 A free trade area Here a number of countries may agree to reduce tariffs and quotas on designated items between themselves, but leave each individual country to pursue independent policies with respect to the rest of the world. Intra-area trade may thus be completely free of all restrictions on goods and services; or (more realistically) tariffs may be reduced but not entirely removed on some, not all, items.

3 A customs union In addition to free trade between member countries, a *common external tariff* may be erected against all outside trade. This barrier will be of different heights for different goods, and erected against some countries and not others, but what makes a customs union different from a free trade area is that it has a common trade policy for all member countries with respect to all external parties.

4 A common market This involves free trade not only in goods and services between member countries, but also in the unrestricted movement and employment of labour and capital. Additionally, a common market usually implies an increasing number of common policies (e.g. in Europe, the Common Agricultural Policy) and – with regard to trade – a progressive reduction in *non-tariff barriers* also. This implies that all the rules and regulations, different specifications and standards embodied in member countries' goods and services become 'harmonised', or that mutual recognition is accepted.

5 Economic union Many common policies are pursued at this stage, in particular a common currency and monetary policy. This would therefore necessitate a common central bank and other economic institutions, co-ordinated fiscal policies, convergent financial performance, an industrial and competition policy and almost certainly a 'structural fund' or regional policy to address the possible problem of differential growth rates between regions/countries.

6 One Nation With an increasingly integrated Union economy, political sovereignty will inevitably be pooled between member countries. Central political institutions tend therefore to parallel the growth of common economic structures. A common parliament and legislature grows up at this stage and, with them, well-defined political and economic relationships are established between member states and the centre. Common social and regional policies will evolve from economic union; a common foreign and defence policy will similarly evolve from a common external trade policy.

(Note that these stages have been delineated as primarily an economic process; the sixth above, however, could be characterised instead as the ultimate stage of a separate political process which examines the degree of integration of political institutions and constitutions.)

It should be emphasised that once started on this process, there is no inevitability in progressing through this sequence of increasing economic integration, nor do these stages themselves represent discrete and well-marked steps along the way. As will be seen, a free trade area may still be rather slow in reducing internal trade barriers yet achieve breakthroughs in other common policies, such as with the mobility of capital, or in exchange rate agreements.

The European Union provides the best example of a regional association of nations that has both deepened and widened its trading relationships through the various stages outlined above. This supra-national development, which first began with the Treaty of Rome in 1957, has provoked different reactions from other countries around the world – from applications to join from near neighbours; to negotiations for concessions from distant partners fearful of being shut out; to the establishment of other regional groupings of countries seeking to rival the EU's growing economic influence.

The most notable recent example of another regional association is the *North American Free Trade Agreement* (NAFTA), signed between the USA, Mexico and Canada in December 1992. It will be instructive to examine NAFTA first as an illustration of the issues involved in the economics of free trade, and then later to look at the EU in more detail as we go on to consider matters related to closer economic integration.

NAFTA

The background to NAFTA is marked by the changing attitudes and economic policies between the three partner countries during the 1980s. There is a long history of unease on the part of both Canada and Mexico of being swamped by a closer relationship with the very much larger US economy. Nonetheless, the oil crisis of the 1970s (see chapter 9), followed by the recessionary 1980s brought about a gradual change in thinking. As has already been outlined in the previous chapter, a growing shift in world economic opinion towards more free-market policies was gathering pace.

For both Canada and the USA, the potential benefits from increasing liberalisation of trade under the latest round of GATT talks were eagerly awaited and the longer the Uruguay round dragged on (thanks to European blocking over agriculture) the more a fall-back position of at least free trade throughout North America became attractive. Negotiations for a US–Canada deal began in earnest in 1986 and, despite fierce opposition from some worried Canadians, a free trade agreement was secured between these two countries in 1987, eventually ratified and carried into effect on 1 January 1989.

It can be argued that the difficulties of reaching accord between Canada and the USA are not great, given that culturally and in terms of living standards these two nations are not so very far apart. Although a vociferous (especially Canadian) minority would disagree, certainly the general mistrust of and resistance to closer Mexican–US ties was greater. Mexican economic history reveals foreign, especially US, dominance of much of its industry, including railways, oil, mining, banks and plantation agriculture – particularly through 'el porfiriato': the 1876–1910 rule of General Porfirio Diaz. After the revolution of 1910 the Mexican economy has been characterised by a fear of dependency on foreigners, a dominant government sector, widespread nationalisations and the promotion of import substitution industries behind a wall of protectionist tariffs. The spiralling debt crisis of the early 1980s, however (see chapter 10), the inefficiencies of much of the domestic economy and the growing need for a vibrant export sector all signalled a sharp about-turn in the Mexican economic strategy. Started in the 1980s by President Miguel de Madrid as a way of negotiating debt relief, the free-market reforms were stepped up by his successor, President Carlos Salinas, who opened the way to NAFTA talks in 1990. The Agreement was finally signed between Presidents Salinas, George Bush of the USA and Prime Minister Brian Mulroney of Canada in December 1992. Newly elected US President Bill Clinton negotiated additional accords on environmental issues and labour laws in 1993 and NAFTA came into effect on 1 January 1994.

NAFTA commits the three participant countries to the elimination of all tariffs and quotas between them within fifteen years. Non-tariff barriers, such as different product safety standards, are subject to decision by a trinational panel of judges. Trade relations with third parties are not affected, however. North America thus becomes a free trade area, not a customs union.

Cross-border investment between the USA, Canada and Mexico is now much encouraged by NAFTA, so the mobility of capital *is* allowed for, as in a common market, though this is not extended to labour. (The contentious issue of increasing illegal Mexican migration to the USA has been one of the alleged advantages supporting the NAFTA accord: insofar as free trade facilitates rapid economic growth in Mexico, the flood of illegals moving north looking for work should eventually cease – which will be to the relief of the authorities on both sides of the border.)

THE THEORY OF COMPARATIVE ADVANTAGE

It is time now to examine in more depth the economic argument for free trade that underlies all the developments outlined above. How is it that reducing trade barriers should lead to increasing wealth and welfare for the countries concerned? Will all benefit equally, or will free trade lead to a widening gap between rich and poor?

The economic theory of international trade and *comparative advantage* is at the heart of this debate and we need to understand this analysis more fully if we are to understand the drive behind GATT, regional associations like the EU and NAFTA and indeed all bilateral and multilateral trade liberalising deals.

We may begin by considering the case of a number of trading countries, each with its own unique endowment of natural resources. It should be seen that instead of each one trying to provide for their domestic needs independently, all countries benefit by specialising in what they are best at and then trading with others in order to purchase, at less cost, what others produce. Free trade thereby enables specialisation, increased production and thus higher standards of living for all participants.

The same principle acts for any individual student: on leaving college a large market society enables the graduate to specialise in his or her chosen employment, selling skills for an income that allows him/her to purchase a far wider range of goods and services than could ever be provided for by the student in isolation.

Although particularly relevant to European nations of similar size and development, it should be emphasised that the theory of free trade as just outlined is also relevant to a small, relatively less-developed country doing business with a larger, wealthier neighbour – say Mexico with the USA.

It might be asked, what has a rich country got to gain in trade with a poorer neighbour when it can produce everything more efficiently itself? Or, conversely, might not a smaller country suffer exploitation from its larger trade partner?

Clearly these arguments are incompatible. They cannot *both* be true.

The same can be said for the following pair of arguments: producers in high-wage countries can often be heard claiming that they can never hope to compete with cheap labour industries in the developing world and so some government support is thus argued as essential. Equally in poor countries other critics can be heard demanding exactly the same sort of assistance because they cannot compete with Western high technology, i.e. cheap capital.

All these arguments are false. Even where trading partners are completely mismatched, economics can demonstrate that both parties may benefit from free trade. This principle was first established in 1817 by economist David Ricardo: the principle of comparative advantage.

Consider again the case of individuals. Why should a doctor, for example, employ a secretary to type letters which she could do more quickly herself? *This is exactly the same question as*: why should the USA buy manufactured goods, clothing and foodstuffs from Mexico that it could just as easily produce itself?

I hope you can see the answer. It is a better, more cost-effective use of resources for the doctor to devote her time to medicine than to waste 20 minutes or so typing a letter. Her less-competent secretary may spend half an hour on the same task but then her time is less valuable and the doctor can meanwhile get on with some more beneficial employment. Similarly, US resources could be devoted to self-sufficiency in clothing, but it is more efficient to import much of this and concentrate on higher tech. products. For their part, the (currently) less-efficient Mexican producers can find a market for their produce, will gain better incomes than if they were confined to domestic sales alone and may start the process of improving their skills and development prospects.

In economics, we say the doctor possesses absolute advantages in both medicine and typing, but a comparative advantage in only one: the former. The secretary has absolute *dis*advantage in both practices but a comparative advantage in typing. Similarly, in trade with the USA, Mexico has a comparative advantage in lower-tech., labour-intensive industries like manufacturing assembly and clothing.

It is this important principle of comparative advantage which determines the direction of trade. Once this is understood, a country is well on its way to concentrating its resources, establishing trade and increasing economic growth.

This point is sufficiently important to warrant further investigation. Consider the case of Japan. There are those who consider this country to be a Far Eastern power-house that can outcompete European and American business in all sorts of world markets. From the analysis just presented you should be able to see that it is impossible for Japan to possess a comparative advantage in *all* its industries. In practice, the growth of Korean, Taiwanese, Hong Kong, Singaporean, Malaysian and Thai manufacturing industries – Asian dragons that have grown up in Japan's own back yard – prove the point. This leads to an important finding: comparative advantage is a *dynamic*, not a static, concept. In 1950 Japan had no advantage in producing cars and motorcycles. Nor in 1960 did Mexico possess any advantage in producing consumer durables like cars, computers and other electronic products; nor even in producing sizable quantities of oil and gas. But in free-market society where: (1) prices are flexible; (2) consumers exercise choice; and (3) resources are free to move their employment, then industries will grow and decline. Comparative advantage will keep changing.

A secretary may not want to be a secretary for ever – she may want to train to be a doctor. Mexico may not want to specialise in cheap-labour industries for ever but may want to secure economic growth and, in time, produce sophisticated high-quality goods and services. Free trade offers a pathway to progress. Countries have to start somewhere. Unless Mexico (and all other countries) can sell its produce in unrestricted markets it cannot begin to reap the benefits of specialisation, trade and growth.

The dynamics of the free market are behind the thrust to implement NAFTA, to enlarge its membership to include others (such as Chile) and in the impetus it has given to other Latin American groupings such as Mercosur (a fledgling customs union between Brazil, Argentina, Paraguay and Uruguay) and CARICOM (the Caribbean Community of West Indian states).

THE COSTS OF FREE TRADE

This analysis of free trade does not deny, however, that there *are* very real costs involved. This chapter started with the assertion that the dynamics of creative destruction impose misery on selected communities in all trading countries. It is for this reason that free trade agreements are usually phased into operation over a number of years. Additionally, public authorities and vested interests in the negotiation process have an important responsibility to monitor the distribution of costs and benefits involved amongst the people affected.

With respect to NAFTA, disadvantages cited include the alleged increasing polarisation or dualism of economic society throughout all of North America. It is argued, for example, that the multinational, Mexican-based *maquiladoras* or assembly plants set up to serve the US market have bled jobs away from north of the border, have generated increased profits for their owners and managers, yet have built few local linkages through which to contribute much towards the host economy south of the Rio Grande (see Harry Brown, *For Richer, For Poorer – Shaping US–Mexican Integration*, Latin American Bureau, 1994).

There is undoubtedly some painful US labour experience behind these criticisms, but even if there is a limit to low-skilled assembly line jobs (which there will not be if free trade stimulates economic growth), it can still be argued that it is better in the short run that they be diverted to those parts of the continent where there is a higher concentration of such workers and where educational, re-training and labour-market opportunities are least developed. That is, even in a stagnant market, redundant US workers would be better placed to find new work than Mexican ones since they have better access to supportive welfare and labour-market infrastructure. (It is, of course, not much consolation for unemployed US car workers to learn that Mexico has a comparative advantage in their type of work and that Mexican workers are more needy anyway. . . . These sort of movements in world economic forces require sensitive management.) In the longer term, these fears are proving groundless as free trade stimulates more efficient deployment of resources, increased growth and more (though changing) job opportunities for all. For example, US exports to Mexico, and domestic employment therefrom, have risen as tariffs have come down since the mid-1980s.

The assertion that new, export-oriented industrial developments in Mexico build few links with the domestic economy is a more serious criticism and strikes at the heart of the principle of comparative advantage with respect to less-developed countries. This argument deserves close examination.

According to theory, as large and small trading partners reduce barriers, separate markets increasingly become one. There can only be one price for each good or service traded in a single market and inevitably the dominant influence on prices will come from the larger, richer economy. That is, Mexican exports – and Mexican labour services – will thus increasingly sell for higher, US/Canadian prices. The distribution of gains from free trade are thus predicted to be greater for the smaller economy. This is known as 'the importance of being unimportant'.

The macroeconomic impact of increasing export earnings will be magnified thanks to the *foreign trade multiplier* – injections to the domestic economy stimulate a rise in national income commensurate with the marginal propensity to consume (refer back to chapter 3). This may at first be regionally focused where export industries are located in certain development zones (e.g. in the Mexican case, in border towns such as Ciudad Juarez, Tijuana and Nogales) but eventually the beneficial effects must ripple through the entire economy as second- and third-round incomes rise.

The most important gains from trade, however, come from the long-term impact of increasing international competition for local industry. Providing the immediate trauma of adjusting to change is phased in carefully, local businesses learn to adapt to international prices, quality standards, and the demands of consumers. Efficiency gains are high. National resources move to employments that are internationally competitive. *Economies of scale* can be enjoyed in selling to far larger markets than are available within the domestic economy alone. Even where such free-market changes are not phased in but impact with a big bang, the evidence from such countries as far apart as the People's Republic of China, Poland and Chile is that short-term costs are eventually outweighed by long-term recovery.

THE CHALLENGE FOR MEXICO

All such benefits require, however, that the economy involved is responsive to market incentives. If, in the case of Mexico, the *maquiladoras* are, indeed, screwdriver plants where skills transmitted are few; if all inputs are imported, and if there is little involvement of the local economy in producing components and providing services then *dualism* results: a rich, westernised enclave co-exists with a poor hinterland but none of the economic benefits mentioned above are transmitted across the barbed-wire fence which divides them. The gulf between the modern enclave and the surrounding community is culturally and economically as wide as the distance between New York and Mexico City.

'Underdeveloped' countries are defined as such in the Western, economic sense. They may be highly developed with regard to their own cultural identity, which has evolved over centuries. They may, however, be relatively unresponsive to modern market signals. Development, therefore, means building bridges across the divide. The early foreign investments in Mexican assembly plants were not motivated by this ideal, and most are still not. But enlightened self-interest on the part of business management and government officials, at local and national levels, can do much to dismantle barriers and to encourage positive economic interchange. Many entrepreneurial talents lie dormant in poor communities, and the appropriate skills and opportunities to develop them require nurturing. Cultural differences, values, hierarchical and dependent social relationships that are embodied in traditional patterns of land ownership and the colonial inheritance cannot be simply wished away and rapidly assimilated into modern industrial structures.

NAFTA can bring, and is bringing, the benefits of free trade to Mexico, but the distribution of these benefits is inevitably uneven. It takes time and a determined sense of direction in government to build bridges to all sectors of the community. The fewer restrictions on social and economic mobility, the more the gains from trade will be widespread. Mexico, however, is a profoundly unequal society where the income gap between rich and poor *widened* during the 1980s. Increasing free trade, liberalising markets, removing exchange controls and privatising state industries without doing more to reform ownership patterns, regressive tax systems and restricted entitlement to education and health programmes runs the risk of further concentrating wealth in a capitalist elite and alienating the rest. Just as NAFTA was being celebrated in affluent districts of Mexico City and in the development zones along Mexico's northern border region, so Zapatista rebels in the southern state of Chiapas forcibly reminded their countryfolk that the national economy lacks the flexible political, social and economic framework to engage all its people in the development process.

In purely economic terms, the arguments in favour of free trade are far greater than those against – any elementary textbook will emphasise this. But all the economic benefits which flow from the application of the principle of comparative advantage are based on the assumption that the countries involved possess the preconditions, the infrastructure, the social dynamism and cohesion to make the necessary changes and enjoy the rewards therefrom. Wherever there are market rigidities – for example, entrenched social attitudes and/or political restrictions that inhibit geographical and occupational mobility – then the gains from trade will bid up wages and profits of those with scarce talents and will increase the sense of frustration and loss of those excluded from the wealth-creating process.

As Mexico is finding out, as weary East Europeans have discovered and also as mature industrial economies such as the USA and the UK know to their cost, opening up free trade is not a fully automatic, value-free economic policy that can be implemented by the central government with a 'hands-off', let-the-markets-decide attitude to the allocation of the country's resources. Microeconomic intervention is necessary to facilitate training, dismantle barriers and to provide access to new employment opportunities throughout the economy, wherever rigidities occur. The process may be slow and in many cases governments may be as prone to failure as the markets they are attempting to reform.

There are no easy answers. How are revolutionary Zapatistas who want access to better land, education, jobs and incomes to be persuaded to lay down their arms and return to their peasant holdings? How are richer middle classes who have voted for the economic restructuring and have appropriated its benefits to be persuaded to identify with the poor and indeed to pay for the improved conditions they demand?

Applying the principle of comparative advantage needs careful management, therefore. This is usually recognised in theory in the case of *infant industries*: that is, granting a level of protection to fragile industrial start-ups that are not yet strong enough to withstand the gales of international competition. The protection is supposedly removed when the infant is strong enough to look after itself and thus free trade may return again to rule. In poorer countries where large fragments of the economy may be underdeveloped, the infant industry argument can be used to justify more widespread protection and intervention. If coordinated in a national, integrated manner, rather than in a piecemeal, business-by-business fashion prompted by powerful interest groups, then the overall result can be a *strategic trade policy*, as used with effect by Japan and certain newly industrialised countries such as South Korea, Taiwan or Singapore.

STRATEGIC TRADE POLICIES

The idea of a coherent trade policy is not to obstruct the workings of free trade but to facilitate them – so as to better exploit the opportunities offered by comparative advantage. Government intervention is urged to raise productivity generally and to help make the country's economy more competitive. Where substantial *external economies* exist in the provision of social infrastructure – educational reform, research and development, transport and communications – where efficiency gains and scale economies require time to learn, and where local capital markets are insufficiently responsive to support developing industry, then properly targeted government subsidies and protection can compensate for the inadequacies of the free market.

Countries with low savings and investment, inadequate capital stock, failing educational systems and poor communications and other public utilities prevent their private business sectors from competing on equal terms with other trading nations. Over time, with such impoverished social capital, a country's comparative advantage is bound to trade down to relatively lower-tech., lower income-earning specialisms. (It is precisely this argument that worries many US and European commentators who fear that their mature, rigidified economies are insufficiently equipped to meet the long-term competitive challenge from fast-developing Asian 'dragons'. Brown and Hogendorn [*International Economics*, Addison Wesley, 1994], for example, quote that one in four students studying for a doctorate in the USA comes from Taiwan – a country with a population 8 per cent of that of the US.)

Japan provides the best-known example of a country which uses a strategic trade policy. Its relevance today may be questioned – Japan's success in world trade now is not just due to overt government direction – but the role of this policy in aiding Japan's development in the past may be instructive for the Mexicos of today.

The typical, developing-country scarcity of entrepreneurial resources and the concentration of economic power in a business elite led in Japan's case to a series of interlocking groups controlling major industrial enterprises, banks, trading companies and government agencies. Rather than promote protection, corruption and the cosy guarantee of personal enrichment, however, the driving ethic of a cohesive and integrated Japanese entrepreneurial class has been to set guidelines for national economic development – a combination of free enterprise and government direction that has existed since the Meiji Restoration of 1868.

Since World War II in particular, government agencies such as the powerful Ministry of Trade and Industry (MITI) have implemented an industrial policy of identifying and supporting winners in international trade: promoting exports, guaranteeing low-cost loans and subsidies, sponsoring research and development and establishing industrial standards which effectively become non-tariff barriers to foreign competitors. During the 1950s, foreign technology was copied systematically in targeted industries. Such technology provided the foundation on which to build successful products. Later high rates of savings, investment and innovation enabled Japanese technology to overtake foreign competitors in an increasing number of industries.

Japan sought first to develop its shipbuilding industry: it had been destroyed in the war, and as an island economy success in trade was dependent on shipping. Rebuilding and modernising the steel industry was also a priority. By 1956 Japan had become the world's biggest shipbuilder and was fast becoming a leading steel exporter as well. The emphasis next turned to developing motorcycles and a car industry. (In 1951 Honda was a small, unheard-of family business. It is not now.) This was followed by consumer electronics which in turn has led to a concentration in computers, artificial intelligence and frontier technologies.

Original protective tariffs on Japanese industry have long since come down. With the exception of agriculture (comparatively inefficient, but protected for social reasons) Japan is now an open economy. Its continuing trade surplus today is a result of a highly efficient manufacturing export sector and, despite criticisms, it is not the result of restrictions on imports, as some would assert.

A less well known, but equally important component of Japan's strategic trade policy has been not only to pick industrial winners, but also to facilitate disinvestment in declining industry. This is because a market economy grows through a process of continuous industrial renewal – creative destruction – which requires *losers* as well as winners. Again, in Japan's case, selected industries have been targeted to be run down. Companies involved are encouraged to diversify into more profitable product lines; depreciation allowances to write off old capital and subsidies for new plant and equipment are granted; labour unions are involved from the outset in planning transfers to alternative employments. Much industrial retraining is undertaken by firms in cooperation with local government. As a result, the Japanese shipbuilding industry in the 1990s is less than half the size it was in 1980, steel is contracting severely, many coal mines are shut down and capacity in other heavy industries has been greatly reduced.

The overall impression created therefore is one of a successful partnership between government and industry. State intervention is devoted not to inhibit free trade but to enhance it. In the case of Japan and other Asian dragons this partnership is the outcome of a particular social inheritance, but even so the impression should not be created that such success is easily come by – it requires hard work on the part of all parties in a bargaining process to reach agreement.

CONCLUSION

The final conclusion offered here is that the principle of comparative advantage provides for substantial benefits in trade, but market economies must be flexible enough to respond to the changing dynamics of international commerce. In less-developed countries in particular, where the geographical spread of the modern market sector may be limited and entrepreneurial resources may be scarce, governments need to work with business to design the appropriate policies in order to establish the infrastructure, the preconditions necessary to secure economic development for all.

In the more mature economies of Europe – flexible in some ways, traditionally resistant to change in others – the gains from trade have so overcome the historical rivalry between these countries that further economic integration has been pursued along the spectrum from free trade areas through customs unions to a common market. It is to this analysis we turn in the following chapter.

KEY WORDS

Economies of scale If a business can increase its scale of operations by, say, doubling all inputs it may make cost savings such that it can more than double its outputs.

Take a simple box. If you double its dimensions you will need four times as much material to make it, but its volume will increase by eight times. The average cost of storing the box's contents falls, therefore, by half. All businesses involved in storing processing and transporting large volumes can exploit this economy of scale. There are a number of other advantages of bigness – for example, a large firm can bargain for discounts on all its purchases – but a business can only benefit from these economies of scale if it has a big market it can sell to.

The European Union A common market of (at the time of writing) fifteen European nations: Belgium, the Netherlands, Luxembourg, Germany, Italy, France, the United Kingdom, Ireland, Denmark, Greece, Spain, Portugal, Austria, Sweden and Finland. The Union will undoubtedly widen its membership and deepen its integration but how and when is the matter of intense debate.

Free rider Where sufficient fee-paying customers exist, trains will run to provide them with service – thus allowing the occasional passenger to ride free if he/she can avoid detection. Obviously the business cannot survive if everyone attempts to free ride. The concept has been widened to include anyone who benefits from cheating when everyone else follows the rules.

Mercantilism A seventeenth-century political philosophy which emphasised the importance of promoting foreign trade surpluses and securing commercial advantage over rival states.

A **quota** is a fixed limit placed on the number of imports allowed into a country. Although the volume of imports is limited, their price may be forced upward (due to scarcity) and thus total spending on them may not fall much, if at all.

A **tariff** is a tax on imports. It raises costs to foreign suppliers, reduces their revenues and thereby reduces a country's spending on imports.

QUESTIONS

1 What are the economic benefits to be gained from removing restrictions to international trade? What are the costs involved?
2 Regional trade blocs are becoming increasingly important in world trade. What are the nature of these trade arrangements; what are the reasons for their growth; and are there any economic dangers in the continuance of this trend?
3 Examine the case for (a) enlarging NAFTA to include other Latin American countries; (b) deepening the economic integration between Canada, the USA and Mexico beyond a free trade area.
4 How can less-developed countries limit the spread of 'dualism' in their economies?
5 Should governments intervene to manage their country's trade or are international markets best left alone?

FURTHER READING

Brown, W. B. and Hogendorn, J. S. *International Economics*. Addison Wesley, 1994.
Browne, H. *For Richer, For Poorer*. Latin American Bureau, 1994.

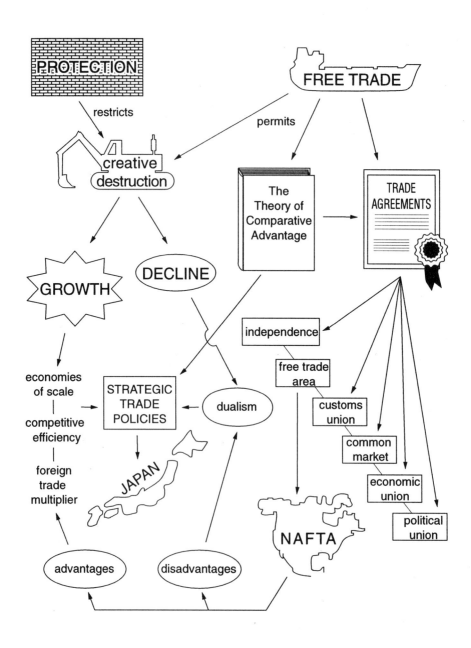

PROTECTION

FREE TRADE

restricts

permits

creative destruction

The Theory of Comparative Advantage

TRADE AGREEMENTS

GROWTH

DECLINE

independence

free trade area

economies of scale

STRATEGIC TRADE POLICIES

dualism

customs union

competitive efficiency

JAPAN

common market

foreign trade multiplier

economic union

NAFTA

political union

advantages

disadvantages

6 Customs unions and common markets

Topics to be considered in this chapter

- The economic theory of customs unions:
  i   trade creation
  ii trade diversion
- Criteria for a successful union
- Common markets and the effect of mobile resources
- The European experience
- Non-tariff barriers

INTRODUCTION

Freeing up trade between partner countries brings increasing economic benefits and such results may thus fuel arguments for even closer integration. In the case of the European Union, this drive for closer relations began on 1 January 1958 with the creation of a customs union between the original six founder members – Belgium, the Netherlands, Luxembourg, Italy, France and West Germany – with the objective to form a common market with overtly political as well as economic aims. The Treaty of Rome, signed on 25 March 1957, committed the participants to the 'promotion of peace', 'increased prosperity' and 'ever closer union among the peoples of Europe'.

Other European countries were not ready at this time to commit themselves to such binding objectives and so the United Kingdom, Norway, Sweden, Denmark, Austria, Portugal and Switzerland preferred instead to establish the European Free Trade Area (EFTA) in 1960. As it turned out, however, the greater economic success of the (then) European Economic Community later drew in the UK, Ireland and Denmark in 1973; Greece became a full member in 1981, and Portugal and Spain joined in 1986. EFTA has now effectively dismantled itself with Austria, Finland and Sweden in 1995 all becoming members of the EU. As for the future, applications to join the European Union include those from Hungary,

Poland and the Czech Republic, and there is talk of them being accepted as members some time after the year 2000.

THE ECONOMIC THEORY OF CUSTOMS UNIONS

The tighter customs union of a group of trading countries all maintaining a *common external tariff* (CET) against outsiders raises important economic issues that are distinct from free trade areas (FTAs) and thus warrant separate analysis.

One of the features of a FTA is that member countries practise independent policies with respect to the rest of the world, and this fact can be exploited by outsiders. There is nothing to stop, say, West Indian cane sugar being imported into one low-tariff country (like the UK when it belonged to EFTA) and then being redirected within the association to a higher-tariff partner (say, Switzerland). Importing countries wishing to frustrate this tariff dodging have to apply costly, complex and (frequently) ineffective ways to identify trade origins. This difficulty of trying to impose rules of origin documentation on EFTA trade actually acted as a form of non-tariff barrier to all commerce between member countries.

A customs union does not have this problem. There is no way into the sheltered market by breaching the external wall at its lowest point, since all member countries have a common tariff. The EC was thus able to enjoy right from its beginnings much freer trade between all its participants.

But such internal freedom comes at the cost of creating a potentially far greater problem – a 'fortress Europe' mentality. Locking-in trade between member countries of a customs union creates a large market place of pooled economies in which all can share, but this is at the expense of denying free access to other countries, and the potential gains from trade that they may bring. How far beneficial trade is created, on the one hand, and blocked, on the other, is difficult to measure in the real world (how can you know what might have been?), but there are a number of guiding principles.

The issue to examine here is *trade creation* versus *trade diversion*.

Trade creation

When countries first join a customs union there is an initial impetus to trade due to the removal of barriers between them. If the economies involved are relatively large and diverse then the efficient industries in each will gain from the enlarged market; the less efficient will suffer from the increased competition.

The consumption effect of trade creation will be that each country now benefits from an increased selection of goods and services provided by a wider range of producers, and prices will be driven down in all member countries to the lowest level that prevailed before the union.

The production effect of trade creation is that, as the sales and profits expand in the more efficient producers, so resources from the less-successful businesses will transfer to this better paid employment. (Assuming a customs union, not a common market, the redeployment of resources at this stage takes place within each member country, not between them.) Increased competition within the union promotes the eventual dynamic gains of more efficient industrial practices, plus the economies of scale available in a larger market.

Trade diversion

Trade diversion, on the other hand, occurs when one member country previously imported commodities from a low-cost, more efficient third-party producer, but subsequent to the introduction of the customs union now finds these imports shut out by a high external tariff. Consumption must now turn to the purchase of higher-cost alternatives provided by a less-efficient domestic or partner-country producer.

The production effect of trade diversion is that resources are now kept employed in protected, inefficient industries rather than being made to search out more productive, more competitive destinations.

It should be appreciated from this analysis, therefore, that not all trade that is generated within a customs union is necessarily beneficial. Some or even much of it may be instead of what could be more economic trading relationships elsewhere.

For example, a new European initiative to produce, say, helicopters or computers in some Anglo-French joint venture is bound to be trumpeted in the press as a great economic benefit by the politicians and industrialists involved. This should not obscure the fact, however, that – depending on the costs involved – it might be wiser for Europeans to purchase American or Japanese products and devote Anglo-French resources to other employments where their technological edge (i.e. comparative advantage) is stronger.

If closer European integration is the result of erecting trade barriers against the USA and Japan, rather than the outcome of fundamental economic compatibilities, then such integration will profit no one. A customs union that promotes internal growth only by reducing its trade links with the outside world will not produce an efficient reallocation of shared resources in the long run.

So long as common external tariffs are maintained, then whether the overall impact of economic integration is a valid cause for increased prosperity depends on the balance of the beneficial trade creating effects versus the harmful trade diverting effects of the union.

If growth in European trade and incomes by itself is no indicator of the benefits of economic integration, what is? Under what circumstances is a given customs union on the whole trade creating or trade diverting?

CRITERIA FOR A SUCCESSFUL CUSTOMS UNION

Competing, not complementary economies

If member-country economies prior to union are similar – that is, they tend to be competing in the same markets at home and abroad – then the eventual customs union will most likely be trade creating. If the original economies are complementary – for example, one being a primary producer, the other being a manufacturer – then closer integration may be trade divertingly inefficient.

This at first sight seems confusing. But think of it this way: market *competition always breeds efficiency*, through a process of survival of the fittest. Two competing countries with rival industries, each with slightly different cost structures will cause the relatively less efficient businesses in both countries to decline, with resources thus switching to the more efficient ones. Note that the initial impact is negative – much publicised unemployment – but in the longer term the size of the united market has grown for all, so the potential for redeployment must be good. There is a beneficial trade creating effect: resources are now more efficiently allocated within each country compared to before.

Now consider the other scenario. A customs union with complementary, non-competitive industries will dovetail neatly together at first – one country perhaps producing the raw materials which supply the other – but neither partner now has any competitive impulse to improve. Both nations are protected by CETs from foreign rivals. Domestic consumers and employers which might have preferred to purchase lower-cost foreign produce/inputs have their trade now diverted to less efficient, more costly domestic goods and services.

Low common external tariffs

Protection promotes inefficiency. Trade diversion will therefore be less the lower the general level of CETs. A customs union is a second-best alternative to all-round free trade. The nearer a CU approaches this free trade ideal, the greater the benefits to incomes and growth for all.

When the United Kingdom joined the EU it had to submit to the community's *Common Agricultural Policy*. The trade diverting effect of this has been to support British and other European farmers at the expense of cheaper foreign producers. The fact that New Zealand can produce better lamb and dairy produce and the West Indies cheaper sugar means that resources are tied up in European agriculture that would be more economically employed elsewhere, and consumers end up paying more. In fact, for at least the last twenty years one of the on-going political struggles within the EU has been to try and reduce the agricultural CET, and, although still discriminatory, trade diversion now is less than it would otherwise have been.

Negotiations within the EU's agricultural commission, and between the EU and GATT have been lengthy and, at times, bitter. The focus has shifted within the EU away from insisting on protective price supports (which act as trade-excluding tariffs) to providing more income and welfare payments to farmers (which have a somewhat less distortionary effect on trade). As a result the European CET has come down, but there is still substantial trade diversion. The losers continue to be farmers in North America, Australasia and numerous developing countries; and European consumers.

More members

The larger the union, the more countries that can join the free trade zone, the larger and more widespread will be the benefits. Clearly the economic resources that can be reallocated and the trade creating benefits that can be generated therefrom depend on the geographical size of the union. The gains from specialisation and economies of scale applicable from the union of the Benelux countries (the forerunner to the EU) were minuscule compared to what is now possible within the European Union. In education, for example, there may not be an enormous demand for specialists in International Economics if the market extends only as far as the borders of the Low Countries. In a unified European market, however, whole university departments are possible as small niche markets become big ones. That is as true in Dresden as it is in Durham; in electronics as well as education. And as the European market widens towards the East so more trade will be created: British manufacturers will be able to sell extra to Hungary, Polish farmers can increase sales to Germany.

Little diversity

In order to best benefit from the economies of large-scale production – where costs and prices can be kept down for all – the market should be homogenous; with little diversity. A large European market is not large if it is fragmented into small product areas where consumer tastes and preferences are diverse and must be separately catered for. The more that participants of a union perceive themselves to be different to other groups, therefore, the less scope there is to profit from a common market.

This important point is very relevant to a continent as culturally varied as Europe. In the Americas, two consumers living 3,000 miles apart speak the same language, live the same lifestyle and respond to the same advertising campaigns. The same is not true in Europe where selling something as mundane as a chocolate bar in northern France requires a totally different psychology to selling it in southern England. Thousands of years of history have bred differences in prejudices that neighbours in the same town in places like the former Yugoslavia, Northern Ireland and Spain still fight, and die, over.

Flexible technology

The need to cater for local differences in consumer tastes can to an increasing extent be responded to using modern, flexible technology allied to an educated and highly skilled workforce. Manufacturing techniques are becoming more and more sophisticated in custom-designing products at relatively low cost. It used to be: 'any colour you want, so long as it's black!' The premium that had to be paid to satisfy individual preference was prohibitively high. This is no longer the case today, thanks especially to pioneering Japanese-style manufacturing innovation. Small runs of production can be as economic as long runs for an increasing array of sophisticated goods and services. Computerised systems can re-tool assembly lines and switch products in minutes today – a process which used to take months and even years in the past.

The difficulties presented by the fragmentation of markets in culturally diverse unions, therefore, can be considerably reduced by modern technology. The gains from trade are enhanced.

Foreign direct investment

High external tariffs – whether erected by individual countries or by customs unions – have prompted in the past much *foreign direct investment* (fdi). Japanese and American multinational corporations, fearful of being shut out of a fortress Europe, have set up their own factories in Britain, Germany, Spain, etc. to serve as a base from which to sell to all of Europe, without restriction. Certain European industrialists and politicians have on occasions complained about allowing such foreign rivals inside the protective union, but in fact the result is greater gains in efficiency and a reduction in trade diversion. Insofar as CETs can be by-passed by foreign direct investment then domestic industry cannot be sheltered from international competition. Philips, for example, the giant Dutch consumer electronics producer, has had to drastically shake up its organisation in order to face up to the challenge from Sony and other multinationals in Europe, let alone in the rest of the world; and so long as Europeans continue to buy Nissan cars produced in the northeast of England then Rover Cars and Ford UK must also revolutionise their production facilities and practices in order to match Japanese efficiency. Wherever incompetence has nowhere to hide it must be cut out.

THE ECONOMIC THEORY OF COMMON MARKETS

This last point introduces the notion of moving capital across national frontiers. Just such an issue separates a customs union from a common market – where not only goods and services but also labour and capital are free to move among member countries. The impact of this next phase of increasing economic integration means that now resources may not only be reallocated *within* European nations but also *between* them.

The free flow of people between countries will inevitably be slowed by social factors – even if there is a complete matching of skills. A lawyer in Madrid, for example, may not wish to leave family, friends and business contacts in order to work in Milan. The absence of a homogenous European market makes such mobility even slower: legal systems in both countries are different. Labour movement will still take place, indeed it is in the process of so doing, but it will take time.

With financial markets, however, mobility is already here. Large sums of liquid capital flow all over Europe and around the world to take advantage of marginal differences in rates of profit. As Europe moves closer to full economic and monetary union we can expect more and more investment to flow in and out of partner countries. What are the implications of such increased capital mobility?

It is important to emphasise at this point that we are concerned here with long-term *investment capital* – that is, money that flows into a country in order to set up an increase in productive capital, a new factory, for example – and not speculative flows of funds that are simply taking advantage of differential exchange or interest rates in order to make a financial gain. (This latter issue is touched upon in the chapter on currency union, below.)

There are contrasting views on the issue of mobility of productive capital and a resort to economic theory is necessary to explain them.

Consider two possible locations for capital investment: one in the heart of Europe, the other in the periphery. One, say, in the lower Rhine valley, the other in the upper Douro in Portugal. It may well be that the opportunities for profitable investment in the Rhineland 'core' are many and widespread; those in the periphery in the Douro are more limited in extent. Be that as it may, assume that the rate of return on investment in the two locations is different: what can we predict will happen?

With no restriction on capital mobility, funds will flow out of the less-profitable investment location and into the more-profitable one. This has two effects: one in each centre.

As capital moves out of the less-profitable site the supply of investment funds dries up and as a result their increased scarcity begins to drive up rates of return. Conversely, funds moving into the more-profitable location begin to satiate demand. Profit rates must fall. So long as any difference in rates persists, funds will move between the two locations until any discrepancy is eroded. The conclusion reached, therefore, is that the mobility of capital between different countries will eventually bring about an equilibrium in profit rates between them.

Actually this theoretical conclusion needs to be amended a little because there are reasons why capital may not be quite as internationally mobile as implied; why differential rates of profit may persist in rival centres. For example, the risk of currency fluctuation may be a disincentive to move funds across borders. Lack of information or uncertainty over cultural differences may similarly impede movement. Nonetheless the analysis can be adjusted to conclude that profit rates in both centres will converge to a differential that accounts for the divergence in risk assessment. Oporto, therefore, may evolve a rate of normal profits that is x per cent above that ruling in Frankfurt to compensate for the perceived higher risk factor.

So far this adjusted analysis supports the general contention that countries have nothing to lose from removing all restrictions on the long-term movement of capital. Donor countries and recipient countries alike both benefit from a more efficient, more profitable employment of European resources. Capital moves across frontiers in pursuit of greater profits; capitalists in periphery countries that are exporting their funds stand to earn greater incomes. There may be a fall in labour employment at first in these sites as capital investments such as new manufacturing plant transfer to the core, but total incomes rise in both countries so winners have more than enough to compensate losers, it is alleged.

There is a powerful argument, however, against this conventional view of the positive outcome of free market forces as applied to capital mobility. Criticism focuses particularly on the limited scope of this analysis: it assumes that only one factor (capital) is mobile and that *all other factors remain constant*.

Given this restrictive assumption, the conclusion is valid. But other factors are very likely to change in a Europe of increasing economic integration. In a dynamically changing environment there may be many forces at work that shift the profitability perspective in both capital-donor and capital-recipient countries.

EXTERNAL ECONOMIES AND DISECONOMIES

Consider firstly the implications of inward investment to a vibrant and innovative core region. As more capital accumulates here there are a variety of reasons why profit rates may *not* fall. Certainly, there will be shortages of land, office space, certain labour skills, etc., which force up prices and act as an *external diseconomy* and disincentive for further capital inflow. Social costs of increased traffic congestion, pollution, possible crime, may also increase.

But these problems may spark off increased efforts to overcome them. There exist many economic benefits to regional concentration: *external economies* of increased competition and efficiency; the establishment of service and supportive industry; research and development; innovative technology; the growth of skills. If these benefits from concentration increase at a faster rate than the costs involved then the profit rate will not fall.

Employment opportunities for capital and labour (especially those with entrepreneurial skills) will not decrease, indeed they may act as a continual beacon to drain these resources away from the periphery.

By the same argument exactly the opposite effects are operating in the periphery (see figure 6.1).

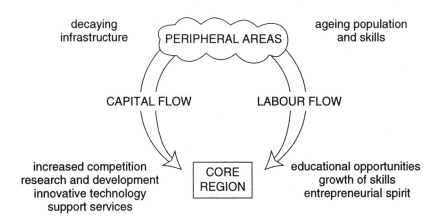

Figure 6.1

The most mobile, employable resources are moving out of the country. What gets left behind are those that are increasingly unemployable: an ageing capital stock; decaying infrastructure; inappropriate skills; out-of-date technologies; a market place of falling incomes and influence. Profit rates are shrinking faster than the attractions of return investment in this depopulating region can reverse.

As an illustration of these themes, British critics point to the problem of industrial decay in certain regions of the UK. Unemployment rates in Northern Ireland, South Wales and northeast England, for example, remain persistently above the national average. That such a phenomenon has lasted for well over half a century despite repeated central government efforts to reverse the pattern of decline is evidence that the centripetal forces which drain the peripheries of resources are strong and they are not easily reversed.

Some have predicted that just such an outcome awaits Europe: the unbridled effect of free-market forces operating on capital employed in Europe will generate cumulative growth in some countries and cumulative decline in others – but due to the severely proscribed powers of the Brussels bureaucracy, such polarising economic effects will occur without the mitigating effects of sufficient redistributive transfers from a strong central authority. Despite its economic difficulties, Northern Ireland continues to enjoy substantial income support from the UK. The same will not be true for poorer areas in a free-market Europe, it has been alleged (by Wynne Godley, of Cambridge University, amongst others).

Such pessimism may be a little overdone. What future awaits a European Union of mobile resources is impossible to predict with certainty. That incomes as a whole will grow is highly likely, notwithstanding the tendency for periodic slowdowns or recessions. That the distribution of incomes will change is equally likely. But to deduce from this that Europe will polarise into richer and poorer regions, accentuated over time, cannot be safely predicted. The centripetal model – where resources drain into the core region – is one possibility. The alternative scenario is a multipolar Europe, where growth centres arise in a number of regions – each exploiting its own comparative advantage. The immensely rich cultural diversity of Europe might be said to support this argument.

THE EUROPEAN EXPERIENCE

It is time now to look in a little more detail at the patchwork quilt of countries that together make up the European Union and examine how far they can be said to form a truly common market (see table 6.1).

No map or set of statistics by themselves, however, can completely capture the true nature of the heterogeneity of Europe. Centuries of commerce and conflict, nation-building and empire-building have bred regional differences that are impossible to simply summarise. Some parts of the continent have enjoyed stability, independence and freedom from dictatorship or invasion for nearly a thousand years; others are still at war, trying to define their national frontiers. Certain states have well-established, mature market economic systems with flourishing, outward-looking industrial and financial sectors; others are still struggling to make the transition out of peasant agriculture and centrally planned command systems.

The objective of attempting to generate increased prosperity via increased economic integration through all the stages from loose free trade areas to tighter and tighter unions inevitably involves so much more than economic issues. Given the enormous cultural, political and economic diversity of European nations referred to above, it is scarcely surprising that promoting the ever closer union of such disparate and partisan peoples is fraught with difficulty and delay.

DISMANTLING THE BARRIERS

The easy part was done first. Eliminating tariffs and quotas and constructing the common external tariff for the original six founder countries was achieved within ten years. The same process was repeated with each successive enlargement of the Union – when the UK, Ireland and Denmark joined in 1973 and again in the 1980s with Greece, Spain and Portugal. By the mid-1980s, therefore, all tariff barriers between the twelve member countries had disappeared. The customs union was officially in place.

Table 6.1 European nations: selected data

Country	Area 1,000 sq. km	Pop. mill. 1993	Pop. density 1993	GDP per head PPP 1992	% growth 1980–92	% export to EC 1992	% inv. 1992	% sav. 1992	Lang.
Belgium	30.5	10.0	329.9	17.1	2.0	74.8	20	23	Fle/Fr
Denmark	43.1	5.1	120.3	16.8	2.1	54.5	15	23	Danish
Germany	356.9	80.6	225.9	16.7	2.4*	54.1	21	28	German
Greece	132.0	10.3	78.4	7.8	1.0	64.2	18	9	Greek
Spain	504.0	39.1	77.5	12.1	2.9	66.3	23	20	Spanish
France	544.0	57.5	105.8	17.6	1.7	63.0	20	21	French
Ireland	70.0	3.5	50.7	12.0	3.4	74.2	16	28	English
Italy	301.0	56.9	189.0	16.4	2.2	57.7	19	20	Italian
Luxembourg	2.6	0.4	152.8	20.5	–	–	–	–	Fr/Ger
Netherlands	41.2	15.2	369.9	16.0	1.7	75.4	21	25	Dutch
Portugal	92.4	9.8	106.7	10.5	3.1	74.6	–	–	Portuguese
Utd Kingdom	244.1	57.9	237.4	15.4	2.4	55.5	15	14	English
Austria	83.9	7.9	94.3	17.0	2.0	66.1	25	26	German
Finland	337.1	5.0	15.0	13.8	2.0	53.2	17	19	Finnish
Sweden	450.0	8.7	19.3	15.8	1.5	55.8	17	18	Swedish

Source: Eurostat, World Bank.
Note: *W. Germany only.

Twelve different national markets still remained, however. The European common market of around 320 million (then) consumers was not a reality since, although internal tariffs had gone, establishing the four freedoms of unrestricted movement for all goods, services, labour and capital, and the 'level playing field' for all competing firms was (and still is) frustrated by national differences embodied in numerous *non-tariff barriers*.

A single market which exhibits different prices for the same model of motor car; which restricts the sale of insurance and financial services in certain regions; where certain governments are allowed to grant hefty subsidies to some airlines but not to others, and grant exclusive public service contracts to domestic suppliers only; where its people still need passports to move around and where differing technical standards, tax regimes and laws all operate together, is quite obviously not a common market in the sense normally understood by the term. And yet all these differences and more are the product of European institutions – despite the fact that eliminating such differences was the original objective of the Treaty of Rome in 1957, and additionally was the specific goal of the Single European Act, agreed in 1985 – that is, to achieve a progressive reduction in *all* restrictions according to a timetable terminating in 1992.

In truth, even without tariffs and quotas there is an infinite range of other factors that can impact on and distort trade between neighbour countries and thus act as forms of non-tariff barriers.

State aid

Nationhood is still officially protected within Europe. The continuation of Air France and Bull computers in 1994 was thought well worth French government subsidy, despite the fact that this contravenes the spirit if not the law of the EU. (Privatised and profitable British Airways attempted to outlaw subsidised competition in air transport. It failed.) This is only one example amongst many – national interests remain inextricably identified with the economic health of certain domestic companies and with the political complexion of certain governments. Lip service to being 'European' is continually being paid in official circles, but the real losers are European taxpayers and consumers who are required, on the one hand, to subsidise the loss-making businesses and, on the other, to continue to pay higher than free-market prices for their products. However, wherever the costs of failing industry are easily identified in terms of the loss of earnings to well-defined groups of workers and the political outcry of numerous citizens, and the benefits are measured in terms of a fractional reduction in future prices to faceless billions of consumers, then the government decision to subsidise national political interests rather than European economic integration will continue to frustrate progress towards a common market.

Public procurement

National governments are extremely unlikely to award highly visible contracts to non-national firms instead of to a domestic producer. When the German Ministry of Transport purchases Fiat cars and French agricultural officials serve banquets featuring Welsh lamb and Rioja wines then the common market will have truly arrived. The public procurement market in Europe is estimated to be very large (approximately 10 per cent of the combined Union GNP) yet only a tiny fraction of this is genuinely open to competition from non-national suppliers. According to the EC Commission's Cecchini report (1988) 0.14 per cent of this trade was won by foreign firms – hardly an open market place. The 1992 programme introduced by the Single European Act has outlawed the more discriminatory practices, so that public authorities are now obliged to advertise contracts widely, and for a sufficient period of time, to allow non-national firms to compete for orders. However welcome, this cannot prevent, of course, the continuation of national preference in public purchasing.

Taxation

Europe's internal frontiers are now more open than ever before to the passage of transport – customs checks on lorry loads of goods have (at long last) all but disappeared – but value added tax differences remain between member countries, as do varying excise duties on such goods as wine, beers and spirits. There therefore continues much costly paperwork to calculate tax charges and refunds and this inevitably inhibits and distorts free trade. (The impact of these formalities is naturally greatest for small- and medium-sized European firms which do not have large outputs over which to spread these fixed costs.)

Technical differences

Rules on the harmonisation of technical standards, or mutual recognition of partner countries' regulations, have been in place since 1992, but there is still a long way to go before all nations accept Community standards for every good and service produced. Many manufacturing businesses across the continent cite differing technical standards between countries as their biggest single impediment to pan-European sales. Consumer electronics products, for example, have to be equipped with a variety of different plugs if they are to be compatible with domestic electricity supplies in every member country. Specific state controls on banking, insurance and finance and restrictions on foreign participation and joint ventures in Spain, Greece and Portugal are another form of non-tariff barrier to free competition in services.

Language

It is impossible to quantify the impact of differing languages as an impediment to trade – obviously they are a major barrier. The lack of a common language is probably the single most important non-tariff barrier to commerce and communication across the entire continent, and yet this is – at the same time – the most important distinguishing characteristic of the European Union. What other part of the world demonstrates such linguistic and cultural diversity? Differing languages *are* Europe. Yet the mobility of resources and the international trade in goods and (especially) services is inevitably greatly slowed by language differences. How can you do business with someone if you do not know what they are saying? Europe now has nine official languages and many other dialects. Translation and interpreting costs in EU administration are immense and selling products across the union involves communication problems that businesses in North America are blissfully free from. *The Economist*, for example, notes that a US company selling computer software packages has access to a domestic market of 57 million home users. In Germany, the biggest European market, there are only 11 million users and those are in a language that has little further sales potential outside the country. Small wonder, therefore, that international trade in software services are dominated by large US firms which enjoy the advantage of home economies of scale. In Europe, less than a third of this linguistically fragmented market is taken up by European firms. Sixty per cent use American software. (Note: despite examples like these, there has never been any suggestion that Europe should attempt to evolve a common language; unlike the increasing momentum towards harmonisation or convergence on other issues.)

Currency

Different currencies have evolved in Europe for much the same reason as different languages. They are the natural outgrowth of people living in different communities, each trading with each other, but distinct from other societies (see the passage on optimum currency areas, chapter 8, below). Weights, measures, units of exchange and the language of commerce all evolved together. Agreement on standardisation of weights and measures has been achieved and, even if much still remains to be done – as referred to above – progress has still gone a long way. Currency agreement is more problematic, however. That differing currencies are a barrier to trade is evident – though exactly how big a barrier they are is open to controversy. Some would say that sophisticated foreign exchange markets, and particularly the ability to deal in currency futures, eliminates nearly all problems of financing trade. Others would argue exactly the opposite: that such currency markets actually destabilise international trade.

To overcome this non-tariff barrier to trade implies moving towards a single European currency – which represents the next stage in economic integration between countries. There is much controversy involved here and it requires, in addition, greater understanding of the particular economics of money and banking. These topics will be treated in more detail in chapter 7 below.

CONCLUSION

We can conclude here that promoting the closer economic integration of countries involves numerous and complex economic, political and cultural issues. Increasing economic prosperity in customs unions is not automatically assured – there may be much trade diversion involved as well as trade creation – and additionally some regions will benefit more than others.

The heterogeneity of many different countries and cultures continues to fragment the common market of Europe, but at the same time it is precisely this quality that provides the immense resourcefulness of the Union.

Over time, the increased union of European peoples will undoubtedly deepen and widen. The growth of competitive forces throughout the continent is meanwhile unstoppable and should overcome any short-sighted protectionist sentiments. The pace and direction of economic integration remains much influenced by the actions of governments and consumer preferences, however.

The *occupational mobility* and adaptability of European lands and peoples will in the long run provide the key to who gains, and by how much, in this process of integration. The more such fractious peoples see their interests in common, the quicker (as well as closer) integration will be achieved and the greater will be the economic benefits enjoyed. But this process cannot be hurried: after thousands of years of separate development, Europe needs time to resolve all its differences. An economic integration of varying speeds for differing countries is both necessary and inevitable.

Finally, let us finish with a global perspective. What is the impact of increasing European economic integration on the rest of the world?

As mentioned in chapter 5 above, one reaction of those left outside a common market is to set up rival *trading blocs*. A desire to emulate the EU's success and a fear of losing out in competition have fuelled the growth of other regional associations such as NAFTA, the Association of South East Asian Nations (ASEAN) and others. The great danger here, however, is that world trade may become dominated by a few, large, rival groups, and – in an atmosphere of mutual distrust – common external tariffs may be easier to erect than to negotiate a general reduction in protection. If this occurs, then world trade may become greatly distorted over time. The potential for much trade diversion exists, rather than trade creation, but this is an outcome which would benefit no one and is a matter of concern that ought to be in the minds of all governments attempting to set up trade deals. Success in achieving a closer European Union would be a hollow victory if this were to take place in a world divided by mercantilist power blocs.

KEY WORDS

The **Common Agricultural Policy** was the first and the central economic policy of the EEC, set up at its foundation in 1957. Its aims were to stabilise post-war agricultural prices and incomes, to ensure market supplies and to increase general agricultural productivity. Its main feature has been to guarantee farm prices at what have evolved as higher than market prices, to subsidise agricultural exports and to support the European farm sector in general. Its effects have been to successfully meet all its aims, but at the cost of creating incentives to overproduce, increasing farm sizes, promoting environmentally damaging farm practices, distorting income distribution and causing widespread trade diversion.

External diseconomies are disadvantages that a business suffers from its locality – such as transport difficulties and high rents in the centre of a busy city which force up costs for shops and offices.
(Note the difference of the above to social costs and benefits – these are the effects *imposed by a business on its surroundings*.)

External economies are advantages conferred on a business from the environment in which it is operating – for example an incoming firm that recruits specialised labour from a region that has built up an expertise in certain skills.

Foreign direct investment   Where a business sets up and directly owns and controls productive capital equipment in another country.

Occupational mobility   This refers to how easily resources can change their employment from one industry to another. A coal miner of many years' experience and with highly specialised skills is likely to be occupationally immobile, for example – he may find it very difficult to retrain as a computer programmer. Land on the edge of a city, however, can be switched from farming to a car park to the site for a housing or industrial estate with comparative ease. Note, that land is typically occupationally mobile but geographically immobile – it cannot get up and go elsewhere in search of a job. (Contrast this with a cement truck . . .)

QUESTIONS

1   Distinguish between trade creation and trade diversion. Using these concepts, examine the case for deepening the economic integration between Canada, the USA and Mexico beyond a free trade area.
2   How might the deployment of resources and the distribution of incomes be affected as a customs union becomes a common market? Who are the winners and losers?
3   Does cultural diversity enrich or impede economic integration and growth? If the EU opts to deepen its integration over time what might be the social costs involved?

4 What are tariff and non-tariff barriers to trade? In your view, which specific barriers are most difficult to eliminate between partner countries and why?
5 As more countries show interest in forming and deepening regional trade associations, should the World Trade Organisation become involved in regulating such agreements? Explain how and why.

FURTHER READING

El-Agraa, A.M. *Economics of the European Community*. Philip Alan, 1990.
McDonald, F. and Dearden, S. (eds). *European Economic Integration*. Longman, 1992.

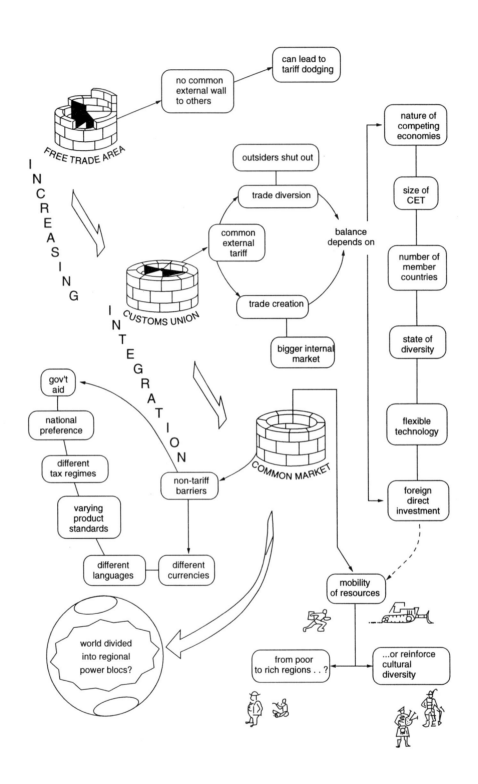

can lead to
tariff dodging

no common
external wall
to others

FREE TRADE AREA

nature of
competing
economies

INCREASING

outsiders shut out

trade diversion

common
external
tariff

balance
depends on

size of
CET

number of
member
countries

CUSTOMS UNION

INTEGRATION

trade creation

state of
diversity

bigger internal
market

gov't
aid

national
preference

flexible
technology

different
tax regimes

varying
product
standards

non-tariff
barriers

COMMON MARKET

foreign
direct
investment

different
languages

different
currencies

mobility
of resources

...or reinforce
cultural
diversity

world divided
into regional
power blocs?

from poor
to rich regions . . ?

7 Money, banking and international finance

Topics to be considered in this chapter

- The functions, forms and qualities of money
- Fractional reserve banking and the creation of credit
- Central bank attempts to control money supplies
- The globalisation of finance: causes and effects
- The impact on government policies

INTRODUCTION

Money is arguably mankind's single most important invention. It has enabled societies all over the world to exchange goods and services, to grow and prosper. Indeed, communities need money in order to function.

In the winter of 1991/2 in the Commonwealth of Independent States, many people lost faith in the value of the Russian rouble. As a consequence the economy disintegrated, living standards collapsed and many people resorted to bartering their belongings in the streets in order to get sufficient food.

The usefulness of money is easily demonstrated, therefore. Without it, people cannot agree to do business and cannot support standards of living much above subsistence level. With money, however, trade can be facilitated and very sophisticated lifestyles may develop. Far from being the root of all evil, money is the foundation stone for trade, economic growth and the development of civilisation. It is certainly worthy of serious study.

THE FUNCTIONS, FORMS AND QUALITIES OF MONEY

The prime *function of money* is to act as a medium of exchange, and any commodity which is held for this purpose – rather than for its own intrinsic value – can thus be defined as money. Money in addition acts to place a price on all goods and services traded, and this includes putting a value on *time*

– the rate of interest on riskless investment indicates how much people are prepared to accept in future compensation for going without their money now. Money should also function as a store of wealth: 'hard' currencies are distinguished from 'soft' ones in that they keep their exchange value for longer – the latter, in other words, are less acceptable as money.

Money at first took many *forms* in the course of its early evolution – salt, corn, sea-shells, etc. – in the many isolated communities where it arose. In all cases, however, in order to function properly as described above any form of money must possess certain *qualities*, such as: portability, divisibility, scarcity, durability and, most of all, acceptability.

In the last resort, *anything* which is acceptable in exchange is money. It is this unique characteristic of money that makes it so different from any other commodity in the global economy – it does not matter what is used, so long as it enables exchange to take place. Hence the old saying: 'money is as money does.' And of course it is this property which makes it so difficult to control by any central authority: as soon as one form of money becomes restricted in its use, another form will immediately evolve. We can call this the phenomenon of *endogenous money supply*. That is, the supply of money circulating in an economy cannot be directly controlled by the state for any long periods, it is determined by the popular institutions and practices of the society itself. We shall return to this important principle again and again.

The earliest, most acceptable form of money that crossed the world was gold. It had all the right qualities, except that it was *too* scarce. As trade grew, the supply of gold could not keep up. The amount of gold thus had an inherently restrictive effect on trade (causing gold prices to rise) and accordingly a new form of money evolved: paper promises.

A promise to pay – *provided it is believed by the recipient* – is as good as gold. Better, in fact, since promises are far less costly to produce than precious metals, and so the supply of banknotes ('I promise to pay the bearer on demand the sum of . . . ') could more closely match the rate of growth of trade.

The catch, of course, is to ensure acceptability. Many banks from the earliest times have therefore had to promote an air of respectability, solidity, stability and all those other adjectives that are embodied in the architecture of banks and the comportment of their managers. How else would they win the confidence of a community and be entrusted with its savings? How else to inspire traders to accept their promises to pay? As Groucho Marx used to say: 'Integrity? If you can fake that you've got it made . . . '

THE MODERN BUSINESS OF BANKING

Modern *fractional reserve banking* demonstrates the importance (and profitability) of generating confidence. So long as confidence holds, banks can issue many more promises to pay (liabilities) than they have liquid funds to cover. It does not matter how little in total a bank holds in its reserves, providing they have just enough to satisfy the next claimant who walks in the door. And, of course, the more respectable the institution, the less likely anyone is to challenge its promises. All the more room, then, for the bank to keep creating loans that it will call in at some future date to be repaid with interest. (It profits the banks to increase the indebtedness of the public.)

The only limit to the money supply now is the bankers' sense of self-discipline. In fact, history shows they have little. Competitive forces drive commercial bankers to create more and more credit in pursuit of more and more profits. But confidence in banks can evaporate as their liabilities expand too fast, outstripping reserve assets. How can so much credit ever be supported? Empires are being built on sand, and a slight shift somewhere in the system can bring everything crashing down. If all claimants simultaneously run to the bank to withdraw their deposits there is little there to pay them. Only promises. And if they are not believed, there is nothing.

The history of money and banking is thus a history of boom and slump – of the overexpansion of credit, of increasing indebtedness and of bank crashes – recent problems being no different from earlier ones, though perhaps they have been bigger and more spectacular of late. Many people around the world, indeed entire nations, have got badly into debt and are now paying the consequences in terms of greatly reduced circumstances. Some lost fortunes in the collapse of savings-and-loans institutions in North America. Similarly, millions of innocent customers suffered when fraud, money-laundering and criminal deceit brought about the closure of the Bank of Credit and Commerce International (BCCI). All affected have naturally asked: 'Why? What did *I* do wrong?' And: 'Isn't there someone reponsible for protecting us?'

TRYING TO CONTROL WHAT GOES ON

In each country it is the role of the state-run *central bank* to control national money supplies, to regulate commercial financial operations and to prevent abuses of the system. It is to the Federal Reserve Bank in the USA, the Bank of England and the German Bundesbank that hard-hit people in these countries turn to complain. The problem is that world financial practices have evolved too quickly for nationally confined authorities to keep up with them. And successful government moves to improve competition and efficiency in financial markets – making it easier/less costly for dealers to move money from one world centre to another – have inevitably made it more difficult for central banks to control what goes on.

Recent experience in the UK, USA and Germany in administering monetary policy has demonstrated that it is extremely hard to directly control the quantity of money circulating in an open, rapidly evolving, modern, market economy. This is because any central government attempt to regulate bank activity according to one target or definition of money simply drives the market to use other forms of money (as predicted by the argument of endogenous money supplies, described earlier). In this case, multinational corporations and others expanded their operations in those markets where the big national banks were restricted. Such *disintermediation* is the result of the institutional and technological changes in financial centres: many more foreign banks and domestic near-banks have set up in London and New York in recent years and have participated in new off-shore and onshore money markets with sophisticated telecommunications technology linked world-wide.

Faced with embarrassing, partly self-inflicted impotence in controlling their own back-yards, monetary authorities in Europe and North America have turned more and more to increases in interest rates (the price of money) in order to rein back consumer demand, thereby indirectly restricting the supply of credit from the banks. This of course means more pain for everyone as borrowing costs more, spending falls, businesses suffer and unemployment rises.

Clobbering the customer in order to get at his supplier seems neither equitable nor efficient. It is, however, the measure mostly commonly resorted to in the attempt to control that most slippery of concepts: modern money.

As different countries lurch from boom to bust there are those who argue that national economies should disconnect themselves from destabilising world developments by unlinking their currency and their monetary affairs from any fixed international exchange rate system. In contrast, there are others who argue for exactly the opposite course of action – that greater monetary discipline is necessary, requiring stable exchange rates, supranational regulation and, in the extreme, monetary union.

These are issues that are complex and need careful analysis. The economics of banking, recent changes and their impact on money supplies – both nationally and internationally – are continued in more detail below. The particular arguments for and against monetary union in Europe are considered in the next chapter and the issues relating to the international debt crisis – which affected many developing countries in the 1980s and still impedes their progress today – follow later on.

THE ECONOMICS OF BANKING: A SIMPLE MODEL

To understand more clearly how the financial world operates, how it is changing and how it affects the lives and livelihood of ordinary people like you and me we need to simplify the analysis of banking with the use of an elementary model, introducing more complex and realistic qualifications later on, once the basics are understood.

Control of the money supply within a country (assuming for the time being the country can be isolated from international events) lies within the relationship which develops between state authorities and private financial markets. This relationship is never stable in any society – it is in a continual state of evolution – but at its simplest level we can begin this analysis by assuming that there are only two forms of money: cash and credit (transferred by cheque).

The institutions of a banking system

Financial market places are where people and institutions buy and sell money – that is, they loan and borrow funds – and in the process determine rates of interest (the price of money) and the money supply (the quantity of funds circulating). Assume that the only traders in this market place are the central bank, several competing commercial banks and numerous private individuals and businesses.

The central bank holds the bank account of the government (it loans and borrows money for the government, amongst others); acts as a banker to all the commercial banks (they all keep their own accounts at the central bank); is responsible for setting the rules and regulations in all financial trade; and is charged with conducting the government's monetary policy within the economy (and internationally).

Commercial banks are *financial intermediaries*, that is they specialise in the business of mediating between those who have surplus money and those who have insufficient. More simply, they accept people's savings and then loan these funds on to others who wish to invest. In the process they make money: creating more or less credit as society demands, subject to the effectiveness of central bank intervention.

Private individuals and businesses of all sizes are customers in these financial markets – they are the many people who save and the not-quite-so-many who invest.

The central bank directly controls the issue of cash (coins and bank-notes) within the country. It is held in the hands and homes of private individuals; is deposited in commercial bank reserves and is also kept by these institutions in their cash balances at the central bank.

The creation of money

A country's *cash base* (defined as M0) is at the heart of its money supply. Commercial banks issue more or less credit to customers (as we shall see) as their cash reserves grow or decline. We can consider how this process takes place first of all in the case of a stable, conservative community where people have no reason to doubt the trustworthiness of their bankers. (Such communities cannot be built quickly – they are the product of lifetimes of responsible financial conduct, where people grow to respect those who hold their money.)

All customers who deposit cash in the banks may come to use cheques as a safe and easy substitute to transfer funds – especially for large purchases. Most people will not cash in their cheques in order to withdraw funds and then transfer this money to someone else. Cheques are handed over instead, and the banks involved subtract the cash involved from one person's account and then add it on to another's. The cash, therefore, never sees the light of day: it stays in the hands of bankers.

The more trustworthy the community, the fewer cash transactions will be necessary, the more acceptable will be cheques. Thus *the form of money changes*: commercial bank promises to pay (cheques) take the place of central bank promises (official banknotes).

Suppose that for every $1 transaction that takes place in the form of cash in this community there are ten times this number of cheques accepted. This means that commercial banks can expand the money supply by ten times the value of the cash base. For every $1 cash deposited by a customer in a bank, therefore, credit can be extended by $10 (by issuing cheques to people asking for loans). The banks are confident that at any one time only one in ten customers will ever come in and demand cash in exchange for their cheques – so cash reserves are sufficient if they only back 10 per cent of all loans created.

The size of the *credit multiplier* (ten, in this example) is a function of the stability and spending habits of the community involved. For politically unstable or economically underdeveloped societies the credit multiplier may be as low as one – that is, every $1 loan is backed by $1 cash, ready to be withdrawn at a moment's notice. Highly sophisticated financial communities, on the other hand, may have very little need for cash. Billions and billions of transactions may change hands daily with an infinitesimaly small fraction ever being converted into cash. It is in these circumstances that numerous financial intermediaries have grown up borrowing and lending credit over varying time periods, and – quite clearly – the direct influence of the central bank as the controller of the cash base is greatly diminished.

Control of the money supply

Theoretically, the central bank can control money supplies of the commercial banks by varying the economy's cash base through *open market operations*. That is, the central bank borrows money from the public through the means of selling *bonds* and *bills of exchange* in the open market place. This means they sell paper (promises to repay loans at some future date) to private individuals and businesses in exchange for cheques. By cashing in these cheques the central bank reduces the commercial bank cash reserves. For every $1 reduction in cash reserves, banks must call in $10 worth of loans (assuming the economy maintains a stable 10 per cent reserves/assets ratio). Conversely, by buying back bonds and bills the central bank increases the flow of cash into the commercial banks, which then can increase lending tenfold.

There are other means by which central banks can attempt to control money supplies. Different countries can use one method, or a combination of methods, depending on what suits their practices and institutions best. For example, instead of operating indirectly through open market operations, central banks can directly reduce commercial bank reserves by seizing or freezing a fraction of their deposits – such cash cannot therefore be used to support credit and, again, loans must be called in to a multiplied extent.

Alternatively, central banks can demand a certain reserve ratio by law, and then *increase* this ratio at times when they wish to restrict money supplies. Thus if banks maintain a 10 per cent ratio of cash to loans and then the central bank insists on a 12.5 per cent ratio, this implies that instead of every $1 cash supporting $10 loans, now it can only cover $8 worth. Twenty per cent of credit circulating in the economy must now be cut back.

Either by reducing banks' cash reserves or by increasing cash ratios, if central banks are successful in curtailing money supplies then they will drive up interest rates in the open market. They may, in fact, decide to operate the other way round: by charging higher base rates on central bank loans (which underpin the money markets) they may drive all interest rates upward and thus choke off demand (and thereby supply) for credit.

All of these measures have been used to a greater or lesser extent over the years as central banks have struggled to assert their authority and thus regulate monetary policy. (Monetary policy is important because it is one instrument used by governments to manage the macroeconomy. Actually, much controversy has burned between economists as to precisely how important this policy instrument is, relative to other controls. The general consensus now is that money supplies and interest rates *do* affect such phenomena as rates of inflation and investment, but the relationship is not as close or as predictable as some have argued.)

The difficulty, however, is that there has been an accelerating number of changes recently that have impacted upon banking practices and – as indicated in the introduction to this chapter – central bank authority and control have for the most part been overtaken by events. Many of the old certainties in this market place have now disappeared.

THE GLOBALISATION OF FINANCE

Central banks are no longer monopolies of the money supply in their own, isolated economies. Thanks to increasing competition and innovation in the banking industry, the widespread application of telecommunications technology and follow-my-leader deregulation of markets in all the world's major financial centres, enormous sums of money can now flow around the world, in and out of different countries, at the press of a button.

The Bank of England estimated that, in 1992, the world's daily volume of foreign exchange dealing was valued at $1,000,000,000,000 ($1 trillion). That was *each day* in 1992; it is even greater now!

By this estimate, international money flows are *over 100 times greater* than all world movements of real goods and services. The buying and selling that these enormous funds are in exchange for, therefore, is in paper promises: all sorts of bonds, bills, securities and derivative financial instruments that private money-makers have invented. The forms of credit are so numerous today that what counts as money – and what does not – is almost a matter of individual preference.

Causes

What has driven this globalisation of finance and what have been its effects?

Trade

The first major impetus to international banking occurred during the Cold War years of the 1960s when foreign (especially Soviet) trade surpluses denominated in US dollars were looking for a place of deposit, free from restrictions of the US monetary authorities. The *Eurodollar* (later Euro-currency) *market* grew up, therefore, with banks of varying nationalities operating in London free from reserve asset requirements and interest rate ceilings demanded either by the Bank of England (because they were not dealing in pounds sterling) or by the Federal Reserve in the USA. Being an 'offshore' market, the banks involved were also outside the exchange controls designed to support the (then) world fixed exchange rate system. Their customers were large, private and public enterprises with international interests and which dealt in large sums of money (e.g. a minimum transaction of US$1 million). By operating wholesale and free from any restrictions, Euromarket banks had lower costs than their US counterparts and so could offer better rates of interest to their clients and could profit on small percentage differences. The first lesson of this new industry was thus well learnt: large turnovers, small margins and fleet-footed avoidance of rigid regulation was the secret of success.

The accelerating internationalisation of finance gained pace in the 1970s when global recycling of petrodollars became the major preoccupation of bankers (see chapters 9 and 10, below). Massive balance of payments deficits of Western, oil-consuming nations had to be matched by opposite movements of large sums of capital financed through the banks. The reverse side of this same coin was that oil-rich OPEC states with small populations and a limited capacity to quickly spend these fortunes needed international banks to place these funds in interest-bearing deposits. Trade imbalances of any kind require financing – these imbalances were the largest the world had ever seen and the opportunities for expansion of international finance were a major boost to the industry.

Deregulation

At the end of the 1970s, the stagflationary effects of the oil shocks on Western economies heralded the ascendancy of conservative economics as espoused by Britain's Margaret Thatcher and Ronald Reagan of the USA. After decades of interventionism, subsidies and controls in all manner of industries, governments in the 1980s seemed to rediscover the dynamism of free markets. Deregulation, privatisation and the liberation of prices became the new orthodoxy. Restrictions on international capital movements were lifted in one country after another (see, for example, UK deregulation in chapter 4, above).

Note that increasing international competition drove deregulation more than anything else. As 'offshore' and foreign banks in London dealt increasingly profitably with large international accounts free of Bank of England controls then UK domestic banks lobbied the government to allow them unrestricted access to this market also. As the amount of business grew in London so the same political pressures built up in New York, Tokyo and Frankfurt: central authorities must lighten the load of their controls or risk the loss of business avoiding their shores. Deregulation rapidly became the dominant political economy, therefore, even in countries with allegedly socialist, or interventionist administrations such as France and Japan.

Innovation

We have met this notion before: any system of heavy-handed regulation drives private profit-seekers to innovate and avoid paying such costs. In banking, with such a slippery commodity as money, the volume of dealing simply changes its form and keeps on growing. If governments resist the tendency towards deregulatory financial policies then they will attempt to exert more and more restrictions on their particular money markets. This will drive interest rates up and make it even more profitable for international dealers to try and avoid regulations and move money around. The opportunities for financial innovation and profitable *arbitrage* increase. Controls cannot succeed in such an international environment – the political movement towards deregulation becomes unstoppable.

Technology

Advances in computing and telecommunications technology provided the means to accelerate these changes worldwide. Round-the-clock, 24-hour trading in a global financial market place is possible with the three largest financial centres of London, New York and Tokyo all linked together. As Tokyo goes to bed, London is waking up and so New York switches from one set of traders to another. And with computers programmed to gather and analyse masses of business data, the *transaction costs* of seeing and acting upon subtle changes in financial information have become greatly reduced. (This fact alone explains why such a lot of international trading occurs: assume 500 dealers each operating in Japan, the USA and the UK. The cost of contacting each one increasingly diminishes as technology improves – banks thus have no economic incentive to restrict the number of contacts. The addition of *one* extra dealer in this network, therefore, will increase the number of trades possible by *1,500*. That is why daily transactions in international money are measured in trillions of dollars.)

The significance of information and transaction costs falling is that the *barriers to entry* to this industry have therefore all but disappeared. Specialist knowledge which used to characterise each segment of financial markets is now widely available to any firm that can tap into the relevant global telecommunication network. Highly efficient and accessible technology has brought increased competition from enterprises formerly unrelated to the industry and, as a result, has been responsible for much *dis*intermediation – the direct matching of buyers and sellers outside the money markets by businesses 'doing it themselves' without the brokerage service of official banks or finance houses.

Risk

Each change mentioned above drives others. Anti-inflationary, conservative governments drive up interest rates rather than expand money supplies. With no restrictions on capital movements, 'hot money' flows in to take advantage of higher rates of return. Domestic currency is in demand, therefore, and the exchange rate must rise. This causes businesses to recalculate their costs and profits in international trade: exports become more expensive and imports cheaper as the price of currency appreciates. (All these events occurred in the early 1980s in Europe and the USA. The business recession created was sharp, painful and costly in terms of business failure and unemployment.)

Businesses are at risk in a world of volatile interest and exchange rates, and risk encourages banks to offer innovative financial packages to help such enterprises to weather the storms. The growth of clever ways to hedge against various types of financial risk has therefore led to an explosive increase in options, futures and all sorts of trading in *derivatives* (and, more insultingly, *junk bonds*), each new financial product being rapidly copied by other banks and centres as soon as it hits the market. Thus dealing in three-month Eurodollar futures totalled US$670 billion at the end of 1989, rising to US$1.1 trillion by late 1991.

Diversification

The appropriate response to a world of increasing risk is for businesses to diversify their spread of assets. As currencies, interest rates and commodity prices have become more volatile, so institutional investors whose profits depend on these prices have increasingly widened their portfolios and purchased assets in a number of different centres. Pension funds, insurance companies and unit trusts have taken a more and more active part in international trading, therefore. For example, in the 1980s decade UK pension funds increased their holdings of foreign securities from 7 per cent to 18 per cent of their portfolios; US funds widened their spread from 1 per cent to 4 per cent and the Japanese from 1 per cent to 16 per cent.

Effects

The implication of all these changes for individual countries is that now it is extremely difficult for governments to use monetary policies to control their economies as they so wish. Any changes they may want to introduce can have unpredictable repercussions, thanks to the volatile and interdependent world we all live in, and so the idea of fine-tuning an economy through regulating the quantity of money or the structure of interest rates is hopelessly impractical.

Multiasset markets

How can central banks control the money supply when money itself can no longer be closely defined? In today's financial markets, dealers work with a whole spread of assets of varying liquidity and security from cash through Treasury and commercial bills of exchange, to all manner of different bonds, securities, certificates of deposits, equities, and longer-term advances and mortgages.

Liquidity is the ease with which any of these assets can be converted into cash. Very short-term loans are highly liquid since they will be repaid quickly. Reliable long-term assets can be very liquid also since they may have a high resale value or *secondary market*. (Government securities of, say, one year to run can be re-sold immediately to any one of a number of interested buyers.) Less reputable commercial bonds and longer-term assets may be more difficult to place a present value upon – they are less liquid – but they carry a higher rate of interest as a result.

With so many different financial institutions holding varied portfolios of income-earning financial assets, which particular ones do you include in the money supply? If the central bank restricts the circulation of those assets it has directly under its own control it will simply prompt the expansion of other financial instruments to take their place. If interest rates on government bills and bonds rise then a whole chain of substitutions may take place as dealers adjust their holdings of these as opposed to other assets. Prices and interest rates on a host of near and distant alternatives will all shuffle up or down accordingly.

As a result of such diversity, central banks have identified an ever-increasing array of monetary aggregates as the money supply: M1, M2, M3, M3c, M4, etc. – each in turn being used for control purposes, only to be just as quickly abandoned as the authorities found that each did not behave quite as it should have done. Experience has produced *Goodhart's law*: whichever measure seems best to represent the money supply will cease to function as such as soon as the central bank tries to regulate it.

Institutional changes

In addition to the vast, innovative spread of assets held by banks, what actually constitutes a bank now is becoming irrelevant. Once upon a time, financial markets were segmented and specialised: commercial or retail banks offered deposit and (relatively short-term) loan facilities to the public; merchant banks, acceptance houses or investment banks underwrote share issues for businesses; building societies and mortgage institutions funnelled many small savings into long-term house loans; discount houses and money market brokers bought and sold very short-term government and commercial debt. All these and more traded in specialised financial products and set their own prices in their own secure worlds.

Now domestic and international competition is rife. The barriers between different financial sectors have come down – so that retail banks have become building societies and similarly they offer wholesale banking services to big business. With cross-border restrictions falling, subsidiaries of foreign, international banks have meanwhile poured into every small financial centre around the world; and, most important of all, many large, national and multinational companies have now entered into the competition as well. As late as the 1970s, US banks controlled about half of the long-term loans made to business in that country. Today that figure is down to around 20 per cent as other institutions have entered the market and, especially, firms are selling their own commercial paper.

Dozens of international mergers and acquisitions have occurred over the last two decades between banks, securities firms and brokerage houses in Europe, the USA and Japan. As a result, which finance house is operating where, dealing in what business is no longer the cosy, predictable affair it used to be. Ten years ago, the international reach of the world's 100 largest banks amounted to over 4,600 offices in different locations – it is certainly far greater today. This remarkable globalisation and opening-up of the banking industry is important because it has made the rapid mobilisation of funds from one centre to another all the more easy and, by the same token, has made the monitoring and control of domestic financial operations by national authorities virtually impossible.

Exchange rate effects

With financial sectors operating increasingly beyond the reach of central banks, government attempts to change money supplies and interest rates within the domestic economy may have little short-term effect on real economic variables such as consumption, investment and employment, but it may have an unpredictable and immediate impact on the exchange rate.

Suppose, for example, that the central bank intends to restrict the money supply, push up interest rates and restrain inflationary expenditure. These efforts may have little impact on the real economy if business activity and expectations are operating in a contrary direction. If official bank lending is tight then, as already explained, large corporations can raise funds by borrowing internationally through a process of issuing their own bonds or securities (though they have to take on the risk of unanticipated exchange rate movements).

High domestic interest rates will anyway attract foreign savers to move their funds into the country, so through a combination of this effect, plus local businesses pulling in cheaper foreign loans, there will be a flow of funds on to the foreign exchange markets and therefore an increased demand for the domestic currency.

Given that the central bank is consistent in wishing to curtail the money supply, the only outcome of increased foreign demand for the currency must be a rise in the exchange rate. Thus the effect of the authorities attempting a credit squeeze is not necessarily to dampen aggregate investment and consumption spending, but to drive up the price of exports and to reduce the price of imports. The country's trade balance will worsen, and industries producing exports and import substitutes will suffer.

All countries have therefore found out over the last decade that they can have *either* an exchange rate policy, *or* a monetary policy, but not both. The domestic interest rate appropriate for one cannot be simultaneously used to control the other. If governments are unhappy that their exchange rate is too high, making exports too expensive and uncompetitive in world markets, then they must reduce interest rates and/or sell more currency to bring its price down. Either way they lose control of the money supply. Alternatively, if they stick rigidly to a monetarist prescription of expanding money supplies according to a prearranged target, they cannot then control interest rates and exchange rates as they so wish, but must leave them to be determined by the free market.

CONCLUSION

In a multi-asset financial world the clear cut distinction between a community's base of cash reserves and its total money supply disappears. There is no simple 1:10 credit multiplier relationship; reserve assets are not easily identifiable nor are they completely within the control of the authorities; and – thanks to institutional changes – official banks subject to central bank regulation now represent a diminishing fraction of financial operators.

All the measures referred to above by which central authorities are supposed to influence monetary aggregates – increasing or decreasing commercial bank reserves through open market operations, direct intervention or changing minimum asset requirements – are now only to be found in out-dated economics textbooks. These measures cannot work in open, deregulated markets since other highly liquid assets can be quickly substituted for those reserves the central bank calls in, and many non-bank financial operators are out of reach anyway.

In effect, most developed countries since the mid-1980s have opted to pursue an exchange rate policy rather than take any overt monetary stance apart from deregulation. For all the reasons given above, monetary policy is too blunt and unpredictable an instrument to serve the needs of governments.

The impact of all these changes on the world economy cannot be easily summarised – we are still in the process of living with them. What is clear is that international financial markets react faster today than ever before and can move such volumes of money that even those central banks with the deepest pockets cannot buy them off. Governments in Mexico and Europe (see next chapter) have recently found this out to their cost.

At such times, when private markets force changes upon public authorities, criticisms typically surface alleging that democratically elected administrations are being held hostage by faceless speculators, profit-hungry conspirators or 'Gnomes of Zurich'. Beware of such politically loaded complaints!

It is true that in interdependent and volatile financial markets, if government policies in one country are not considered trustworthy then both national and international wealthholders will quickly desert those shores and look for safer havens. In these circumstances it is probable that local capitalists, and not faceless international speculators, will be the quickest to move – they are likely to know local conditions best and have most to lose. For example, domestic and *not* US and other foreign investors were the first to jump ship in the 1994/5 Mexican crisis. (The same was true in the economic turmoil that accompanied the end of the Allende government and preceded the Pinochet dictatorship in Chile in 1973. Although international monetary movements were much more restricted then, that did not prevent much of the blame being heaped on foreign – and especially US – interests.)

This does not mean that governments have any less power these days – it is just that they cannot fool people for so long any more. The penalty for implementing unsustainable economic policies is now a financial crisis sooner rather than later. The implication here is wholly positive:

governments cannot pull the wool over the eyes of their electorates and so they must make a better job of communicating what it is they want to do and how they intend to pay for it. Any attempt to fudge the issues will be penalised.

The better the quality of information fed to financial markets the more efficiently – and less harmfully – they will react. One major worry still remains, however. Are the interests of money market dealers the same as those of the people in whose country they operate? Are their priorities shared by simple farmers, industrial labourers and the average person in the street? Maybe elected governments with a social conscience (especially left-wing ones) that want to build more public hospitals/housing and implement more redistributive incomes policies will be subject to far more demanding financial terms by distrustful, right-wing capitalists?

This is an understandable and recurrent concern. The answer is twofold. Firstly, the large sums of money that move across international markets are not likely to be those of individual capitalists, they more often feature pension and savings funds that are protecting the interests of millions of ordinary workers and people in the street. And, secondly, professional fund managers are less interested in the politics of governments than in their financial credibility. No matter if socialist administrations want to build public hospitals and tax the rich – if they borrow the hard-earned pennies of countless ordinary citizens, will they pay back on time?

Financial markets, therefore, operate similarly to all others. The more competition and the more quality information they act with the better they will function. Their limitations are no more nor less than those of the market economic system in general. But note: the more globalised they become, the more they will link the fortunes on one side of the world to those on the other. They are just one dimension of our interdependent, international economy.

KEY WORDS

Arbitrage This refers to the exploitation of marginal differences in prices of financial assets between different markets. If the price of a given currency, commodity or bond in Frankfurt or New York is higher than in London then it pays to buy in the cheaper market and sell in the other. The smallest price differentials can yield significant profits if large volumes are traded. Risks are low since arbitrage implies simultaneous transactions at known prices. Its economic effect is to secure price equivalence between rival centres.

Barriers to entry These are the restrictions imposed on any new enterprise wishing to start up business in a given field. Such barriers may be legal, bureaucratic, financial or economic. Governments may restrict foreign firms from buying domestic industrial assets by law; the process of acquiring all the necessary licences may be exhausting; the costs of insurance or borrowing local funds may be excessive, or the capital equipment necessary to start business may be highly expensive.

Bills of exchange These originated centuries ago as three-month trade deals. You give me capital on the understanding that it takes me three months to equip a ship, sail out to the South Seas, buy lots of exotic goodies, come back and sell them off at a profit and then pay you back the agreed amount. A bill of exchange is now a promise to pay a given sum in three months' time. The cheaper you buy this bill, therefore, the more you stand to gain. Note that if a private bill, or bond, is guaranteed by a reputable third party (e.g. a well-known bank or business) then you have little risk of loss – the price of this paper is likely to be higher. Such is the case also with Treasury Bills, which are issued by the government. The riskier the dealer, however, the cheaper he will have to sell his paper – the more profit he has to offer to attract a buyer. (See junk bonds.)

Bond   Old English for promise. A bond is a written promise, a legal contract – usually a promise to pay a fixed rate of interest on a given loan. For example: you pay me $1 million and I will promise to pay you 10 per cent for as long as you have my 'bond'. My bond may be returned to me and cashed in at an agreed date; or you may decide to sell it to someone else (at whatever price you can get) in a 'secondary market'.

Central bank   The government's bank, charged with the responsibility to run monetary policy, which includes making loans to and accepting deposits from private, commercial banks and thereby determining the rate of interest on government debt. *Open market operations* is the term used to refer to the central bank's dealings with free-market banks and credit institutions – especially when it attempts to influence the quantity of money they hold.

Credit multiplier   Most private, commercial banks will hold a given proportion of their total assets in the form of a reserve – liquid funds that they can use to meet customer demands. A 10 per cent reserve implies that for every $1 in the till they have $10 in longer-term loans circulating. A given increase, say $100, in the reserve base of such a financial community can thus lead to a tenfold increase in longer-term loans – up to $1,000 in this case. Total credit is thus a multiple (e.g. ten times) of bank reserves.

Derivatives   Any tradable paper which derives its market value from that of some underlying asset is a derivative. This would include a promise to buy a certain security at an agreed price at a given date in the future ('futures'); or the option to buy certain shares at a given price within a certain time period ('options') . The enterprise which buys a derivative from a financial institution is in effect paying the seller to take on the risk of a change in economic conditions and prices over the lifetime of the business. For example, a plantation company may be unsure of the income it will earn from sales of a future harvest and thus be unable to make required investments today. An astute bank will offer to sell derivatives on the company's behalf, guaranteeing capital to the plantation, taking on the risk of a commodity price collapse but making a nice profit if it calculates correctly.

Disintermediation   Commercial banks act as intermediaries between savers and investors. Increasingly, however, buyers and sellers of money have met each other outside banks' doors. Big businesses can sell their own paper promises in financial market places to whoever is willing to accept them. This is *dis*intermediation: the matching up of funds that does not feature on the balance sheets of recognised financial institutions.

Endogenous money supply   This is where the supply of money in a country is not created and directly controlled by the central authorities but is determined by the actions of private individuals, businesses and banks. The form of money and the nature of credit-creating institutions can change where state attempts to restrict commerical banking activities bite hard – thus leading to an endogenous money supply.

Fractional reserve banking Commercial banks traditionally keep a relatively small sum of liquid funds in reserve in order to meet customer demands for withdrawals. That is, if a bank possesses $5 million in cash deposits from savers it may decide to create $50 million in credit to loan out to needy investors. The bank's reserve:assets ratio is thus 1:10. That is, it figures that out of the $50 million of its cheques circulating no more than one tenth will be cashed in.

Goodhart's law Charles Goodhart, who went from the Bank of England to the London School of Economics, claimed that any observed statistical correlation betweeen two variables would break down as soon as public authorities attempted to use it for policy-making purposes. This comment is as relevant for central bank attempts to control the money supply by restricting trade in certain reserve assets, as it is for relying on a Phillips curve relationship to control unemployment by opting for a bit more inflation. Goodhart's law recognises the fundamental uncertainty of social science.

Junk bonds These are commercial bonds *not* guaranteed by first class banks or acceptance houses and they thus carry a lower price and higher risk factor than other market instruments – though they may turn out to be perfectly reputable, despite their name.

Liquidity Forms of wealth that can be quickly turned into cash without loss of value. Banknotes and coins are 100 per cent liquid. Some bonds and short-term loans can quickly be sold off in the markets and thus converted into cash without much loss of face value. If you own a vintage car, some old paintings, certain shares and longer-term commercial loans, however, you may have difficulty in finding buyers unless you sell at a discount – these are illiquid assets.

Secondary markets No one would buy a very long-term promise to pay if it meant that they could not get their money back in emergencies. Ploughing millions into buying shares, bills or bonds would not occur if there were no market place where you could sell them off second-hand to other willing customers.

Transactions costs This is how much it costs to make a certain trade. If it requires time and effort to find out about asset prices in a neighbouring market; if governments restrict access to foreign currencies or charge a tax on the value of trades, then the cost of doing business may be prohibitively high. Why invest in Country X if the transactions cost involved is higher than in Country Y?

QUESTIONS

1 How and why have the forms of money changed through history? What difficulties has this presented to central authorities trying to control the money supply?
2 Commercial banks hold only a fraction of their assets in reserve. Explain the reasons for this and its relevance to their ability to create money. How has financial innovation affected this ability?
3 How can central banks attempt to control the money supply in their domestic economies? What are the costs involved in so doing?
4 Why does so much money move around the world?
5 'The more globalised (financial markets) become, the more they will link the fortunes on one side of the world to those of the other.' Consider the implications of this statement.

FURTHER READING

Hallwood, C. Paul and MacDonald, Ronald. *International Money and Finance.* Blackwell, 1994.

The Economist publishes annual surveys of International Banking and The World Economy. See, for example: 'The myth of the powerless state', 7 October 1995.

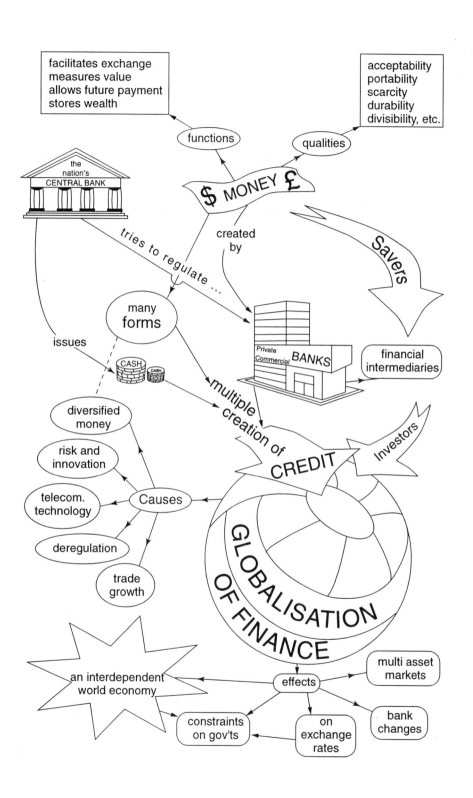

facilitates exchange
measures value
allows future payment
stores wealth

acceptability
portability
scarcity
durability
divisibility, etc.

functions

qualities

the
nation's
CENTRAL BANK

$ MONEY £

created
by

Savers

tries to regulate ...

issues

many
forms

CASH
CASH

Private
Commercial BANKS

financial
intermediaries

multiple
creation of
CREDIT

Investors

diversified
money

risk and
innovation

telecom.
technology

Causes

deregulation

trade
growth

GLOBALISATION
OF FINANCE

an interdependent
world economy

effects

multi asset
markets

constraints
on gov'ts

on
exchange
rates

bank
changes

8 Exchange rates and currency union

Topics to be considered in this chapter

- Separate currencies
- Fixed and floating exchange rate regimes
- Costs and benefits of a currency union
- European currency crises, 1992–3
- An optimal currency area
- A European future

INTRODUCTION

Money – at its most perfect extreme – is invisible, costless to produce, environmentally neutral, has no intrinsic value but is exchangeable for anything. It allows the construction and trade of productive assets and the creation of great art, science and civilisation.

In less-than-perfect everyday practice, however, money occurs in a variety of different forms in a number of different market places and is only imperfectly exchangeable. Some currencies are a significantly better store of wealth than others, and a certain price must be paid to persuade people to transfer their holdings from one form of money to another. At worst, *hyperinflation* can occur – destroying the credibility of a currency – and when this happens the domestic economy breaks down, as has happened a number of times to different countries in Europe this century.

In one part of Europe a currency union has recently broken down. The economy of the old Soviet Union was bound together by the Russian rouble which formed the common medium of exchange for a currency area that stretched from Tallinn to Tashkent, Kiev to Vladivostok. Now the Union has dissolved under the pressures of separatist and independence movements; and the hyperinflation of the rouble has spawned a number of breakaway currencies, some successfully (as in the Baltic States), others less so (in the Ukraine).

Meanwhile, in another part of Europe currency unions are in the ascendant. Belgium and Luxembourg have had a common currency for years; on 1 July 1990, the unification of East and West Germany brought about the integration of the Ostmark and the Deutschmark, with the latter replacing the former; and, despite all the difficulties with the *Exchange Rate Mechanism* (ERM) during the latter part of 1992 and 1993, the political momentum towards monetary union is being revived between members of the European Community.

What is the rationale behind currency areas? Why do some parts of the world use one distinctive form of money and other parts use others? What are the stages involved in enlarging a currency zone and what are the costs and benefits for those communities entering a union that previously used their own, separate means of exchange? Let us consider each of these questions in turn below.

DIFFERENT COMMUNITIES: DIFFERENT CURRENCIES

Look quickly at the variety of forms of money that have existed through history: commodities, for example, such as salt, goats, corn, precious metals and even cigarettes. The fact that some societies traded with sacks of corn or livestock and others with a variety of different metals seems bizarre to us today, but perhaps this sentiment will be no different to some future European observer who looks back to the twentieth century and sees some communities trading in pounds, others in francs and others in pesetas. Why cannot Europe bring together its fragmented national markets to form one continent-wide currency bloc for the increased wealth and welfare of all?

Currency areas, like linguistic zones, evolve principally for social, and not economic reasons, and – like languages – the lack of a common currency in a large, populated land mass isolates individual communities and ties them into their own social confines. A currency becomes, therefore, the economic boundary to a social grouping. It is like saying: 'We only trade with these people, not those . . . '

Of course, with improved political and social relations between countries, increased economic growth and steady progress in telecommunications and transport technology there has been rapid expansion in international trade in the second half of this century.

The economic benefits realisable from international trade are in fact driving the move towards European currency union. After two 'hot' world wars and one cold one, political relations between (most) European neighbours are now more harmonious; incomes and consumers' buying power have increased steadily and, thanks to the falling cost of transport and telecommunications exchange, people know of goods and services produced elsewhere, can gain access to them at reasonable prices and – with the globalisation of banking services – can get the foreign exchange necessary to make their purchases.

Barriers to international trade have always existed and, at first, it was the natural barriers of mountains, seas, rivers and geographical remoteness that were the most difficult to overcome. It is still costly to transport Mediterranean fruit and vegetables long distances to northern Europe, for example, and Welsh lamb back in return, but continuous transport innovation since the Middle Ages (culminating in the Channel Tunnel and the integrated network of high-speed road and rail links today) has been devoted to overcoming this problem.

The greatest obstacles to trade this century have been the man-made, nationalist barriers. The intervention of governments has never failed to create more and more complex tariff and non-tariff barriers to reinforce political and social prejudices. It has therefore taken immense efforts on the part of individual political idealists and institutions like GATT and, within Europe, the European Commission to counter these mercantilist, isolationist tendencies.

Thanks to the EC's success in eliminating intra-European restrictions on trade (see chapter 6), the single, most important economic barrier to trade within the common market that remains is the lack of a common currency. The Maastricht treaty, signed in 1991 by all member countries, was centrally concerned with this issue and it laid down strict criteria that European currencies/economies must fulfil in order to bring about currency union.

Europe today is engaged in a journey towards full *economic and monetary union* (EMU). This pathway is steep and set about with pitfalls; some European partners have stumbled on occasions and in consequence are going along it more slowly than others; some have been complaining loudly about where it is leading and certain critics even assert (they hope) that the way is now completely lost. The momentum along this pathway nonetheless continues and by the end of this century some countries should have reached their destinations in an irrevocable and binding currency union. Others will most likely get there later.

STAGES TOWARDS CURRENCY UNION

What are the stages involved in this journey? The route to increasing monetary integration has travelled through many twists and turns since the end of the Second World War.

1 European nations, like all others, firstly pursued *independent monetary policies*. Governments were free to control their own money supplies; to borrow and lend as much as they wished; to run budget deficits and charge whatever interest rates they could get away with internally.

From 1944 to 1971 such independence was subject to the international system of *fixed exchange rates* agreed at Bretton Woods, USA, in 1944. This was effectively a dollar standard system where all world currencies were tied to a dollar price with very little room for movement (maximum fluctuations were to be contained within 1 per cent either up or down). A balance of payments deficit incurred by any trading country was cancelled by a payment of dollars. If the dollars required were greater than existing reserves, then the deficit country in these circumstances was forced to sell its own currency to buy the necessary foreign exchange, thus automatically deflating domestic money supplies, incomes and spending. If such deficits were recurring and the country concerned wished to escape from a continuous cycle of deflation then realignment was possible by refixing the relevant currency's dollar price at a lower value. (This was described as *'the adjustable peg'*.) With this system, certainty and stability of trading rules was thus established after the chaos of the 1930s and the 1940s and individual countries were free to conduct their own policies within this disciplined framework.

The slowly increasing economic strength of Germany and Japan since the Second World War, and the sudden leap in economic importance of the Organisation of Petroleum Exporting Countries (OPEC) in the 1970s, could not be contained within a fixed rate system frozen since 1944. International exchange rates were therefore floated free throughout the seventies, although – in order to moderate some of the wilder fluctuations involved – most countries attempted a form of *managed floating*. This involved national authorities intervening in foreign exchange markets, buying and selling their own currencies in the attempt to limit the extremes of price movements. The US Federal Reserve Bank would, for example, start selling part of its foreign reserves and buying overseas-held dollars in order to defend a target floor in the price of its own currency. Conversely, if it thought that the price of dollars to yen was increasing too much – putting US exports at risk compared to cheaper Japanese goods, for example – then the Fed would start selling dollars and buying yen on the international money markets.

2 An additional or alternative means of managing exchange rates is to institute some form of direct control: traders cannot bid down the price of a particular currency if the authorities concerned restrict their access to it. With *exchange restrictions* imposed, importers, for example, would have to apply to their central bank for the purchase of the foreign money required to buy the goods they desire. The bank can thus ration out foreign currency slowly, to preferred customers and at the official price, as a means of delaying import penetration and protecting the exchange rate.

Removing exchange restrictions allows a free market in a country's currency and thereby makes that nation vulnerable to any changes in international trade. This measure may be introduced, however, to signal to the international financial community that the government has instituted a fundamental shift in its policies – as in the case of the incoming Thatcher government of the UK in October 1979 – and it can also be used, as in a widening group of EU countries during the 1980s – to promote the tighter integration of a number of economies together.

3 Closer integration is secured by *tied floating*. The countries concerned agree to fix their respective exchange rates to each other within a confined range of values and allow them to float up and down more or less as a whole – or rather as a flexible 'snake' – against all other world currencies.

In March 1979 the European exchange rate mechanism was set up to overcome the problems encountered with the floating international exchange rate system of that time. For European countries that conducted a lot of trade with one another, the short-term speculative fluctuations in exchange rates that were possible under the floating regime of the seventies were a destabilising disincentive to trade. (For Europeans with a population similar to the USA, this is rather like businesses and consumers in New York trying to trade with others in Washington and Los Angeles yet having to cope with forever fluctuating currencies and price levels in both cities.) Agreement was thus secured between contributory partners to fix exchange rates within bands of movement of 2.25 per cent (6 per cent for Italy, Spain and the UK when they first joined). To keep currencies tied to this restricted range of movement, all members of the ERM had to commit themselves to follow broadly *similar monetary policies* and to secure, therefore, convergence in economic performance.

The system instituted was similar, on a regional scale, to the Bretton Woods 'adjustable peg' system of fixed exchange rates. The anchor currency, however, which evolved was the Deutschmark (DM) rather than the US dollar and the system could be characterised as a '*crawling peg*' – the wider bands of currency movement and, smaller, more frequent realignments made for a more flexible regime (during the 1980s) that was less liable to the sudden shocks experienced when currency devaluations occurred (see figure 8.1).

4 The ERM was part of the European Monetary System that also included the European Currency Unit – the Ecu – *a parallel currency*. This is the next stage in increasing monetary integration since once currencies have been fixed in price in relation to one another then they can clearly be valued in terms of a common unit of exchange.

The Ecu is a 'basket' of European currencies, each weighted in accordance to their importance in intra-union trade. It was introduced as the official unit of account for EU finances, for intergovernmental exchange of debt, and with the hope that it would become an increasingly important denomination in the international bond markets and eventually the currency for Europe. In the event, less than 1 per cent of EU trade today uses the Ecu and relatively little paper in the Eurobond markets is quoted in Ecus, either. The main reason for this failure is that – like that other pure fabrication, the 'international' language Esperanto – the Ecu has no natural constituency, and additionally it is composed of some currencies that have been subject to unsettling amounts of inflation, and thus has been perceived as a risk.

5 To consolidate the next step towards currency union it is important to move towards *irrevocably fixed exchange rates*, assuring financial markets that there can be no further realignments within the system.

For Europe, this would mean that member currencies are tied into narrow margins for movement and thus the composition of the Ecu could be frozen. The Maastricht treaty envisaged that a *fledgeling central bank* – the European Monetary Institute (EMI) – would come into being at this stage to promote progress towards a single EU monetary policy and the convergence of European monies to a full currency union.

At present in 1996, for a number of reasons enlarged upon below, the international money markets are not convinced that Europe is ready for the final, no-turning-back commitment to fixed exchange rates that will be linked together forever. Despite well-publicised claims of unshakeable faith in their currencies by various political leaders in Europe, they were unable to prevent major devaluations of the lira and peseta and the withdrawal of sterling from the ERM in September 1992, and the 1993 crisis over the franc which blew apart the bands of movement to 15 per cent, effectively dismantling the fixed rate system.

6 *A single currency* is the final stage in monetary union. This simply confirms that a group of currencies with irrevocably fixed rates are as good as one. It has been argued that there is no theoretical difference, for example, between the existence of two separate units of exchange circulating at a fixed price – say one Deutschmark equalling one guilder – and the introduction of a common currency, say the Ecu, which represents the same thing. While this statement is absolutely correct, it is another thing, however, to convince the money markets of this equivalence, as we shall see later. So long as two currencies are representative of two different communities, two different political and economic realities, then money markets are unlikely to accept that any exchange rate between the two is irrevocable. A single currency, then, is the ultimate expression of an integrated, common market.

CONTROL OF THE MONEY SUPPLY

Money's value and usefulness is derived from its liquidity or flexibility: it can be turned into almost anything. (Who, after all, would place any value on money that cannot be quickly exchanged for anything else?) The more easily it can be used, however, the more easily it can be abused: money loses its value if too much of it is created. It is for this reason that, in all communities and throughout history, there have been continuing efforts to control the supply of money.

The relationship between state authorities and private financial markets is the key to understanding how money supplies are determined. This relationship is never stable in any society – it is in a continual state of evolution. On some occasions, for example, private commercial banks have created too much money in order to fund their own ventures or lend to their preferred clients and when carried to excess this led to a collapse in credibility with markets refusing to accept that bank's money. (Innocent bank customers who thus lose all their deposits can criticise central authorities for failing to regulate bank activities here.)

In other cases, governments have created money in order to pay for their own spending (on wars, massive public works, to repay debts, etc.). This leads to debasement of the legal tender, economic dislocation and, in the extreme, markets will again turn to another form of money.

Germany, which has experienced two destructive hyperinflations in the twentieth century, has learned the hard way that social cohesion is dependent on monetary discipline. Bitter experience has shown that government budgets must not be spendthrift and public sector borrowing should not be excessive. (This is because government credits – bonds and bills – quickly become accepted in the markets as a form of money; thus lending can get out of control and only after the crash do societies realise their mistake. It is not just one bank's customers but everyone who loses money in these circumstances.)

If there is to be one common currency in Europe in the future, its reliability and thus its acceptability must be assured. In order to guarantee this, all countries embarking upon the road to monetary integration agreed at Maastricht to meet five convergence criteria. By 1 July 1998, the EMI is supposed to confirm which member states' currencies meet these criteria below, and by 1 January 1999, for those who wanted it, the single currency was agreed to come into being.

THE MAASTRICHT CRITERIA:

1 *Price stability* Inflation in each country concerned must not be more than 1.5 per cent above that of the three lowest EU countries.
2 *Budgets* No government should run a budget deficit beyond 3 per cent of that country's National Income (GDP).
3 *National Debt* Public sector borrowing must not build up over the years to exceed 60 per cent of a country's annual income (GDP).
4 *Interest rates* The market rate of interest for long-term government bonds of each country must not be more than 2 per cent above that of the three lowest EU countries.
5 *Currency fluctuation* National currencies must not be devalued two years previous to union and must stay within the narrow bands instituted by the ERM.

It has been argued that the key criterion here is number 4: interest rates. This is because the price on government bonds is the valuation that independent money markets place on the respective authorities concerned. If government credibility towards currency union is at all suspect then this price will rise with the perceived increasing risk. Alternatively, where a currency's interest rate is in line with others, then the market accepts it is on course for union.

Much has happened since these criteria were agreed upon. Of the twelve signatory countries, not one now satisfies all of these conditions, and the ERM itself has redesigned itself almost out of existence in response to speculative attacks in 1992 and 1993. There is an ongoing debate about the suitability of these criteria and it is now unlikely that they can be used alone to determine which countries will go forward to the stage of full economic and monetary union (EMU) at the end of the century.

The enthusiasm for the Maastricht accord was driven partly by political forces – the desire for a closer European union – and partly by economic argument – if there was to be a common currency it had to be 100 per cent reliable. The alleged economic benefits, however, must be balanced against the costs of achieving monetary integration.

BENEFITS AND COSTS OF A SINGLE CURRENCY

- One direct benefit of a common currency easiest to appreciate is in *the elimination of transactions costs.* Any trade between European partners involves paying the cost of exchanging one currency for another. All tourists know this problem – travel from the north of Italy through Austria and into Germany and in half a day you have lost a considerable sum of money in commission charges changing cash from lire to schillings and then into Deutschmarks. Monetary union will eliminate this deadweight loss: that is, the significant cost that consumers have to pay and for which they receive nothing. The EU commission has estimated that such transactions costs are between 13 and 20 billion Ecus per year.

- The indirect benefit of removing transactions costs and *increasing the transparency of European prices* is more difficult to calculate. European consumers will be able to compare prices of the same good on one side of the continent to the other and make their purchases accordingly. Note that price discrimination between different countries is easier to conceal when people use different currencies – it has been calculated that during the 1980s, buying the same Ford car in the UK has been up to 30 per cent more expensive than in Belgium, for example. Hiding such differentials would be impossible with a common currency. This is an undeniable gain, though quantifying the stimulus this will undoubtedly give to freer trade and increased consumer welfare is difficult to predict.

- A common currency will *remove any uncertainty over future exchange rate movements.* Cross-frontier investment is impeded by the risk of a change in currency prices. Estimated profits from an investment in another country can be reduced or even wiped out if the currency in which those profits occur unexpectedly devalues. Such exchange rate uncertainty can be partly reduced by hedging in currency futures – paying others to take on this risk – but, again, this cost is another deadweight loss which businesses can well do without. A single currency will thus lead to an increase of marginal projects in cross-border investments.

These three benefits are all related: they result from the increased workings of a pan-European price mechanism. Wider, freer trade across the whole continent, it is alleged, will secure a more efficient allocation of combined resources.

- The dominant cost that is raised over currency union is the considerable *loss of economic and political sovereignty* involved. With only one pan-European currency, there can be only one monetary policy. National governments must cede this instrument of their control, therefore, to an independent European bank. No country will be free to increase or decrease their money supply, devalue or raise the price of their currency, and adjust the level of interest rates to suit their own particular circumstances. Thus if one European nation grows faster or experiences less inflation than another, and as a consequence is able to sell a surplus of exports to its neighbour, then before EMU the deficit country could correct the trade balance by choosing either to devalue its currency or it can deflate (i.e. reduce) its national income. Both ways restrict a country's ability to purchase foreign goods, but most would agree that the latter option is the more painful. With monetary union, of course, this policy choice will not be available: only deflation is possible.

Only one cost of currency union has been mentioned here, but this is the major stumbling block. What will be the solution to this problem in the future if there is a single European currency? What policy options do national governments have if they feel that their country is losing out in competition with other European states?

The answer at the national, macroeconomic level is: not a lot. If monetary policy is designed to suit a common European market then differences between existing nations obviously cannot be accommodated. When forced to choose between national interests and a fixed European exchange rate mechanism, therefore, speculators have bet that individual governments will put national interests before European ones. They have not been wrong. Centuries of cultural differences cannot just be assumed away by Euro-enthusiasts.

A SINGLE MONETARY POLICY

How, in theory, could a common monetary policy between a group of countries be constructed? There are two possible means of achieving this: (i) by negotiation and agreement between all partners, or (ii) by the dominance of one major player.

(i) Assume a fixed exchange rate union with capital mobility and no exchange restrictions between three countries: Germany, France and Italy and their three currencies: the Deutschmark, franc and lira. If the interest rate in one country, say Germany, is higher than in the other two (taking into account any risk differential) then this will cause funds to transfer from France and Italy. There will be net sales of francs and lire as holders of these currencies in these two countries switch their savings into Deutschmark in order to enjoy the higher rate of return involved.

Assuming that there is agreement between the three nations involved, as currency-holders in France and Italy switch out of francs and lire and buy into Deutschmark so the money supply of all three countries must change: Germany's will grow and the others' will shrink. This will happen so long as the central bank in Germany makes the Deutschmark required available to buyers in France and Italy. These money movements will continue between countries until interest rates in all cases have moved into line – Germany's will come down a bit and the other two's will move up. (Note that this implies some increased expense for people living on borrowed funds in France and Italy, but the more Germany allows its money supplies to increase and its rate of interest to come down, the less its neighbours will suffer.)

(ii) Now consider the scenario where there is no negotiated agreement between the three countries concerned, or that any such cooperation has broken down. A common monetary policy can evolve in this case where one dominant economy sets its own interest rate or money supply and all other countries adjust their decisions around that.

Suppose Germany has a high interest rate as before. This will again attract funds from the other two countries, but if the Bundesbank in this situation is unwilling to increase its supply of Deutschmark then the other two partner countries have no choice but to adopt the same interest rate – and suffer the much greater contraction of their money supplies and domestic economies – if they wish to preserve a common policy.

In this scenario, so long as Germany is recognised by the international financial markets as possessing the anchor currency in the union then its partners have no option other than to follow its lead or abandon the system.

Just such an analysis applies to the European ERM. Thanks to its strong, anti-inflationary track record ever since it was founded, the German

Bundesbank has inevitably earned the reputation as Europe's key monetary authority. The Bundesbank is independent of German political influence and is constitutionally required to prevent inflation of the Deutschmark. Money markets know this.

Throughout the 1980s, all other member countries in the ERM pursued policies to reduce their inflation rates to correspond to German levels. The deflations this required have been substantial for some countries, and to ease this adjustment process relatively small and frequent devaluations were resorted to (see figure 8.1). Such realignments were allowed within the system and indeed were essential to its survival, given the structural differences between member countries. Additionally, for much of the 1980s, France and Italy maintained controls on the movement of capital in and out of their countries. Some European governments had a reputation for being softer on inflation than others and speculative attack on those currencies would have been inevitable had these measures not been taken.

THE CURRENCY CRISES OF 1992 AND 1993

What doomed the ERM was the rigidity of the mechanism after 1987. Just as it had brought down the Bretton Woods system before, so political inflexibility and the pegging of government reputations to currency prices caused the ERM to eventually blow apart. The build up of international speculative forces against the fixed European exchange rates in the 1990s simply became too great to withstand.

By the early 1990s the ERM had evolved to become a truly fixed rate system. The Maastricht treaty had emphasised the importance of eradicating fluctuations of exchange rates at least two years before union (see criterion 5 above) and it therefore became a sort of virility symbol of governments to achieve this stability as early as possible. Having identified the conditions required for countries to enter the select monetary integration club, it obviously became easy to compare the success of each nation in reaching these goals. Newspapers in all member countries published charts grouping those nations closest to meeting the essential criteria – the pressure was on all governments to improve their position in the rank-order. A currency that devalued in this rarefied atmosphere would indicate an apparent economic weakness and thus lack of political influence for the nation concerned in the councils of Europe.

Unfortunately, at the same time as this convergence in performance of different member countries was becoming an inescapable political strait-jacket, the external economic forces defining Europe were undergoing radical change.

The collapse of communism at the end of the 1980s resurrected the ambition of unifying East with West Germany. Hopes that had been buried for a generation were in the space of a few months astonishingly realised.

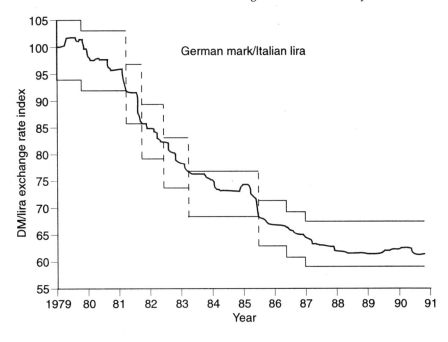

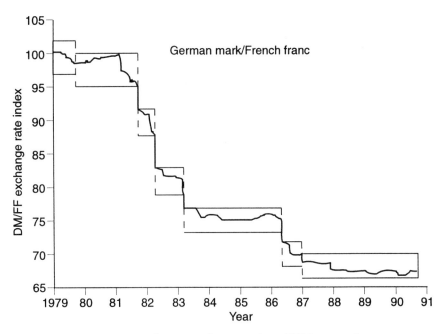

Figure 8.1 'Crawling peg' adjustments between three ERM currencies
Source: P. de Grauwe.

Scores of thousands of East Germans were voting with their feet to adopt the economic system that operated in the West and, especially with Western politicians anxious to stimulate these demands and win votes, the pressure for rapid unification was unstoppable.

What was politically imperative, however, was economically impossible: the sudden opening up of the East German economy and the overvaluation of its domestic currency brought almost immediate economic collapse. Large tracts of East German industry had no markets in the West and were uncompetitive at anything but the lowest possible prices; converting the Ostmark into the Deutschmark at a one-for-one exchange rate bought the support of millions of Eastern voters who had their savings in Ostmarks but grossly overvalued all East German products.

The traumatic contraction of the old East German economy that occurred was only endurable with massive *fiscal transfers* from West Germany. It says much about the importance of their sense of political and social identity that Westerners were prepared to pay the increased taxes required to support their neighbours. In the event 60 per cent of East German income came from this source in 1991–2.

Taxation alone, however, could not pay for all this – government borrowing had to rise. With the Bundesbank unwilling to increase money supplies (it would have been inflationary) increased government borrowing meant that German interest rates rose.

Meanwhile other countries of Europe at this time were characterised by recession. The spending boom at the end of the 1980s decade (prompted by supply-side tax cuts, amongst others – see chapters 3 and 4 above) had led to inflation, increased indebtedness and, consequently, the imposition of deflationary cut-backs. Falling incomes and rising unemployment were the inevitable inheritance at the beginning of the 1990s.

All the elements necessary for a European currency crisis were, by 1992, now in place:

- The ERM had become a rigidly fixed exchange rate system.
- EU governments were anxious to prove their anti-inflationary, pro-Maastricht credentials.
- Due to the shock of unification, the Bundesbank had independently set its interest rate at a relatively high level within Germany.
- Deflation and unemployment were becoming increasing problems for a number of Germany's partners.
- Popular support for the Maastricht agreement and its stringent conditions was by no means overwhelming.

It is not difficult to see the incompatibility of these features. In order to ease the widespread recession (which affected the USA, Japan and many other countries too) there was much talk of the need to reduce interest rates. With German intransigence, however, this was impossible without undermining progress to European currency union. Critics, nevertheless, were not slow to point out that US interest rates were far lower than European ones and this country was rapidly recovering from the recession.

Pressure to devalue was greatest on those European states who had most to gain from so doing and where internal political criticism of the Maastricht agreement was known to be strong.

Given fixed exchange rates plus the prediction that they may not stay fixed for very long and you have the perfect scenario for heavy *speculation*. Sterling fund-holders, for example, have little to lose if they convert all their money into Deutschmark: if there is no change of currency prices then they can simply buy back later when all the fuss has died down; but if sterling is devalued then they can repurchase far more than they had before. This is not just greedy speculation against a particular country's interests: no responsible manager of insurance or pension funds, for example, can sit idly by if those funds are about to be devalued.

In 1992, the Italian lira was thought to be inflation-prone. In contrast, inflation in the UK was no different (if not lower) than in Germany, but it was suffering from the recession and political support for the pound's membership of the ERM was questionable. Heavy selling of both currencies took place in September of that year and, with the Bundesbank unwilling to supply Deutschmarks, devaluations were inevitable. Additionally, the UK left the exchange rate mechanism entirely (rather than just realign the pound's price at a lower level) and brought its interest rates down.

A year later, it all happened again when the French franc came under attack. Similar to the UK, France's inflation record was not in dispute – it satisfied more of the Maastricht criteria than Germany – but now it was deep in painful recession and speculators were betting that the country could not go on any longer without taking the medicine of reducing interest rates. This time, speculation embraced not only the French franc but also the Belgian franc, Spanish peseta and the Danish krona. The ERM could not continue in its present form. The 2.25 per cent narrow band of movement allowed between currency prices was widened to 15 per cent – as good as returning the currencies of Europe to independent, managed floating.

CAN EUROPE HAVE A COMMON CURRENCY?

All these events appear to be very persuasive evidence that squeezing very disparate economies into one currency and one common monetary policy is impossible. But this is not quite the whole story – there is a growing appreciation that it is not at the level of macroeconomic monetary policy where the all-important flexibility is required. Microeconomic occupational and geographical mobility of resources is more necessary, and thus it may be that responsive supply-side policies can compensate for macro-money rigidity – if not straight away, than in the future with increasing economic integration.

Already the trade-creating effects of a common market have led to increasing integration of the economies of Europe. Each country's economic health and welfare is tied into each other's, and though this level of integration varies amongst them (see Figure 8.2), it is increasing for all. National sovereignty is thus becoming increasingly irrelevant. No one European nation can conduct an effective, independent, macroeconomic policy – the fortunes of all member states are inextricably entwined.

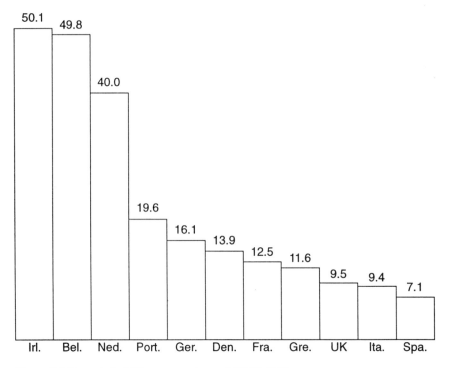

Figure 8.2 Exports to EU as percentage of GDP, 1990
Source: EC Commission in P. de Grauwe.

The costs of any monetary union will be lessened, therefore, and the benefits maximised, the more integrated and flexible the contributing national economies become. This argument leads directly to the question: how flexible and internationally integrated must a group of economies become before a common currency brings more benefits than costs? What is an *optimal currency area*?

THE ECONOMICS OF AN OPTIMAL CURRENCY AREA

Consider the situation, referred to earlier, where one country (Country A) experiences an increasing deficit in its trade with another (Country B). Over time, if the unequal demand for these countries' products persists, Country A will move into deepening recession, while B's economy will boom.

How can this disequilibrium situation be resolved in a single currency area where realigning exchange rates is not an available policy option?

1 Microeconomic, 'supply-side' *flexibility of labour markets* is required. Where wages are flexible and/or labour is geographically and occupationally mobile in and between the two countries concerned then there is no need for separate currency price movements.

A slump in demand for A's goods will produce a fall in demand for A's labour. Where wages are flexible (downward) then, it is argued, there will be no unemployment since labour is retained at lower cost. The cost and thus price of A's exports will fall, winning back an increase in demand. The opposite effect operates in the case of Country B. Booming demand bids up the wages of B's labour. As costs and prices rise so B is not likely to sell as many exports. The trade imbalance between A and B rights itself.

If wages in both countries are 'sticky' and do not move smoothly in response to changing conditions of demand (they tend not to) then unemployment will result in A, overfull employment and perhaps inflation might occur in B. Where labour is mobile, however, A's unemployed workers simply migrate to B, thus removing unemployment in one country and reducing the inflationary pressure in the other.

If neither conditions hold, if wages are sticky and labour is immobile, then differential economic conditions in both countries cannot be alleviated without exchange rate movements. An optimal currency area is thus one which enjoys flexible labour markets.

2 The problem of deficits and surpluses is hardly a matter for concern between large, mostly self-sufficient countries where only a small fraction of goods and services are internationally traded. In contrast, where a group of countries exchange a high fraction of their produce then they have much to gain from a single currency. Frequent changes in exchange rates between them would trigger far-reaching shocks throughout their economies. Open economies with a high *proportion of tradable goods and services* exchanged between them, therefore, benefit more and suffer less in a currency union. It makes less sense to include those neighbours who are less integrated within the group or have stronger trade links with countries outside the region.

THE CASE OF EUROPE

If we apply this analysis to Europe now we can see how far these countries concerned make up an optimum currency area.

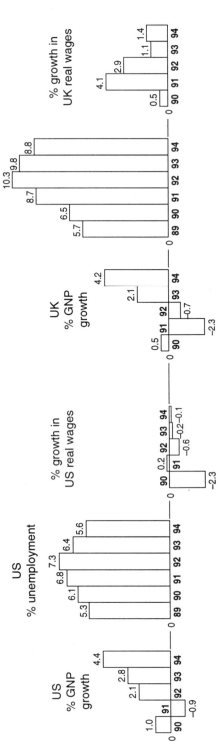

Flexible labour markets should show unemployment positively correlated with real wages and (after a time lag) negatively correlated with GNP growth. Compare the workings of US labour markets with those of different European states. Real wages have fallen throughout the early 1990s in the USA whilst unemployment was rising then falling even whilst growth was recovering. European unemployment rates were generally higher yet their rates of growth of real wages have stayed stubbornly positive also – a clear indication of inflexible, unresponsive markets.

Figure 8.3 USA and Europe: economic growth, unemployment and wage increases, 1989–94
Source: The Economist.

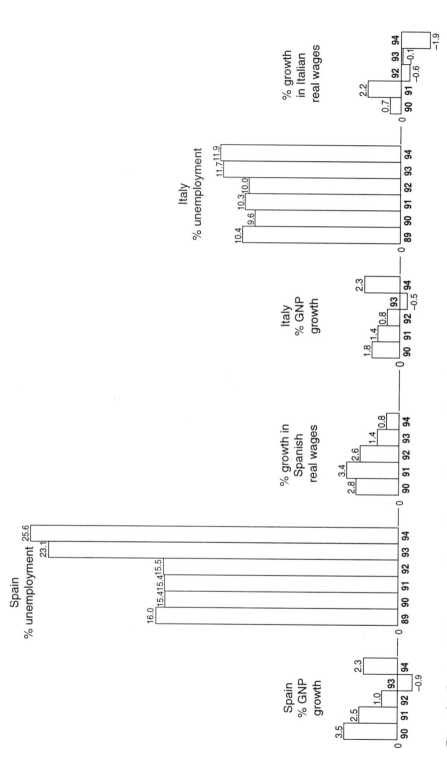

Figure 8.4 Spain and Italy: economic growth, unemployment and wage increases, 1989–94

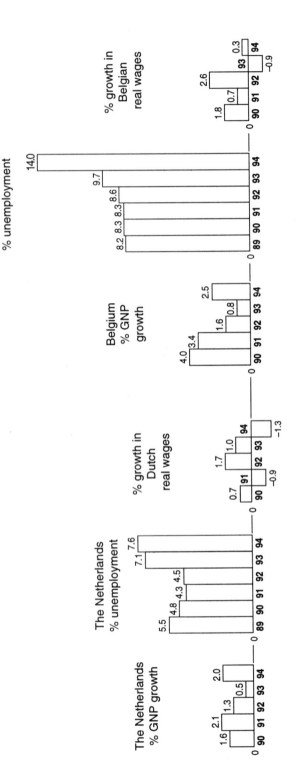

Figure 8.5 The Netherlands and Belgium: economic growth, unemployment and wage increases, 1989–94

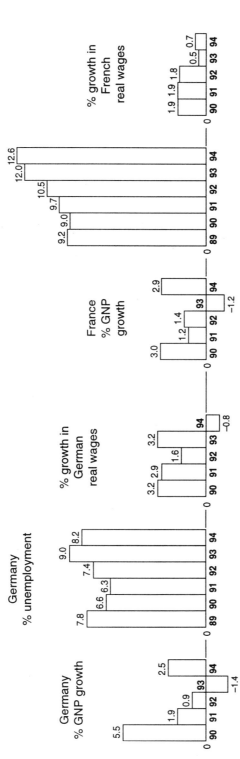

Figure 8.6 Germany and France, economic growth, unemployment and wage increases, 1989–94

With regard to labour markets there has been growing concern that European labour is far less mobile than in North America. This is true geographically – it is more difficult for labour to move around Europe where different cultures, languages and laws act as a disincentive, compared to the homogeneity of North America, for example – and also occupationally, where social welfare legislation and government minimum wage laws (such as embodied in the 'social chapter' to the Maastricht agreement) are argued to reduce labour mobility. Workers are less keen to change jobs if they have accumulated many non-wage benefits in their present occupation; employees are less willing to take on extra labour if it will be difficult and expensive to sack them. Such market 'distortions' have been blamed for a European average unemployment of persistently over 10 per cent in the early 1990s: almost double that of the USA which has far less protective labour legislation.

The argument that social welfare legislation distorts labour markets and is responsible for unemployment is by no means accepted by all. But for whatever reason, wages and labour do appear to be generally less flexible in Europe than in the USA.

Consider the accompanying graphs on rates of economic growth, unemployment and real wage movements for selected European countries and the USA (see Figures 8.3–8.6). The latter has had consistently lower rates of unemployment than in Europe during the early 1990s recession, and its rate of growth of real wages has been close to zero or negative, even when recovery from the recession has been rebounding strongly. Compare this with the European countries. Few seem to be able to show that deepening recession and their much higher unemployment levels have had any noticeable effect on containing wage rises. Clearly, on this evidence, labour markets in Europe appear to be far less flexible and responsive to economic realities than those in the USA.

Insofar as integration within a European common market is concerned, some countries are much more tied into the economic fate of their neighbours than others (see Figure 8.2).

For the Netherlands, Belgium and Ireland, large fractions of their exports are sold in Europe, so clearly any change in exchange rates will significantly affect their export revenues – with knock-on effects for the domestic economy. (This is the *foreign trade multiplier*: any change in export demand has a multiplied effect on domestic incomes.)

For countries such as the UK, Spain and Italy, however, a far lower proportion of their exports are sold in Europe and so the argument for these countries joining a single currency as soon as possible is less convincing. If eventual monetary union remains their goal then they can afford to move more slowly – and maybe work at loosening internal markets, eliminating structural unemployment – until their trade patterns are more tied into the rest of Europe and the balance of costs and benefits shifts more emphatically in favour of integration.

A CONCLUSION FOR EUROPE

The conclusion offered here, therefore, is that the European Union is not an optimum currency area at present. The striking economic diversity of European nations indicates, at best, a multi-speed approach to currency union – the cost of converging towards a common monetary policy has already proved to be too great for many.

A number of European states may feel they already have enough in common to press ahead with integration: possibly a 'greater Deutschmark area' embracing Germany, the Netherlands, Belgium and maybe Denmark and Austria, following a single monetary policy along the lines of the dominant partner model analysed above. Introducing a new, single currency for Europe, however, is beset with problems of political credibility, quite aside from the economic arguments involved. Germans will not want to lose their trusted Deutschmark in favour of an untested Ecu; France and the UK will not join any union that does not give them significant influence over a common monetary policy.

It was stated at the beginning that currency areas were the economic expression of social groupings, and so the argument for currency union, in the end, stretches beyond economics. The experience of German unification is instructive in this regard. Only when the peoples of Europe (or any other combination of countries contemplating monetary integration) see their economies and thus their destinies inextricably entwined, such that even the most myopic nationalists are willing to pay the costs involved to secure the common good, will a single currency successfully come into being.

KEY WORDS

Adjustable peg   Where a currency's exchange rate is fixed, or pegged, in terms of another and then it is decided to re-fix or adjust the price to another level. The fixed exchange rate system continues but with a different central rate. A *crawling peg* implies a system where the prices are adjusted in small steps on a monthly basis over a longer period of time, rather than a big, once-and-for-all readjustment.

The Exchange Rate Mechanism   was set up as one component (along with the European currency unit, the Ecu) of the European Monetary System in 1979. The ERM tied the (then) European Community currencies together at fixed rates within agreed tolerances for movement (2.25 per cent, except Italy: 6.0 per cent. The UK opted not to join). Realignments of the currencies' central fixed rates were allowed for through negotiation with other partners, and indeed were a common feature through the early part of the 1980s – the French franc was devalued three times and the Deutschmark upvalued seven times from 1979 to 1987.

Exchange restrictions   Any attempt by governments to restrict free trade in a country's currency.

Fiscal transfers   The transfer of tax revenues from – in this case – West German taxpayers to East German development funds.

Fixed exchange rates   This is where a currency fixes its price in terms of another within strictly defined limits, e.g. 1 per cent movement up or down. To fix a price in a free market means the supplier must buy back any quantity surplus to requirements, or increase the quantity if there is a shortage. That is, if the price is fixed, supplies must adjust to secure equilibrium.

Foreign trade multiplier   An injection of increased spending in an economy will lead to a multiplied growth in the circular flow of income (see chapter 3). Increased spending, for example, can come from foreign customers buying more of a country's exports. Any given impulse of spending raises incomes many times since increased first-round earnings for exporters are then passed on in the form of more spending on business supplies; this increases second-round incomes for a whole range of producers, who then spend this, and so on. The larger the fraction of exports to total production in an economy, the more important the foreign trade multiplier, i.e. the impact of export demand.

Hyperinflation   This is where the rate of growth of prices increases so rapidly that people lose confidence in the value of money. The local currency then ceases to become acceptable as a medium of exchange and traders either turn to another form of money, if available (e.g. foreign currencies), or they resort to barter.

Managed floating   Exchange rates, like any prices, can be left free to let the markets decide what they should be. Governments may wish, however, to limit any excessive swings in their currency's price by entering the market to buy it when they think the exchange rate is too low or sell it if it is considered too high. They thus attempt to 'manage' or control the floating price at an acceptable level.

An optimal currency area   Some relatively small communities have their own currency and set themselves apart from larger neighbours (e.g. Bahrain Dinar – population 0.4 million); whereas, in contrast, some extremely large populations share a single unit of exchange (the Chinese Yuan – population 1,134 million). The economics of optimal currency areas considers what size of trading community is best to have a common currency.

QUESTIONS

1   Explain how the Bretton Woods fixed exchange rate system operated. What are the advantages of fixed rate regimes and why did this one break down?
2   In 1991, European governments agreed to move towards a common currency and they committed their economies to satisfy certain convergence criteria. What are the *economic reasons* for these Maastricht conditions?
3   What policy options do national governments have if they feel that their country is losing out in contrast to other partners in a currency union?
4   What caused the break-up of the European Exchange Rate mechanism in 1992–3? How can different countries' currencies move closer to a union *without* suffering speculative attack?
5   Should the European Union adopt a single currency?

FURTHER READING

De Grauwe, Paul. *The Economics of Monetary Integration*. Oxford University Press, 1994.
Hallwood, C. Paul and MacDonald, Ronald. *International Money and Finance*. Blackwell, 1994.

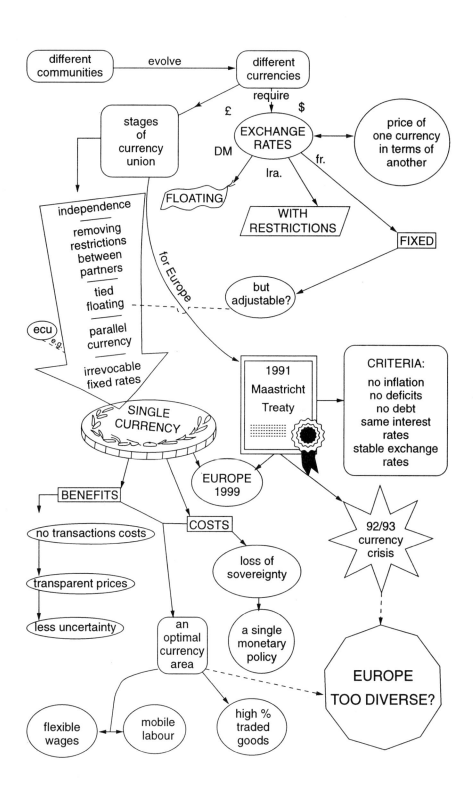

9 The economics of oil

Topics to be considered in this chapter

- Factors influencing oil demand:
  i derived demand
  ii incomes and income-elasticity
  iii complements, substitutes and cross-elasticity
- The oil industry: competition, monopoly and oligopoly
- Exploration; production; transportation; refining; and distribution
- The costs of production; diminishing returns; economies of scale; vertical integration
- The major oil companies, OPEC and the struggle for ownership of supplies
- The history of oil prices

INTRODUCTION

Oil is a very important twentieth-century product. It is a vital source of energy, an irreplaceable transport fuel, and an essential raw material in many manufacturing processes.

Crude oil is a source of great economic power. Since its production cost in many places is far below its selling price in world markets, so the ownership and control of oil reserves has been a means by which great wealth has been earned and lost.

The countries that export and import oil are – for the most part – geographically, economically and culturally separate. Oil has thus become the world's most important internationally traded item – both in volume and value terms – and changes in this trade have had enormous financial, political and socio-cultural repercussions on the parties involved. (Wars, revolutions and mass migrations are only perhaps the most visible manifestation of these.)

Understanding oil prices proves the key to understanding these issues. As oil prices change, so this impacts on consumer desires to use one form of energy or another; what sort of car to buy, or whether to use a different mode of transport altogether. The implications of changing consumer demand spread throughout the industrialised world causing classic microeconomic reallocation of resources. Oil prices affect decisions to invest billions of dollars in different industrial projects: whether to build major highways or rail networks; high-speed trains or electric cars; offshore drilling platforms or nuclear power stations. Industries grow and decline; workers get laid off and seek employment elsewhere; certain regions and countries earn more, others less.

Oil prices also affect macroeconomic variables such as the levels of national incomes, aggregate spending and the balance of payments of different countries. The enormous sums involved affect countries' rates of economic growth, levels of international debt and the overall functioning of the world's financial system.

Finally, oil prices affect how quickly the various forms of energy are exploited – whether we use nuclear power, renewable sources of energy, or whether oil, gas, coal or forests are burnt – and how, therefore, global environmental degradation will be affected.

All these decisions are influenced, one way or the other, by whether the price of oil moves significantly up or down.

OIL DEMAND AND SUPPLY

A study of oil prices involves study of three major areas of interest – the consuming countries, the producer countries and the international oil industry which mediates between them. This relationship has been described as a *trilateral oligopoly* (Roncaglia, 1984); that is, each of the three parties referred to above is dominated by an important core or oligopolist element: the wealthy OECD countries amongst the world's consumers, OPEC amongst the producer countries and the major international oil companies in the industry. How the nature of oligopoly relationships within each power group has changed and how this has affected the interaction of the three parties together leads to a greater understanding of the determination of oil prices and the myriad of other issues that spill out from this.

Consumption

The three biggest consumers in 1993 were: the USA (16.4 million barrels per day [mbd]); Western Europe (13.7 mbd); and the ex-USSR (5.5 mbd, down from 8.4 mbd in 1991). As a group the OECD countries, which include North America, Western Europe, Japan, Australia and New Zealand, exert most pressure on world markets at present since they have the highest incomes yet produce insufficient oil to satisfy their own needs. OECD countries consume 57.7 per cent of the world's oil, yet produce only 24.4 per cent. The early 1990s recession in these countries has brought flat demand and as a result this has influenced a fall in world oil consumption of 0.8 per cent in 1993. This average hides wide disparities, however. The unprecedented collapse in incomes, industrial output and energy demands of the former Soviet Union, for example, meant demand for oil fell 19 per cent in Russia and 29 per cent in Ukraine. In contrast, less-developed countries – which of course contain three-quarters of the world's population – consume comparatively little (31.9 per cent) of global oil supplies but it is here that the rate of growth of oil demand is now growing most strongly, and the future impact of, particularly, Asian demand is likely to be of increasing importance.

The industrialised world has grown up through the twentieth century dependent on cheap oil. Note that consumption of this fundamental raw material is a *derived demand*, that is, it is derived from people's demand for such essential, everyday products as electricity, and transport services. As world incomes, trade and travel have increased at an accelerating pace this century, so has consumption of all energy supplies – from 7.7 billion barrels of oil (bboe) equivalent in 1925 to around 59.7 bboe in 1993. Of this, oil consumption has increased from approximately 1 bboe to 23.9 bboe over the same period. That is, the actual *growth* of the world economy has been fuelled mostly by oil (and very recently, by natural gas – a related energy source); demand for other forms of energy has changed, by comparison, relatively slowly.

Revealed by these figures is the finding that demand for oil is *income elastic*, that is, as incomes rise so consumption of oil increases at a faster pace. While this has been true of general world demand during the first half of the twentieth century, because of the enormous changes in oil markets since the 1970s this is no longer the case today for the richest countries (for example US oil consumption grew by 0.7 per cent during 1993, while its economy expanded by 3 per cent). Income elasticity of oil demand can still be high, however, for developing countries where in the early stages of growth, human and animal effort and primitive energy supplies (like burning wood fuel and animal dung) are replaced by more efficient oil-driven machinery. (China's oil consumption grew by over 11 per cent in 1993; Thailand's increased 13.8 per cent).

Quite apart from this structural change in energy demand for countries in the early stages of development, the sheer force of numbers involved in population growth drives the accelerating demand for oil in countries like India and China. There is a huge potential demand building up in these countries where, at present, energy consumption per head is a tiny fraction of that in the developed world. With increasing populations, increasing industrialisation and increasing incomes we can predict that the less-developed world will, by the end of the century, be competing strongly to command a greater share of the world's oil.

At the time of writing, rates of growth of industrial production in China (population over 1,200 million), India (population over 850 million), Indonesia (population 180 million) and Brazil (population over 150 million) were 28.1 per cent, 10.6 per cent, 18.2 per cent and 12.5 per cent, respectively. (This compares to USA industrial growth of 5.8 per cent and Japan, 6.7 per cent.) Growing industry needs energy. Workforces need transport to and from work; raw materials need to be brought into factories, transformed into finished products and then distributed throughout the country and abroad. As cities and industrial areas grow, more roads need to be built, more houses and factories go up, more lighting, heating and transport is demanded. At present, energy consumption per capita of poor Asians and Latin Americans is less than an eighth of rich North Americans, but this only goes to show what growth potential there is locked up in continents with the fastest growing incomes and most of the world's population.

As well as income, an important determinant of oil demand is the price (and thus availability) of *complementary goods*. In particular, so long as humankind's love affair with the motor car continues, so will its dependency on oil. There is no sign yet that there is a limit to this particular market. As technology improves, and increasing world competition between motor manufacturers stimulates efficiency, the relative price of cars is falling. Thirty years ago, the cost of buying a standard family car in Western Europe was equivalent to the average annual real wage. It is half that now. Car ownership per head is thus increasing everywhere.

The most saturated market is the USA, which has more cars than drivers, but even here – although sales growth has slowed and environmental concerns are becoming ever-louder – vehicle numbers and miles travelled are still both increasing. If this is true of North America, small wonder that the big, multinational producers are competing strongly to get a foothold in the potentially huge markets of Asia. Vehicle sales in East Asia (excluding India and Japan) are predicted to double to over 8.7 million vehicles per year by 2005, and this is based on the assumption that these will be principally lorries, vans, buses, pick-ups, etc. The dynamic growth sector of private car consumption is not scheduled to take off until next century!

Based on the evidence so far, the demand for oil thus looks like being buoyant well into the future, given the assumption that no catastrophic slump in world incomes or vehicle consumption occurs. This is not yet a complete picture, however, since there is still a third influence to consider: the price of *substitute fuels*.

The lower the relative price of substitute energy sources like coal, natural gas, nuclear power, etc., the more competitive they become as alternatives to oil. The future demand for oil therefore must take into account what is likely to happen to prices of these competing fuels.

The change in consumption of one good in response to the change in price of another is measured by the *cross-elasticity of demand*. In transport, for example, the cross-elasticity of demand for alternatives, compared to oil, is close to zero. There are *no* closely priced alternative fuels in sight as yet for road and air transport. In power generation, however, long-term cross-elasticities are high between oil and gas, wherever supplies of the latter are relatively easily attainable (i.e. at low cost). The technical difficulties of transporting gas nonetheless mean that it is still not a competitive substitute fuel for *all* oil-fired generators, though clearly as gas technology improves it is pricing itself into more markets.

Consumption of gas is predicted to grow strongly into the next century, driven by demand for its use in power stations and by the increasing investment in gas supply infrastructure in a number of developing and developed countries alike. In the past, the ease of use of gas in substitution for other fuels has been held up more by political and social considerations than by economic factors. In a number of European countries, for example, there has been a comparative lack of government interest in gas, despite discoveries of large reserves. Where power generation has been under public ownership there has been a tendency to support traditional, labour-intensive, coal mining rather than the more economically efficient (but less employment-creating) gas industry. With increasing deregulation, however, this public sector restraint has diminished

The long-term demand for oil in power generation will therefore be subject to competition from gas, wherever low-cost supplies are available. The graph of the world's primary energy consumption, 1968–1993, already shows this trend (see Figure 9.1). It is almost certain that natural gas will continue to steal the market share from oil in OECD power markets, but substantial declines in oil use for this purpose are now highly unlikely, since the massive substitutions in favour of gas after the 1970s oil price hikes have already taken place. Note that the cross-elasticity of demand for gas as opposed to oil-powered energy *in the short run* is low – since it takes an enormous amount of capital to switch distribution networks and electricity generating capacity from one power source to another.

The power supply for the future was once popularly considered to be *nuclear energy*. During the 1970s when oil prices were rising sharply and there was a general fear that the world was running out of fossil fuels, nuclear power was held up to be the saviour of the modern Western economy. Cheap electricity produced by the alleged non-polluting, peaceful use of nuclear technology was seen as the only viable means of getting the OECD countries off the hook of OPEC dependency. The strategic incentive to invest in large programmes of nuclear power expansion was thus all-persuasive. Given the one-sided political debate of the times, the purely *economic* arguments for such actions were never properly evaluated.

Privately owned, profit-seeking nuclear power stations that must sell their electricity at competitive rates or go bust are a rarity. Few countries that have invested massively in nuclear power have put their decision to the test in a free market place. West and East European nuclear industries which produce significant fractions of their countries' total energy needs are all in public hands. (40 per cent of France's energy is nuclear powered; the figure for all of Western Europe is 15 per cent.)

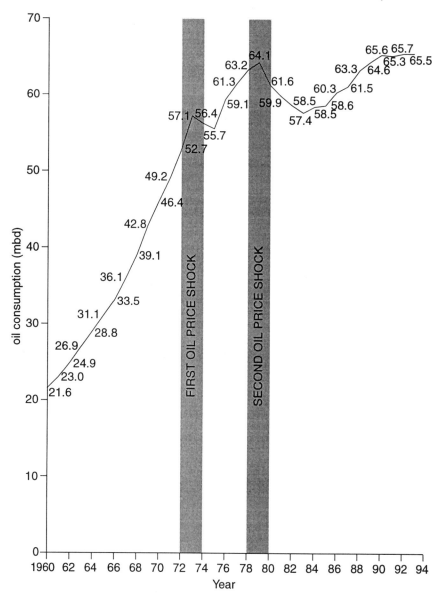

Figure 9.1 Oil consumption, 1960–93 (mbd)
Source: BP Statistical Reviews.

During the 1980s decade, however, after the oil shortage panics of the 1970s and the rush to find alternatives, a number of private electricity generators in the USA had a good, hard look at the economics of nuclear power stations. They did not like what they saw. With low oil prices now asserting themselves in the market place there was no economic case for expensive nuclear energy. Contracts for building new nuclear facilities were cancelled.

Into the 1990s now, with both construction and running costs for nuclear power stations much higher than was originally estimated; with research costs that have always been extremely expensive (though normally funded by government research grants for security reasons); with growing public anxiety over safety precautions; and awareness of the earlier, over-optimistic view of reprocessing and storage costs of spent fuel, the enthusiasm for nuclear energy has evaporated. It is revealing that in the late 1980s privatisation of the electricity generating industry in the UK, the nuclear sector was the only one not offered for sale to private buyers. It has never made a profit. No profit-seeker would ever invest in it.

We can safely conclude that the world's growing energy demands cannot be economically supplied through nuclear power. The demand for oil is unlikely to be significantly reduced by any effective competition from this industry.

Total world consumption of *coal* has been falling slowly but steadily through the 1990s, due to the twin forces of recession (especially in the former Soviet Union) and substitution for more competitive fuels in power generation (gas in Europe). The political and social arguments to support coal have been strong in this traditional, high-employment sector, but as government subsidies continue to lose out to market forces in Europe and further east in Poland, Ukraine and Russia, the demand for coal will be constrained by its rising real price, even as these economies recover their growth.

In the developing countries, where labour is cheaper and strikes less likely, coal industries remain economic where reserves have not already been overexploited. China is now the world's biggest coal producer and its output increased by 2.7 per cent in 1993, in contrast to declines in East and West Europe and North America. Coal consumption figures for LDCs are set to continue rising – but they are unlikely to compensate for falling OECD demand in the near future, though they may prompt increasing growth beyond the year 2000. If growth in LDC and particularly Asian incomes continues apace into the twenty-first century, however, it is unlikely that coal supplies will be able to keep up with demand. Oil is most likely to be the marginal fuel that will be required to fill the gap.

Conservationists argue that *renewable energies* must eventually replace fossil fuels if the world economy is to have a sustainable future. This is an important argument that deserves fuller coverage below (see chapter 13). The demand for oil as compared to alternative, renewable energy, however, will depend on at what price these fuels are delivered to the market place.

There is no doubt that demand for renewable energies is growing strongly, but it comes from a very low base (e.g. hydro-electricity – the only economically significant renewable energy source – satisfied only 2.5 per cent of world demand in 1993); there is no low-cost, environmentally friendly supply that can come anywhere near to meeting total world consumption needs; and no renewable energy is environmentally costless anyway (huge dams and reservoirs required to supply industrial amounts of hydro-electricity are notoriously damaging to local ecologies).

We can conclude, then, that the cross-elasticities of demand for renewable energies in comparison to oil will be close to zero for the foreseeable future.

To summarise, consumption of oil is greatest in the world's developed, market economies though growth here has been flat through the early, recessionary 1990s. Demand in less-developed countries has been increasing steadily and if this trend continues they will pay an important role in determining the future price of oil.

Demand for oil in transport looks unshakeable; in power generation oil faces increasing competition from gas in a number of OECD countries and, to a lesser extent, from coal in the developing world.

There are a number of unknowns facing future oil demand. This section will finish with questions involving three different parts of the world, starting with the biggest.

The extent of the collapse in the former Soviet Union is still unpredictable. It is the world's third biggest consumer *and* producer. With economies still in convulsions it is difficult to see when, and in what form, this commonwealth of states will recover. The old Soviet Union was a net oil exporter, but production has since contracted faster than consumption. How will they rebuild? What relationship will evolve between Russia and its neighbouring states? Will oil be exported or imported in the future? What influence will this commonwealth have on world markets?

China is the world's most populous state and its economy has recently been booming with market reforms. The early 1990s has seen China become a net oil importer. Will these trends continue, post Deng Xiaoping?

Growth in the less-developed world can never be taken for granted. International debt crises seem to recur with disturbing regularity, but assuming these do not erupt into world-wide panic, and assuming that governments do not turn the clock back on the successes in economic policy that they have enjoyed recently, it is the argument here that Asian and Latin American consumers will play an increasing part in determining the future movement of oil prices. But just how fast will LDC incomes and consumption continue to grow?

The oil industry

There are a number of different players in the oil industry – six major international oil companies (the 'majors': Shell, Exxon, BP, Mobil, Texaco, Gulf/Socal); a number of middle-sized companies like the 'independents' (e.g. Phillips, Marathon, etc.) plus various state-owned enterprises (e.g.

ENI, Petrofina, etc.); many relatively small, specialist, contract companies (e.g. in prospecting, engineering, undersea diving, transport, etc.); and, finally, a few increasingly large and competitive OPEC state companies (such as Saudi Aramco/Samarec).

All these businesses operate at various stages along the production line of a liquid – from 'upstream' exploration and discovery, through production and transportation, to 'downstream' refining and distribution. In the industry, only the majors have traditionally been heavily involved all round the world in all stages of this production process.

An examination of the constraints that define business practice at every stage in the oil industry provides a fascinating series of examples of microeconomic principles at work, and they eventually build up to determine the nature of the relationship that has evolved between industry practitioners and the producer countries that are host to much of their operations.

Exploration

Oil exploration started in the USA in the hands of the independent, speculative 'wildcatter' where test drilling on land was not technologically difficult, where capital threshold costs were comparatively cheap, where chances of discovery were entirely random, where competition was rampant, and where US property law emphasised the 'rule of capture'. These conditions in effect programmed the sort of oil industry that was to emerge in the USA and they still have an important influence today.

Oil exploration is now technologically complex, expensive, but still a random, financially risky business. Seismological search techniques and computer data gathering and interpretation are infinitely more skilful and sophisticated compared to past methods of finding the appropriate geological structures below ground, but ultimately, whether a given rock formation bears oil or not can only be determined by digging for it, and the likelihood that one test bore will strike it rich are as good as any other. A cheap, independent wildcatter who sets up his rig one day, drills quickly, then cuts his losses, up-roots and moves elsewhere tomorrow is being very economically efficient. A multi-million mega-buck operator who invests a fortune in investigating all the possibilities of one specific location is employing a far less productive exploration strategy.

US oil exploration at the turn of the twentieth century illustrated the *'tragedy of the commons'*. Where an underground oil reservoir was common to a number of different properties, US law held that the oil belonged to whoever could get it out. Each individual landowner, therefore, had an economic incentive to drill holes all over his property in a mad rush to extract as much oil as possible before anyone else could do the same. The more holes are drilled, the more rapidly the oil could be depleted, the more the landowner could capture at the expense of his neighbour. As all tried to do the same, of course, the landscape was desecrated, the common resource exhausted and there was an inevitable excess supply of oil, falling prices and thus falling profits. Success or failure in such a competitive environment depended in the end on the number and cost of test drills, the percentage success rate and the market price at which the oil could be sold off. For many operators, profits were negative.

The economics of exploration today still illustrate many of these fundamentals, though the rush to capture a common resource is no longer applicable in most areas. Instead, risks are compounded by political factors – in many parts of the world, the search for oil goes on in disputed territory. Probabilities of a change in governments, taxes, exchange controls, policies regarding nationalisation of foreign assets, and – worse – guerrilla action, wars, etc., must all be calculated. The total cost of drilling activity must be compared to projected yields and the price of oil. The lower the oil price, the less exploration will take place in risky, marginal areas. It is not worth the expense of looking for future supplies if the rewards involved in present exploration are less than can be earned by placing those same funds in non-risk-bearing bank accounts.

Note the converse implication of this principle: oil reserves are a direct outcome of exploration activity, and the higher the price of oil, the more supplies will be looked for and brought on-stream. The world's oil is thus *not* fixed in supply (as so many conservationists insist) – it increases with its price.

This principle is true even for one given reservoir: how much oil is there, in economic terms, depends on how far it pays to extract the oil from all the other junk that surrounds it: water, mud, gas, etc. If it is too fragmented, too messy a cocktail, then it does not pay to pump up much other than the purest, most accessible deposit. But if the price of oil increases, then it becomes worthwhile to extract more from this same source. What counts as the total of commercially viable reserves in the world (see Figure 9.2), therefore, *immediately* increases as oil prices increase – the economic boundary of all existing reservoirs shifts out (and this does not include all the other unknown reservoirs that now become worth looking for).

Production

Once a test drill has struck oil, immediate clues are given with respect to the quality of the deposit and the pressure it is under. Further wells give information on the geological spread and characteristics of the underground structures, indicating the optimum location for a production platform.

The nature of oil in the ground varies immensely. Some reservoirs may contain many unstable gases which are best flared-off at the well-head; others may be highly polluting – rich in sulphur, heavy with tar, etc. Deposits can be very fractured and technologically complex to exploit. Pressure and depth vary. Each complication adds to the costs of production.

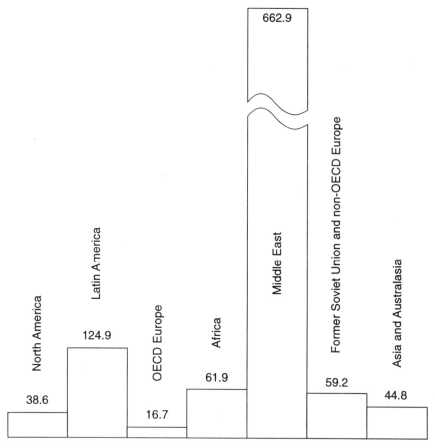

Figure 9.2 World oil reserves, 1993 prices (measured in thousand million barrels)
Source: BP Statistical Reviews.

For certain sites the geographical, technical and political environment may be relatively uncomplicated and small operators may be just as cost-effective as bigger ones. With other sites, however, where the natural environment is difficult, where distances are long and supporting infra-structure absent (e.g. in the North Sea and Alaska) then investment requirements are much greater. Add to this the hostility or unpredict-ability of the political scene (e.g. in Azerbaijan, Nigeria, Colombia, etc.) and here oil production is subject to substantial economies of scale. Only the large, multinational oil companies have the resources to manage the risks involved. Small companies cannot afford to compete.

Once all investment is in place for the production of crude oil – once government approval has been negotiated; percentages agreed; contracts signed; production platforms installed; pipelines and storage facilities constructed, then finally the taps can be turned on. The economics of production are then characterised by the following:

- The *marginal cost* of producing one more barrel of oil is *very small* compared to the *fixed cost* of negotiating the way in and installing all the necessary production capacity.
- Production is subject to *the law of diminishing returns*. The more the taps are opened, the faster oil is depleted, the quicker pressure drops and the more investment is necessary (in pumping, water drives, etc.) to secure each additional barrel. This production decline curve ensures that returns diminish: the rate of increase of marginal costs depends on the speed of the depletion of the oil reservoir.
- The production rate will depend on the market price of oil. If current oil prices are higher than bank interest rates, then it pays producers to sell oil rather than leave it in the ground. If, however, oil prices and thus rates of return fall *below* market rates of interest, producers are better off withholding investment, depositing these funds in a bank and waiting for prices to recover before they produce more.

Transportation

This involves transporting crude from well-head to storage facility, from here to a refinery, and finally taking petroleum products to retail outlets. The location of production sites and markets for consumption determine the pattern of transportation needs. Generally the transportation of oil is highly specialised and this thus falls within the domain of the oil industry rather than becoming a sub-division of the transport industry.

The most efficient way to transport a liquid is via pipelines, rather than in discrete units by sea, road or rail containers. Pipelines, however, represent a huge investment in occupationally and geographically immobile capital and this can only be commercially profitable if a regular flow between producer input and market output can be assured. This way, if dealers both ends of the pipeline keep to the bargain, average and marginal costs of production can be minimised.

Pipelines are a form of *natural monopoly*. That is, it is quite clearly most economic to have one large supply line leading from oil fields to market, rather than have different oil companies construct a number of smaller ones. Such economics supports the creation of a monopoly, or a *cartel* of a group of producers where agreement between them over use of a common pipeline can be negotiated. In the ocean-going tanker market, however, competition is the natural outcome where *barriers to entry* to the world's seas are few and a large number of rival carriers can thus compete over any designated tanker route.

Note, lastly, that the transport of crude oil out from a production region is necessarily more cost-effective than the distribution of petroleum products from a refinery. There are hundreds of different products, all requiring specialised treatment, and with dispersed markets there is thus no potential to exploit economies of scale.

Refining

Oil refineries are the factories of the oil industry – manufacturing finished products for the consumer. They thus have to be responsive to changing consumer demand on the one side and match this up with appropriate inputs on the other. As with all manufacturing industry, however, capital equipment is highly specific. Once built, refineries are tied in to a particular composition of crude, and to the production of petroleum products in a relatively restricted range. There is limited tolerance for changes: costly investment is necessary for any up-grading of product or process (e.g. to build in cleaner, more environmentally friendly technology). Fixed costs, as elsewhere in the industry, are very high and profits are maximised when the plant is operating at capacity with a regular through-put at very low marginal costs.

Individual refineries tend to have a degree of market power according to the geographical region in which they are located. This is determined by the costs of distributing products – often in comparatively small road or rail tankers. Some oil companies dominate in some world markets, others in others. Profit margins vary according to the degree of competition versus market power that reigns. In all cases, guaranteeing secure inputs of crude is essential, hence the importance of *vertical integration* (extending the business upstream and downstream), and/or signing long-term contracts or agreeing to joint ventures with low-cost suppliers.

Distribution

There are numerous petroleum products derived from crude oil, including gases (such as butane, acetylene); light oils (gasoline, aviation fuels, paraffin); fuel oils (for heavy goods vehicles, heating, ships); heavy lubricating oils; residuals (asphalt, bitumen, wax), and waste products (e.g. sulphuric acid). Athough the fractions concerned will differ according to the particular crude being refined, they are all in *joint supply*.

Maximising profits in conditions of joint supply is complicated since, although the demand for the lighter oils may be high, for example, there may be little interest in consuming any of the heavier fractions that are produced with it. Prices and profit margins may be slimmed right down on these other products in order to gain sales. Additionally, the state of competition in some product markets may be greater than others, which is another reason for weak margins on some jointly supplied products.

In the market for petrol/gasoline and diesel fuels there are extensive distribution networks where the majors have a strong presence. Some regional markets are more competitive with independents and local state companies represented. Advertising, branding and all forms of *non-price competition* are important.

Gas and oil distribution for power generation is frequently highly competitive with direct contracts being secured between large *monopsony* buyers, on the one hand – electricity generating companies (often publicly owned) and big sellers, on the other – the major oil oligopolies.

In other product markets, like for domestic and commercial heating oils, bitumens, etc., a local refinery may serve a territory where transport costs confer upon it a *local monopoly*.

Considering all the above stages of the production process of oil, we can now conclude the following:

- It is an industry characterised by massive *economies of scale*. As we have seen, huge investment in fixed capital is necessary even before production can take place. With highly capital-intensive production techniques at all stages, the average and marginal costs of production can only be brought down to acceptable levels if overheads can be spread over a very large output.
- Since oil is a liquid, production through all stages is most economic if *a regular flow* of inputs matched to outputs can be assured. Variable flow and fluctuating levels of capacity mean fixed costs have to be paid over smaller ranges of output – profit margins are immediately eroded.
- The need to maintain a regular flow means the industry has a tendency to produce *excess supplies*. With huge fixed costs, a continual need to increase outputs and the marginal cost of producing just one more barrel being relatively low, it will always be tempting to try and sell more than the market can take.
- Reconciling the need for a regular flow with an unstable, unpredictable world means access to crude supplies is essential, as is safeguarding outlets. Vertical integration is one way of minimising uncertainty, since a business can thus bring all stages of the production process under its own control. Securing long-term contracts, combining in joint ventures and entering into a cartel with rivals are all other means of managing a risky business environment, *eliminating competition* and ensuring regular throughputs of oil are achieved.
- Putting all these features together it is not difficult to see why the international oil industry has been dominated by *oligopoly*. With massive capital entry/threshold costs and the desire to exercise control over an unstable but potentially highly profitable industry, the actions of the majors have demonstrated classic oligopolistic behaviour: long periods of comparative market stability interspersed with fierce price wars; cycles of managed oil supplies and then gluts or surpluses, booms and recessions.

Producer countries

Trying to give a picture of the world's most important oil-producing countries is like taking a snapshot of traffic in a busy street. There have been so many changes in the rank ordering of the top oil producers that it all depends on when you choose to view the picture.

Russia was the world's largest producer during the 1980s, but economic and political upheaval have significantly reduced its influence in the last years of the twentieth century. In 1993 it produced 6.9 million barrels per day – 10.9 per cent of the world's production, well down on the 11.5 mbd only six years earlier.

The USA has always been a significant producer but its mature oil fields have been in slow, steady decline since the mid-1980s. Nonetheless, it was the second biggest producer with 8.5 mbd, 12.7 per cent of the world's total, in 1993.

Middle Eastern countries are big producers and, more importantly, major exporters (since, unlike the USA and the former Soviet Union, their consumption needs have been comparatively slight). The wars, revolutions and political changes in the region have, over the years, greatly affected the relative standing of differing Middle Eastern states, but generally Saudi Arabia has always been the dominant partner. In 1993 it was the world's number one producer with 8.6 mbd, 13.4 per cent of the overall total, but perhaps of greater significance is that it holds by far and away the greatest volume of the world's reserves (over 25 per cent, compared to Russia's 4.8 per cent and the USA's 3.1 per cent) and, in addition, its oil is *cheap to produce*. In 1985, Saudi oil was estimated to cost less than US$1 a barrel to extract, compared to $7–8 for Alaska and the North Sea. Its actual production of oil in any one year, therefore, really depends on how much it wants to open the taps (which in turn depends on just how much such a dominant supplier wants to affect the oil price).

The changing pattern of oil production since the early 1980s is given in Figure 9.3, but a much longer view is necessary to pick up just how the role of the Middle East has changed to become the world's most important exporting region and thus the most important influence on the international trade in oil.

In 1920 the Middle East provided approximately 12 per cent of the world's oil needs. By 1973 this proportion had grown to 50 per cent. In between these two dates, however, the control of Middle Eastern production and prices passed out of the hands of the major oil companies and into those of the host country governments. The history of the power struggle involved and its impact on the rest of the world is fascinating – only a very brief account is possible here.

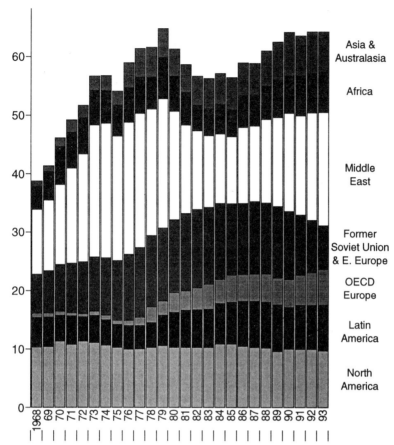

The Middle East's relatively low-cost oil producers have acted as the world's safety valve: increasing output rapidly when world demand has been accelerating and reducing supplies when consumption has fallen. The early 1990s have seen a continuing slow decline in US oil production; a rapid contraction in supplies from Russia and its neighbours; and a complete halt in oil sales from Iraq and Kuwait thanks to the Gulf War. Nonetheless, Middle East (and especially Saudi) production has compensated for such cut-backs so that world oil output has been relatively constant through these years

Figure 9.3 Oil production, 1968–93: by region
Source: BP Statistical Review of World Energy, 1994.

THE STRUGGLE FOR CONTROL OF SUPPLIES

In the first decades of the twentieth century, as the use of the motor car was growing and the world's navies were switching from coal to fuel oil propulsion, the Middle East was dependent on the international oil industry for the exploration, discovery and development of its oil resources. Only the majors possessed the necessary capital and expertise to carry out this work.

Additionally, the nature of the political relationship between the fledgeling states of the Middle East and the Allied Powers was one still locked into colonial protectorates. Long-term concessions were thus granted by host governments to the majors to produce oil for a fixed royalty: the first big concession was made in 1901 by Iran to the Anglo Persian Oil Co. (later BP). Similarly, Iraq in 1925 awarded its oil rights to the Iraq Petroleum Company – a consortium of BP, Shell, CFP, Exxon and Mobil. In the 1930s the big Arabian Gulf fields were discovered and concessions were given to the Kuwait Oil Company (jointly owned by BP and Gulf) and in Saudi Arabia to Aramco (Exxon, Socal, Texaco and Mobil).

The world's oil supply was thus effectively controlled by the oligopolistic majors. Classic cut-throat competition between them ended in 1928 in a cartel agreement to supervise joint production and to apportion down-stream market shares. (Note that cartels work best where there are few parties involved, each one's actions are observable to all and penalties for cheating hurt. These three conditions were all met in the joint concessions on production: any one major trying to take off more oil from a joint source could not hope to go undetected and unpunished by its partners.) Prices were stabilised by a unique pricing agreement where oil sold any-where in the world was equal to that of Gulf of Mexico oil plus transport costs – irrespective if it had come from the Middle East at half that figure (such outrageous exploitation was amended slightly by 1945 at the insis-tence of UK and US navies which were fuelling up in the Arab Gulf yet paying as if the oil had been shipped across the Atlantic).

The 1930s up to the 1960s, therefore, saw an unparalleled control of the world's oil market where stability of flow, market shares and *joint profit maximisation* were all secured by the majors. With the main producer countries' sources of supply at their disposal and with vertically integrated business empires stretching forward to every market place there was, in effect, no free international trade in oil. Majors that were 'crude long', i.e. with a supply of crude oil greater than their market outlets (such as BP), were tied in to 'crude short' companies (such as Shell) by long-term contracts and so the scope for competition from any other suppliers was strictly limited.

Producer countries were increasingly unhappy with this arrangement. Western businesses were seen as being rich and powerful thanks to poor countries' oil. In 1951 Iran unilaterally nationalised its oil fields, but such was the power of the majors' cartel at this time that they could close down all Iranian production and compensate for this loss by producing more from other sources. Iran was thus forced into signing a humiliating, 25-year further concession in order to start up producing again.

Such a victory for the majors, however, proved to be their last. Iraq in 1961 similarly nationalised 99 per cent of foreign oil capital and subse-quently got involved in a long drawn-out series of negotiations with the oil companies which were never concluded to the satisfaction of the latter.

Meanwhile, Libya had shown the way by excluding all majors from tendering for concessions in its newly developed oil fields. In limiting the bidding only to the less-powerful independent oil companies, Libya had wrung from them a higher share of the profits and, simultaneously, had increased the downstream competition for the majors.

On 14 September 1960, OPEC was born. Iran, Iraq, Kuwait, Saudi Arabia and Venezuela were the pioneering members of this organisation which was formed in reaction to the oil majors deciding to reduce prices and with them producer countries' revenues. Although its initial impact was limited, OPEC became the forum through which producer countries could exercise increasing bargaining power, where follow-my-leader nationalisations could catch on and where eventual control of oil supplies could be wrested from the grip of the majors and passed into the hands of host country governments.

As well as increasing success in gaining ownership and control of their own oil supplies and in weakening the competitive strength of the majors *vis-à-vis* the independents, two other events strengthened the producer countries' resolve to become more active players in the world oil market. The first was the floating of the dollar in 1971, which effectively devalued OPEC revenues since oil has always been denominated in dollars. The second highly significant development was the shift of the USA in 1972 from being a net oil exporter to a net importer. Low prices relative to other fuels had stimulated post-war Western dependence on oil and now tight world demand coincided with OPEC being, at last, in control of its own supplies.

The political trigger was the 1973 October War between Israel and its Arab neighbours. OPEC shut off all oil supplies to the USA and the Netherlands (Rotterdam was Europe's major oil port) in retaliation for the West's alleged support of Israel. In three months the price of oil shot up 400 per cent and the shock waves reverberated around the world.

Western oil demand was *price inelastic* – there were no short-run alternatives to buying OPEC oil if modern industry and trade were to continue functioning – and as a result the OPEC economies quickly accumulated enormous wealth at the expense of the OECD consumer countries.

In 1979, the Iranian Revolution which deposed the (pro-Western) Shah and ushered in the rule of fundamentalist Ayatollahs caused the second oil cut-back and shock to oil prices. Again OPEC incomes leapt upwards, while the consumer countries were faced with *stagflation* – a slump in growth, large trade deficits and double-digit inflation.

This time OPEC was in danger of killing the golden OECD goose which was laying the golden eggs. Whereas the 1973 price shock did not choke off world demand, by 1979 its effect had brought onstream North Sea and Alaskan oil fields, and simultaneously stimulated Western industry to invest in smaller cars, more fuel-efficient technology plus research into alternative energy supplies. The 1979 shock provoked a further slide into world recession so that now, after decades of a relentless rise in oil consumption, Western demand went into decline.

Oil prices fell in the 1980s. OPEC thus attempted to exercise the same control over supply as the majors' cartel had done before so successfully for all the time up to the 1970s. They failed. The three criteria for a successful cartel mentioned earlier did not apply: the producer countries are greater in number, have widely diverging interests and their actions are less open to observation and joint control than was the case for the majors. The temptation to sell the marginal barrel remains as ever, and for those OPEC countries with pressing development needs and smaller reserves there is always a strong case for trying to maximise revenues now, rather than later.

OPEC has therefore never succeeded as a cartel. Quotas to restrict oil production have been set regularly for member countries and just as regularly broken. In the early 1980s, Saudi Arabia was willing to act as OPEC's controlling safety valve – always cutting back on its own output as others cheated on theirs – but in 1985 it refused to keep sacrificing its own income for others. It opened up production again and the world oil price collapsed (see figure 9.4).

CONCLUSION: OIL AT THE END OF THE TWENTIETH CENTURY

Producer countries

The economics of oil have now changed again. The squabbling between Middle Eastern oil producers erupted into war on 2 August 1990 when a demanding and financially impatient Iraq invaded Kuwait which it had alleged was overproducing and driving oil prices down. World oil prices scarcely blipped as Iraqi and Kuwaiti oil was taken out of circulation – an indication of plentiful supplies and an absence of consumer concern.

As a result of the war, the differences between the Arab states widened considerably. The southern Gulf states are relatively oil rich, under-populated and now deeply suspicious of their northern neighbours. Their need to maximise current revenues is not so great as northern states like Iraq which have large populations, are war-damaged and have urgent development demands. Saudi Arabia, in particular, has reserves which will last over eighty more years at current rates of exploitation and it has no interest in restricting production, driving up prices and stimulating Western consumers to conserve demand, develop alternatives and to reduce their dependency on Saudi oil.

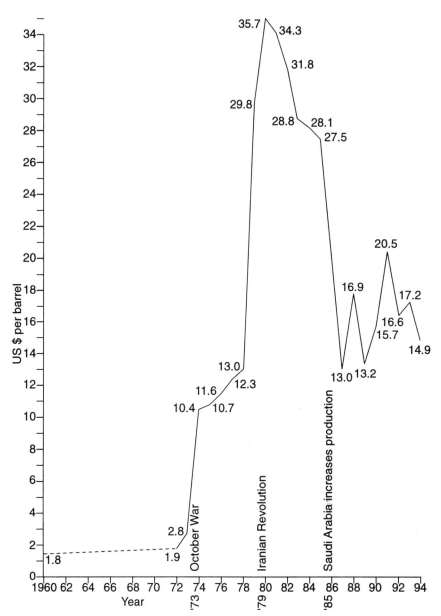

The price of oil is determined by the tightness of world demand compared with world supply. Political events in the Middle East are only important in so far as they affect this market balance. Thus the 1967 Arab–Israeli 'Six Day War' had no economic significance and the 1990 Gulf War had only a limited impact. Saudi Arabia's decision to increase production in 1985, however, caused a major economic upset.

Figure 9.4 Crude oil prices (Arabian/Dubai: light)
Source: BP Statistical Reviews.

The oil industry

The majors, meanwhile, have lost access to cheap crude and have consequently been tireless in their search for downstream efficiency, cost savings and protection of market share. More oil is now traded than ever before as oil companies buy and sell between them, wherever a margin can be made. The majors can no longer behave as oil production lines, running their own crude through to their distribution networks and denying all others access. They buy in the cheapest oil at whatever the production stage, from wherever its source (BP calculated in 1991 that confining its refineries to its own supplies of crude could cost up to 25 cents per barrel in some places – a recipe for inefficiency and uncompetitiveness). As a result the industry is now *de-integrating* downstream – each business unit must act as an independent profit centre if it is to survive.

The biggest cause of concern is with future sources of supply. At present, with the last big oil discoveries now 25 years behind them and most fields under their control maturing rapidly (e.g. in the North Sea and Alaska), the majors are anxious to develop other resources. There is massive potential in many underexplored parts of the world that remains to be tapped, *but not without an increase in the price of oil.*

In the Russian Federation and neighbouring states such as Azerbaijan, Kazkhstan and others there are large known reserves that are waiting to be got out, but the political risk is high, much capital needs to replaced and upgraded and the distances to Western markets are great. Much production potential is here – but it is for the long term only.

A second cause of concern is growing downstream competition from OPEC state oil companies. They are the ones now with the access to cheap Middle East crude and, just as it was for the majors before them, the incentive is to vertically integrate forward into the market place. A case in point is the merger in 1993 of Saudi Arabia's two state oil companies – Aramco and Samarec – which brought together the world's largest producer with a big refiner. Although this giant has yet to make its move overseas, Gulf producers have been looking for some time to gain refining footholds in Europe and Japan. Kuwait had already begun this process in Europe (with 'Q8') just before it was invaded. The situation today is different from the growth of the industry in the past, however, in that Western multinational oil companies are now well established in all world markets so any growing competition will be bloody.

Consumption

Finally, as we have seen, the rate of growth of world demand will not be excessive for the last years of the twentieth century but it is projected to pick up strongly thereafter. Oil prices, we can conclude, will not increase markedly in the short term, but the longer they stay flat, the longer the oil industry is discouraged from exploring and bringing new fields onstream, the longer the Western world is kept dependent on existing OPEC supplies, the more explosive the price rise will be when it comes. The economics of oil continue to be a fascinating, controversial and immensely important centre of academic, political and military conflict!

KEY WORDS

A **cartel** is a small group of rival producers that decide to act together, formally or informally, legally or illegally, as if they were a monopoly or single seller. In the case of oligopoly, price competition can be unpredictable, costly, even fatal to the interests of one or more of the rival producers. In such situations, *non-price competition* may be safer: rivalry in advertising, packaging, special gift promotions and other marketing gimmicks. Cutting prices to win sales can always be matched by a rival. A really clever advertising campaign and slogan, however, can be unanswerable in the short run.

Complementary goods are those in joint demand – for example an increase in demand for cars will lead directly to an increase in the demand for petrol. **Substitute goods**, in contrast, are in competitive demand – an increase in the demand for natural gas is likely to lead to a decrease in the demand for oil.

Joint profit maximisation Where oligopolists agree they can increase prices together, or at least refrain from price cutting, such that revenues and thus profits are maximised for the group as a whole. The temptation always exists, however, for one producer to break ranks, cut prices and win a larger market share at the expense of its rivals. Hence the typical oligopolistic outcome is long periods of price stability and joint profit maximisation where competition takes place in the realm of advertising and marketing – interspersed with shorter, violent price wars where the relative standing of the rivals is reassessed.

A **local monopoly** can increase prices up to the point where it pays consumers to travel elsewhere to buy from an alternative supplier. The greater the travel costs involved, the greater the power of the local monopoly.

A **monopsony** is a large, single buyer. A big business which buys its inputs from any one of a number of small, competitive suppliers can drive the price down since it can choose to award its custom to whosoever it wants. Rival suppliers, on the other hand, have to sell to the monopsonist or not at all.

In an industrial situation where a monopsonist is buying from a monopolist then the outcome is unpredictable – a balance of countervailing power prevails (as first described by US economist J. K. Galbraith).

A **natural monopoly** occurs where the most economically efficient form of business organisation is for one, large, sole producer to provide all of the industry's supply. The economies of large-scale production are such that it pays one large enterprise to dominate the industry, rather than have several competing firms try to operate where none can reduce costs sufficiently. This is typically the case in the distribution of water, gas, electricity and (sometimes) rail services where one pipe/rail/transmission line can link major towns rather than the wasteful competition of many competing lines.

The Organisation of Economic Cooperation and Development This was set up to promote economic growth and financial stability amongst countries of the developed world. Its members include: Australia; Austria; Belgium; Canada; Denmark; Finland; France; Germany; Greece; Iceland; Ireland; Italy; Japan; Luxembourg; the Netherlands; New Zealand; Norway; Portugal; Spain; Sweden; Switzerland; Turkey; UK; USA. The OECD is therefore a club of rich countries.

Price-inelastic demand This is where the price of a product changes greatly yet its demand changes proportionally less. If consumers are dependent on oil, for example, then producers can hoist up its price, sell not much less than before and thus enjoy much greater revenue.

Vertical integration A company who owns a pipeline and buys an oil field concession in order to safeguard supplies is vertically integrating backwards (to its sources). If it constructs a chain of filling stations to sell its products it is vertically integrating forwards (to the market).

Vertical integration can be contrasted with **horizontal integration** – where one firm attempts to dominate one process only (e.g. a pipeline owner which takes over all others in the region) – or **lateral integration** – where the firm moves out of the industry altogether (e.g. a refinery business which combines with a petrochemical plant, a producer of fertilisers and a coal mine). The major, multinational oil companies have practised all of these business strategies at one time or other in their history.

QUESTIONS

1 Why is the price of oil important? Explain the consequences of a significant rise in the price of oil at the end of the twentieth century.
2 What factors influence the demand for oil? How are these factors likely to change over the next decade?
3 What determines the level of investment in the exploration, production and development of new oil reserves?
4 Explain how and why the competitive structure of the oil industry has changed over its history.
5. What makes for a successful cartel? Compare the fortunes of the majors' cartel with that of OPEC.

FURTHER READING

BP Statistical Review of World Energy, June 1994.
Roncaglia, Alessandro. *The International Oil Market*. Macmillan, 1985.
Stevens, Paul. 'Oil prices – an economic framework for analysis', in G. Bird and H. Bird, *Contemporary Issues in Applied Economics*. Edward Elgar, 1991.

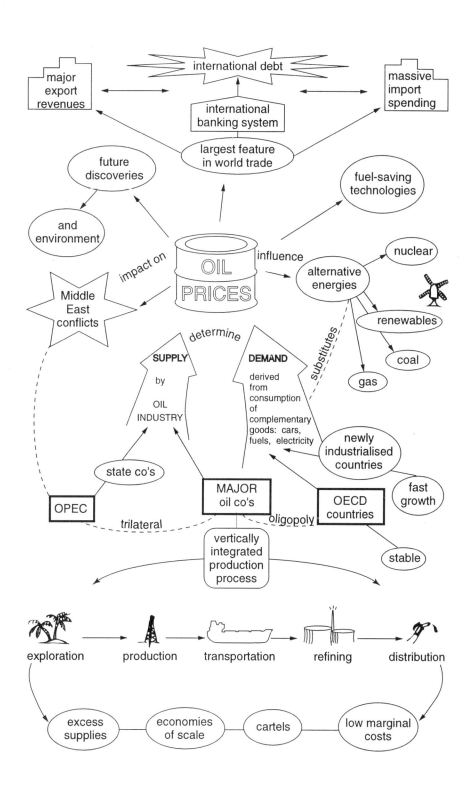

10 Foreign debt, Western banks and international policemen

Topics to be considered in this chapter

- The causes of the 'debt crisis'
- Characteristics of the crisis for:
  i the international banks
  ii developing countries
- The debt rescue packages
- The International Monetary Fund
- Debt and the world order at the end of the twentieth century

INTRODUCTION

The 'International Debt Crisis' describes the situation during the 1980s when a number of developing countries were close to defaulting on the loans they owed to international banks. The banks were so overextended at this time that there was a real danger that a major default would spark a crisis in confidence. If a sufficient quantity of worried depositors had then tried to grab their money and run for cover, any one of a number of banks might have been forced to close, thus triggering a chain reaction of other bank collapses that would have led to a full-blown international financial crisis and quite possibly a 1930s-like world-wide depression.

Fortunately, despite a lot of nervous nail-biting in Western financial centres, things never got that bad and now commentators can look back on these times as a crisis that passed, as a battle that was won (William Cline, *The Economist*, 18 February 1995). The 'crisis', however, was always defined in terms of the danger it posed to the developed world and the financial institutions that underpin it. In the sense that now the richer, creditor nations feel less vulnerable to a massive haemorrhaging of the international financial system, they are right – that crisis has passed. But severe indebtedness of developing countries still remains with us and struggling with this burden continues to be a major problem for many of the world's poor. This is a battle that continues to be fought.

The mountain of money owed by developing nations in the mid-1990s currently exceeds the debt that was accumulated by these same countries during the worst years of the 1980s. The reason for this is that the structure of this financing is now far less threatening to the international financial system, so that many developing countries have been re-admitted into the banks that not so long ago were closing their doors to them. Renewed lending has taken place in the 1990s. Debts are rising again.

There is no doubt that, emerging from the 1980s, a number of indebted countries have put into place economic reforms that have improved their prospects and met the approval of international financiers, but if that battle has been won, it does not mean that peace has yet returned. The skirmish over the Mexican peso at the beginning of 1995 which spread jitters through stock markets in Brazil, Argentina and even in places as far away as Sweden shows that confidence is a volatile mixture that can nowhere be taken for granted. In this particular case, it was a relatively simple, old-fashioned currency crisis where the Mexican peso was overvalued, rather than fundamental concern over the country's international debt and its ability to pay its way. But this is small compensation now for many poor Mexicans whose cost of living has just jolted upwards again. Global money markets can panic over any one of an infinite number of reasons. The shock waves this latest affair has caused have thus rippled the brows of many a public and private official in Latin America and elsewhere: the world is an unregulated financial market place where at present money can flow faster than attempts to impart order and control over it. And without a fair-minded international policeman, it is always the weakest who get hurt the most.

The continuing growth of developing countries' debt need not be a problem, however, providing it does not outstrip those nations' ability to generate income, or panic their creditors. As anyone who has bought a house, car or fancy hi-fi equipment knows, it is not the absolute total of debt that matters so much as the ability to keep up with the payments. The prospects of keeping current levels of debt within manageable proportions we shall return to later; let us first look in more detail at how the 1980s debt crisis originally came about; what were the dimensions of this crisis; what actions were taken to address it and what issues remain with us to this day.

OIL SHOCKS AND THE ORIGINS OF DEBT

The origins of the debt crisis can be traced back to the first oil shock that affected the world economy and brought about a 400 per cent increase in oil prices from September 1973 to January 1974.

Major oil consumers had little option but to pay this price at the time. Western industry and transport were dependent on oil supplies and there were no short-term alternatives.

Massive oil revenues crossed the globe, therefore – real incomes fell in the West and rose for the Organisation of Petroleum Exporting Countries (OPEC).

Large readjustments in the distribution of world incomes are not achieved painlessly. Falling incomes in consumer countries brought rising rates of inflation and unemployment in the 1970s. While the political and social impacts of these changes were bad enough for wealthy Western countries, for poorer countries in particular the long-term developmental implications looked far worse – without some form of external assistance.

The problems of the oil-exporting nations were of a different sort. With small populations and a limited capacity to absorb funds quickly, there was an embarrassment of riches. What was to be done with all this money? The bulk of their surplus oil revenues were placed in short-term bank deposits in the offshore Eurodollar market – earning interest at competitive rates.

The problem of finding a useful outlet for these funds was thus passed on to the international banks. With billions of petrodollars pouring into their accounts, the pressure was on these multinationals to find profitable destinations – how else could they repay the interest on these rapidly accumulating deposits? *Recycling* the petromoney was all the talk of the day.

The world economic backdrop to these events of the late 1970s was one of recession and readjustment. Oil-consuming nations were faced with huge import bills and the need to cut back on domestic consumption and real standards of living. No government was happy with the political implications of these events and many tried to obscure these painful realities by increasing domestic money supplies and cloaking the facts of economic life behind *money illusion*. Slow growth and double-digit inflation was the inescapable result.

For the poorest of the poor in the less-developed countries (LDCs), at the bottom of the world's list of priorities, this meant that official, inter-government aid flows were drying up at the same time as Western markets for their exports were slumping. Governments in the more developed nations were generally too worried about the falling incomes of their own people to devote increasing sums to others suffering in foreign lands.

The outcome of this unique combination of circumstances is not hard to see. Resource-rich but underdeveloped countries are a valid destination for surplus petrodollars. Wise investment could employ these funds in emerging, productive industries. The channel for the distribution of these funds, however, had now become private, profit-seeking international banks and not Western governments and their aid agencies. The loans being placed were increasingly in the form of short-term credit (not long-term development capital) and quoted at floating, free-market rates (not on fixed, concessionary terms). But then beggars cannot be choosers.

Mistakes were made on both sides of the bankers' desk. Some borrowers were too eager to accept cheap credit and lacked clarity over how most productively to employ these funds. Lenders were too keen to off-load their cheap money and too indiscriminatory in their choice of customers.

No one could see the emerging danger in the situation.

On the debtors' side, borrowing to invest in public services and improve *human capital* – e.g. via health and education projects – is socially desirable and economically beneficial; but such investments clearly cannot pay back quick returns. However, so long as cheap petromoney was flooding capital markets and world inflation rates were moving upwards then the *real rate of interest* on loans was very low and even negative. Low private yields on social investment projects were thus no problem; maintaining consumption levels at pre-oil shock levels could also be supported; expensive government and military projects of dubious economic value could still be funded.

On the creditors' side, all the international banks were competing to get into recycling, so confidence in the commercial wisdom and social necessity of this action was thus unquestioned. 'If everyone was doing it, it must be OK.'

Since the majority of loans were tied up for short terms only, bankers were less nervous about getting their money back. Risks were minimalised, it was further believed, by syndicating each big loan – that is, by sharing it around a number of major banks such that no single institution felt over-exposed. Finally, much of this money was loaned to national governments so there was the assumption, again, that risks were reduced since private commercial debtors might go broke, but whole countries do not.

A fundamental weakness is that in the global market place there is no overall regulatory agency responsible for recording and approving inter-national affairs. There is no world central bank or government that has the right or opportunity, even today, to see all that is going on with multi-national money flows. Neither the United Nations, nor the International Monetary Fund nor the World Bank possess any such authority. The global economy is thus a truly 'free' market with no all-powerful central adminis-tration. Banks and businesses operating across frontiers enjoy all the advantages of freedom from restriction, therefore, but at the cost of having no international policeman to turn to if things go wrong.

In 1979 came the second oil shock. Prices leapt again, OPEC incomes boomed and the world economy staggered. The Western political fall-out this time had important economic policy implications: governments changed in the UK and USA and the era of Thatcherism and Reaganism arrived. Right-wing conservative economics was in the ascendancy.

What this meant was renewed government determination to cure Western inflation by resort to monetary stringency, i.e. cutting back money supplies and increasing interest rates. This was accompanied in the US by an aggres-sive defence posture which implied increasing government spending/deficits, more borrowing to balance budgets, which in turn reinforced the excess monetary demand and upward pressure on interest rates. In addition, high dollar interest rates in international money markets meant there was a flow out of other currencies to get into high-interest-earning dollars. The price of US dollars moved upwards, therefore.

Biting the bullet of high interest rates to cure inflation in the West at a time when oil prices were peaking meant the 1980s began with a steep recession. The impact on the world economy affected some more than others. As the saying goes: when the USA sneezes, Europe catches a cold and the rest of the world dies of pneumonia.

In the late 1970s, with money markets awash with cheap petrodollars and anxious to loan, short-term Eurodollar interest rates averaged 6 per cent. Additionally, with inflation rising these interest rates in real terms were – in some cases – actually negative. There was no real cost involved in borrowing. In 1981, however, with all the changes listed above those same rates now averaged 16.8 per cent in a world where inflation was falling/money values rising.

Less-developed countries had taken on massive loans at floating-market rates and denominated in dollars. Between 1980 and 1982 the interest payments now required to service these debts more than doubled. The only way they could earn the hard currency to pay these off was by selling exports, but Western markets were now in recession and putting up the barriers. The *terms of trade* for primary producing countries thus fell. LDC export prices and revenues slumped while the price of dollars and the size of interest payments being demanded by creditors surged. The crunch had come.

THE DEBT CRISIS

Measuring the nature of the debt crisis depends on the yardstick used. In absolute terms, the outstanding debt in LDCs grew as shown in table 10.1.

As mentioned earlier, the absolute size of debt is less informative than data on a country's ability to pay. The key variable here is a country's earnings of foreign exchange, gained mostly from export sales. Thus a crucial indicator is the *debt–service ratio*, which records the amount of interest-plus-principal repayments as a fraction of export revenues. It changed as shown in table 10.2 for selected LDCs.

That is, in the early 1980s, these debtor countries were having to hand over half their export earnings to pay increased bank interest charges.

In August 1982 Mexico became the first country to say that it could not pay. Large loans that had been contracted in the expectation that continually rising oil revenues would bail them out of any future trouble now were a major embarrassment. Demand for oil was contracting, prices were tumbling and Mexican export earnings were insufficient to meet all the country's commitments. This was not just a case of being unable to pay off the principal of the loan in time, it was a declaration that it could not even keep up with the interest payments.

Table 10.1

			(*US$ billion*)		
	1978	*1979*	*1980*	*1981*	*1982*
Africa	71.9	83.7	93.9	102.8	117.1
Asia	93.4	112.1	134.7	151.4	180.1
Latin America	155.8	188.0	230.6	288.4	333.0
TOTAL	321.1	383.8	459.2	542.6	630.2

Source: World Bank.

Table 10.2

	1970–9	*1979–81*	*1982*
Debt–service ratio	27.3%	35.7%	51.9%

Other countries shared the same precarious financial position. Argentina and Brazil, in particular, were big debtor countries that were in deep trouble with domestic growth rates slumping and inflation rates soaring. Smaller economies with less absolute debt in Africa and Latin America experienced even greater hardship. In the case of Peru, President Alan Garcia stood up and unilaterally declared that his country could not and would not pay the full measure of the debt service charges that they owed.

The international banking community went into shock. Many European and American banks were heavily extended in these countries and if any of their depositors panicked and came in to withdraw their funds then these institutions were now in grave danger of going bust.

Terrified of this outcome, the banks first put pressure on the big debtors to come up with the cash. But if LDCs cannot sell sufficient exports during a global recession the only way to find money is to cut back on consumption. Imports had to be forsaken; standards of living had to fall. Heavily in debt and failing to keep up with their interest payments, LDC governments could hardly hope to borrow more in order to pay off urgent demands. Capital inflows into these countries dried up. Meanwhile, anyone with access to funds or who could liquidise any accumulated wealth in these countries was funnelling it out as quickly as possible to safer havens. *Capital flight* was rampant. At a time of increasing hardship for the poorest of the world's poor, the net flow of private funds from 1983 onwards was thus *out* of LDCs and into the wealthy creditor nations (see table 10.3).

The senselessness of this situation took a little time to sink in. Creditors were not going to get their capital back in the long run by driving debtors into the dirt. Pressures on deficit LDCs were going to be self-defeating so long as richer countries refused to expand their economies to accommodate

Table 10.3 Net capital transfers (selected LDCs)

(US$ billion)				
1979–81	*1982*	*1983*	*1984*	*1985*
13.2	9.3	–21.2	–38.0	–37.3

them. No one country could right its financial position by selling exports if there was no other country in the world willing to import them. Meanwhile Western exporters were going bankrupt and laying off workers because international trade was slumping. No-one wins if everyone plays beggar-my-neighbour.

But still they played the game. IMF teams visited chronic debtors and recommended traditional deflationary policies of restraint on consumer demand, devaluations, export promotions and *rescheduling* of debt to pay off the interest over longer time periods.

Ouch! Cutting back incomes and consumption of people who are already poor hurts. Social and political unrest were inevitable, as were hyper-inflations where governments lacked the commitment to increase taxation officially (see table 10.4).

Table 10.4

		% Inflation per year	
	1983 *% Debt/GDP*	*1978–82*	*1983*
Argentina	70.6	121.5	343.8
Brazil	41.1	95.2	142.0
Mexico	60.5	37.0	101.9

People who are in debt are never in a strong position to argue their case. Creditors want money, not excuses. In the mid-1980s, international creditors were demanding repayments and insisting that conservative monetary policies be implemented by debtor countries before any help was to be offered. The fact that most of the changes that had precipitated the crisis were not of the LDCs' making (the rise of the dollar; the change in interest rates; the closing of export markets and the collapse of primary product prices) was of no consequence. With the international financial system threatening to fall apart, somebody had to pay up quick and that somebody, it was judged, had to be the poor debtor.

PAYING THE PRICE – THE IMPACT ON LDCs

The effect of these demands was to bring about a vicious economic readjustment. Between 1982 and 1985 developing countries were forced to cut back on incomes, consumption, imports and investment (see table 10.5). Consumption on essential goods and services could not fall much, but spending on imports and on vital long-term investment crashed. For example, the major Latin American debtors had *Balance of Payments deficits* totalling US$51 billion in 1982. With no chance of expanding exports the cost of readjustment had to be borne by cutting imports – within three years this US$51 billion deficit had been reduced to zero. Investment similarly contracted fiercely such that not only was no new capital construction taking place but there was insufficient replacement of existing equipment. These countries were thus not escaping from financial difficulty but spiralling down deeper and deeper into it. The real economic foundation of debtor countries was being eroded, and with it the prospect of creditors ever getting their money back.

The situation was worse for other debtor countries like Nigeria, Peru and smaller, sub-Saharan countries like Côte d'Ivoire. Here although the absolute size of debt was lower and their threatened default was thus less 'important', less threatening to the international financial order, these countries were much poorer and therefore much worse affected by demands for deflation and the shrinking of world trade. Their economies were savagely affected and real hardship was involved for the bulk of their populations (see table 10.6). Without external assistance, prospects for their recovery looked grim. Unfortunately, they were not big enough debtors to attract sufficient attention. As the saying goes: if you owe the bank a hundred thousand, that's your problem; but if you owe the bank a hundred million then that is the bank's problem. . . . Smaller debtors were likely to get less help to cope with their difficulties than big debtors like Brazil and Mexico which could not be allowed to fail.

It should be noted that not all debtor countries suffered such extremes. Despite the fact that interest rates and dollar exchange rates were now – in the 1980s – much higher than anticipated when the bulk of the debt was incurred, a number of countries, such as South Korea, Indonesia and Turkey (see table 10.7), had invested their loans successfully and had earned rates of return sufficient to pay off increased service charges without recourse to rescheduling and the drastic financial stringency that that entailed.

Maintaining their debt payments was clearly not without some cost to current incomes and consumption in these countries but, most importantly, investment and thus future growth was not sacrificed for these newly industrialising nations – unlike many other developing countries which were forced to run down current consumption and their capital stock in order to pay their debts.

By 1985, the continuing problems of most debtor nations – the drag this was imparting on world trade and the impossibility of individual countries escaping the mire without some form of multilateral rescue package – could not be ignored any longer. Since the destinies of debtor and creditor

Table 10.5

	1981	1982	1983	1984	1985
BRAZIL					
GNP/head (1987 US$)	2,030	2,050	1,820	1,710	1,640
Imports (US$m.)	24,073	21,061	17,233	15,209	14,329
Gross Dom Inv	2,481.6	2,257.8	1,747.8	1,813.0	2,116.0
(1987 Cruzeiros m.)					
MEXICO					
GNP/head	3,170	2,910	2,410	2,240	2,300
Imports	24,853	14,910	10,797	14,458	16,152
Gross Dom Inv	67.5	51.1	37.3	39.6	43.7
(1987 pesos m.)					
ARGENTINA					
GNP/head	2,720	2,670	3,000	3,400	3,150
Imports	9,430	5,337	4,504	4,585	3,814
Gross Dom Inv	5.24	4.38	4.35	4.20	3.45
(1987 Arg. pesos m.)					

nations were linked, a coordinated effort to solve the international debt crisis was necessary – which must involve some effort to: (a) reduce the demands on debtors and (b) increase their access to Western markets. The Baker plan (named after the US Treasury secretary of the time) and its successor the Brady plan (ditto) were put together with these ideas in mind.

THE 'RESCUE' PACKAGES

What rescue measures were therefore attempted during the 1980s to relieve the debt crisis for the most seriously affected countries? It must be said that the actual practical policies put into effect did not go far to meet the two points above; most were concerned with reshuffling commitments and protecting the world's financial institutions rather than prioritising the needs of the poor. The bulk of the costs of readjustment thus remained with the LDCs:

Rescheduling. One way to reduce the size of a country's debt–service burden is to negotiate the payment of smaller sums but over a longer period – that is, stretch out the period of debt dependency for longer.

New loans. Similarly, granting new loans allows debtors to pay off urgent claimants, thus enabling the LDC time to meet other demands later. Both this and rescheduling, above, allow debtors breathing space to support essential consumption but only at the cost of putting off the evil day for repayment to a later date.

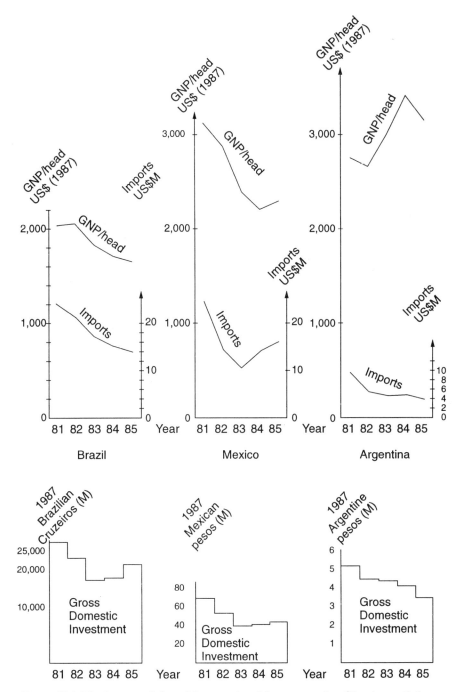

Figure 10.1 The impact of the crisis on major debtor countries. (Precise statistics are given in table 10.5.) Declining GNP/head illustrates the change in average living standards; falling imports are an indication of collapsing consumption; the reduction in investment means less capital stock for the future.

Table 10.6

	1981	*1982*	*1983*	*1984*	*1985*
NIGERIA					
GNP/head	1,130	1,120	990	920	990
Imports	20,455	16,061	9,029	5,868	6,205
Gross Dom Inv	48.3	37.7	29.3	20.5	18.6
(1987 Nairu bn)					
PERU					
GNP/head	1,240	1,350	1,100	1,070	930
Imports	3,160	2,940	2,234	1,881	1,767
Gross Dom Inv	1.36	1.24	0.75	0.69	0.59
(1987 '000 Soles)					
CÔTE d'IVOIRE					
GNP/head	1,190	970	730	670	660
Imports	2,393	2,184	1,814	1,497	1,734
Gross Dom Inv	627.8	568.1	421.1	166.5	306.5
(1987 francs bn)					

Debt/equity swaps. This is where a creditor is offered the opportunity of exchanging debt for shares in LDC enterprises at knock-down prices. For creditors, short-term loan capital is thus converted, at a discount, into long-term investment capital. For debtors, dollar-denominated interest payments are swapped for foreign ownership of domestic shares which pay dividends in local currency. Debt is reduced – but by transferring a country's productive assets into foreign hands.

Secondary debt markets. Not so much assistance to a debtor country, these secondary markets sprung up as a way for the international banks to offload some of their risky loans to others. Debts were offered for sale to other banks in secondary markets – in many cases debt-for-debt swaps were set up as a way for each individual bank to reduce its exposure on any particularly sizeable loan. The price that a particular debt could be sold for was an indication of its real income-earning power to any potential buyer.

The Baker and Brady plans were centrally concerned with brokering such arrangements on a case-by-case basis between debtor governments and the international banks. To secure these deals, the debtor countries had to agree to a standard deflationary, devaluing, trade-liberalising package of economic policies aimed at promoting exports and curtailing consumption and imports – typically monitored by the *International Monetary Fund* (IMF).

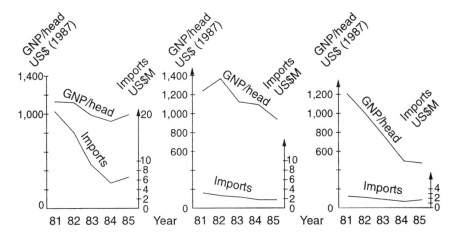

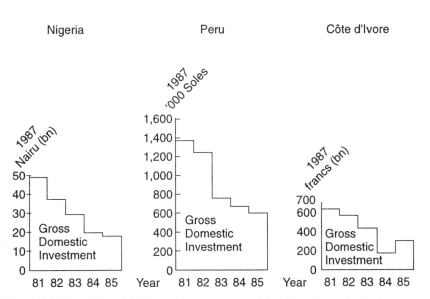

Figure 10.2 The debt crisis for certain poorer countries. Less 'important' than bigger debtors, their change in economic circumstances was more extreme. (For details, see table 10.6)

Table 10.7

	1981	*1982*	*1983*	*1984*	*1985*
SOUTH KOREA					
GNP/head	1,840	1,930	2,110	2,250	2,340
Imports	26,028	24,236	26,174	30,609	31,119
Gross Dom Inv	16.76	18.06	20.51	23.57	24.48
(1987 Won trln)					
INDONESIA					
GNP/head	550	610	610	590	550
Imports	13,008	16,530	16,346	13,865	10,256
Gross Dom Inv	32.28	30.62	31.60	32.21	37.18
(1987 Rupiah trln)					
TURKEY					
GNP/head	1,450	1,300	1,180	1,110	1,080
Imports	8,864	8,794	8,548	10,663	11,341
Gross Dom Inv	11,335	10,801	10,754	10,940	12,427
(1987 Liras bn)					

THE ROLE OF THE IMF

For severely indebted countries, successful negotiations with the IMF were essential – the private international banks wanted IMF approval of debtor government's financial policies before they would offer any assistance in rescheduling the time-pattern of existing debt–service demands or agree to any further financial support.

But the IMF was no impartial international policeman sensitive to the needs of the LDCs as well as to those of the developed world – it was really no more than the first and most important representative of the rich world's banking community. This is shown by the nature of the traditional *stabilisation policies* that it imposed on all countries that called on it for help:

(i)   Conservative, anti-inflation measures were firstly required to generate confidence in the domestic currency. This involved cutting back on local bank lending and increasing interest rates; reducing excessive government spending (especially on social services and subsidies for the poor); increasing government revenues via taxation and controlling wage demands.

(ii) Freeing up prices and removing barriers to trade were required to improve the efficiency of the free-market mechanism. This meant abolishing all fixed prices (e.g. on cheap foods, minimum wages, etc.); letting exchange rates devalue; removing import controls and restrictions on foreign investment and generally opening up the domestic economy to the world.

It is not hard to see who are going to be the immediate winners and losers in such a 'rescue package'. The IMF was repeatedly criticised for

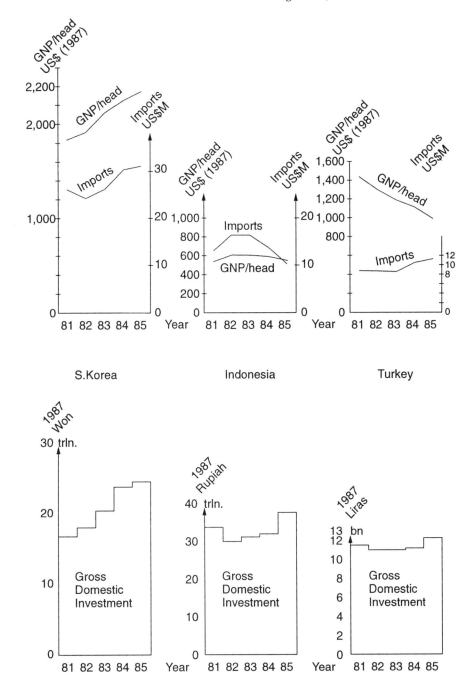

Figure 10.3 Not all debtors shared the same fate. Despite difficulties, these countries managed their finances better, with less cost to their current and future living standards. (For details, see table 10.7.)

Table 10.8 LDC debt–service ratios

	1985	1986	1987	1988	1989	1990	1991	1992	1993
All LDCs	20.9	22.5	20.1	18.8	16.3	14.3	14.2	14.5	13.2
Sub-Saharan Africa	27.6	27.8	23.4	25.8	25.1	25.5	26.7	28.3	26.8

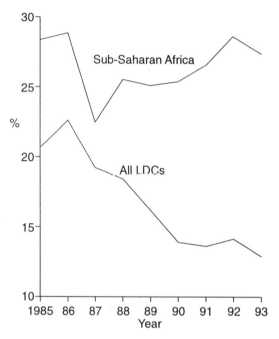

Figure 10.4 Debt–service ratios, 1985–93
Source: World Bank.

imposing the greatest pain on the poorest income groups and on defence-less small traders, and for prising open the LDCs for greater exploitation by the rich capitalist classes. The unpopularity of the heartless deflationary measures recommended made them impossible to implement in some countries, which subsequently led to political as well as economic chaos. Equally, it did not go unnoticed that the IMF was profoundly silent in the face of the massive budget deficits, excessive borrowing and punishing interest rates of the world's greatest debtor – the USA.

To be generous, the IMF did not act in any conscious way as the instru-ment for the industrialised nations to prolong LDC debt dependency and to maintain the existing world order of power relations between rich and poor. It was simply acting in accordance with the orthodox financial criteria by which it was originally set up. It was concerned with countries' short-term monetary stability and an 'orderly' world trade system. Where enacted, its policies certainly have improved debtor countries' inflation

Table 10.9 Per cent rate of growth of GDP, selected countries

	81	82	83	84	85	86	87	88	89	90	91	92	93	Debt-service ratio 1993	US$ GNP/ head (1992)
Argentina	-5.9	-3.2	3.8	1.8	-6.6	7.3	2.5	-1.8	-6.3	0.2	8.9	8.6	4.5	47.6	6,050
Bolivia	0.9	-4.4	-4.5	1.0	-0.7	-3.2	2.6	3.8	2.9	2.4	6.7	3.8	–	39.0 (1992)	680
Brazil	-4.4	0.6	-3.4	5.4	7.8	8.4	3.3	-0.3	3.3	-4.6	0.4	-0.9	6.0	24.4	2,770
Chile	4.8	-10.4	-3.7	8.0	7.0	5.6	6.5	7.3	10.1	2.9	6.1	10.3	3.9	23.4	2,730
Colombia	2.1	1.0	1.6	3.6	3.3	6.1	5.4	4.1	3.4	4.1	2.0	3.7	–	36.4 (1992)	1,330
Jamaica	2.4	0.9	2.4	-1.4	-4.8	2.0	6.4	1.9	6.2	4.1	0.7	2.0	–	27.9	1,340
Mexico	8.8	-0.6	-4.2	3.7	2.7	-3.9	2.0	1.3	3.4	4.6	3.6	2.6	4.5	32.9	3,470
Peru	7.4	-0.4	-12.5	5.8	2.1	9.3	8.3	-8.2	-11.8	-4.4	2.7	-2.8	–	63.7	950
Indonesia	7.4	-0.3	8.9	6.7	2.6	5.8	4.9	5.8	7.4	7.0	6.7	6.3	6.5	32.6	670
South Korea	6.9	7.4	12.1	9.2	6.9	12.3	11.8	11.4	6.1	9.0	8.4	4.8	7.7	9.2	6,790
Philippines	3.4	3.6	1.8	-7.3	-7.3	3.4	4.8	6.3	6.0	2.6	-0.8	0.0	5.1	24.9	770
Côte d'Ivoire	3.8	-0.1	-3.0	-2.7	4.5	3.4	-1.6	-2.0	-1.0	-1.6	-0.4	-0.3		31.9 (1992)	670
Nigeria	-9.2	-0.8	-6.6	-4.3	9.3	1.7	-0.2	9.8	6.7	5.6	5.1	4.1		29.4	320
Uganda	–	–	–	-6.1	-2.6	-1.4	5.5	6.8	7.4	5.8	3.2	2.1		40.2 (1992)	170
All sub-Saharan Africa	2.2	1.4	-0.9	1.7	1.5	2.4	1.6	3.7	3.5	0.8	0.8	0.0		20.0 (1992)	530
All high-income	1.7	-0.1	2.7	4.5	3.3	2.8	3.3	4.4	3.4	2.5	1.0	1.7			21,960
Latin America and the Caribbean	-0.2	-1.2	-2.4	3.7	3.0	4.9	3.2	0.7	0.9	0.0	3.4	2.8		29.5 (1992)	2,690

and balance of payments records. The fact that the burden of LDC debt has continued to increase and for many their development has stalled, and that it helped generate greater overseas earnings for richer countries is the unintentional but inevitable result of its narrow role and blinkered vision.

WHERE WAS THE POLICEMAN?

Why was the focus of 'rescue packages' on rescheduling and on inventing novel ways of shuffling commitments around, instead of actually forgiving substantial fractions of the debt? Why were LDCs forced to open up their domestic economies to greater foreign penetration rather than Western markets being made more accessible to LDC exports? Why could not any one of the international players in this drama have taken a more active lead in promoting the long-term development needs of debtor nations instead of emphasising the primacy of short-term monetary balance?

The answers to these questions are both economic and historical. The main economic difficulty is concerned with the notion of *market failure* in unregulated world trade. Free markets 'fail' where individual decision-makers, acting independently, bring about outcomes that are socially inefficient/sub-optimal. Hence the need for regulation or intervention by central authority. Take the example of an individual, profit-seeking bank: what incentive does it have to forgive a particular debt if the LDC concerned uses the money it saves to pay off other banks' interest charges? The forgiving bank loses out to its main business competitors. Another example: what incentive does any welfare-maximising country have to put into effect painful, import-reducing/export-promoting remedies if the main beneficiaries of any dollars earned will be foreign creditors?

Economic philosophies move in historical cycles and, as has already been explained, the international debt crisis was played out in a period when free-market, neoclassical economics was in the ascendancy. The conventional wisdom that dismantling restrictions to trade was the right policy for *all* countries gained evidence to support it all the way around the world from the USA to China. But freeing-up global markets can only benefit LDCs if their productive resources can respond rapidly enough to the price signals that the markets send them. It does not help if international resources are quicker to seize the business opportunities that are presented than LDC industries, and if richer, creditor countries are not pressured as much as debtors to reduce their tariffs.

The outcome of these inconsistencies in the 1980s was that, on the one hand, creditor nations continued to demand more sacrifices from LDC debtors than they were prepared to make themselves; on the other hand, a number of poor countries found it politically impossible to put into effect those policies asked of them; and there was no international arbitrator to bring both sides together to negotiate a more balanced and practicable solution.

FOREIGN DEBT TODAY

What has happened to the international debt crisis of the 1980s? Has it gone away? Well it has from the West in the sense that there is less danger of debtor default and international financial collapse now. Meanwhile, in the less-developed world, some nations are doing better than others. Much effort has taken place on a country-by-country basis to reschedule payments and to restore confidence in debtor countries' financial policies and institutions. Also, some debt forgiveness has at last occurred: Brady plan deals have been slow to set up, but by the early 1990s they were eventually beginning to bear fruit (e.g. US$51 billion forgiven in eighteen different countries).

Success has been gained in a number of areas: satisfied that their balance sheets are in order, the banks have re-opened their doors to LDCs and begun re-issuing loans; and although the absolute size of debt has been growing, debt–service ratios for most of these countries have been falling – that is, international debt has become more manageable (see table 10.8 and figure 10.4).

Observers have even commented that the painful 1980s of trying to cope with debt forced LDCs to effect a historic shift in economic policies away from heavy-handed, restrictive, protectionist and ultimately inefficient import-substitution strategies to free-market, liberalising and export-oriented reforms. It could therefore be argued that the pain was necessary – such readjustment would not have taken place without it.

This success can be celebrated in some countries in Latin America and Asia where the policies seemed to have worked. They must be questioned elsewhere in the Americas and in Africa, however, where the legacy remains one of faltering recovery, struggle and hardship. The debt–service ratios of sub-Saharan African countries show little improvement.

The World Bank reports growth rates of GDP for selected debtor countries as shown in table 10.9 and figure 10.5. Such a broad picture, of course, captures the impact of an infinite number of variables. There are all sorts of country-specific reasons for these growth rates. What seems clear, however, is that not all these nations have been able to shrug off their debt demands and secure steady growth. Their debt crisis is far from over.

CONCLUSION

What are the final impressions that remain from considering all of the above?

One overwhelming conclusion from this evidence is how interdependent all countries are. The world economy swings up and down as one. Clearly, some individual economies are more resilient than others. The developed countries and successful rapidly industrialising nations can better weather external shocks because they have a wider range of industries and skills

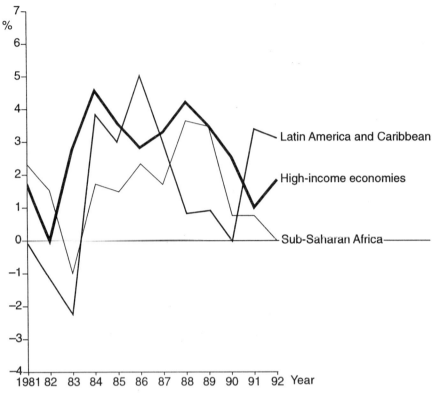

Figure 10.5 Per cent of GDP growth, 1981–92
Source: World Bank.

which support them. It is the least-developed countries that have the most unstable growth rates, and are the most vulnerable to any change in world economic fortunes.

This does not mean the poor are helpless. Domestic policies make a difference. Good government and wise investment are the best recourse to unnerving external shocks. South Korea and Indonesia have both maintained growth in the face of debt. And despite a paralysing monetary crisis in 1982 in Chile, a determined effort to reform internal financial markets, to promote exports and to diversify the industrial base has been pursued throughout the debt-ridden 1980s – under both dictatorship and democracy – such that this country's growth prospects are now the soundest in Latin America. Argentina's reforms have been more recent and are much more fragile, but cutting down on overprotected and oversubsidised public and private sector enterprise and controlling the money supply are bringing benefits here too.

Alternatively, borrowing which is used to finance consumption, buttress extravagant government spending and protect the status quo only delays essential (though maybe difficult) moves towards development. Structural changes such as reforming taxation systems, transforming education and training and allowing people greater participation in the productive process via land reforms and privatisations need disciplined domestic governments more than they require supplies of foreign money.

But implementing sound development policies is not painless, especially in times of global economic difficulty. Rich countries can do more to facilitate growth amongst the poor. Those who advocate outward-looking, export promotion policies, on the one hand, and seemingly cheap loans, on the other, cannot turn away when world events beyond LDC control turn sour. Fragile, emerging market economies that have been encouraged, even bribed, to liberalise trade then find they have opened all their doors only to let in a debilitating recession and let out flights of capital.

Debtor countries' prospects at the end of the twentieth century are made more difficult to manage, more volatile and are allowed less room to safely manoeuvre thanks to the internationalisation of finance. Global money markets magnify the risks and accelerate the time scale of events that occur, given any change of government or economic policy on the part of debtor countries. Despite having implemented many free-market reforms and having signed an agreement which gives them unrestricted access to the world's richest market place, the Mexican authorities delayed a little too long in tackling their balance of payments deficit – with the result that financial markets panicked, the peso plummeted and the government has had to increase interest rates, cut spending and increase taxes in order to restore international confidence. For millions of hard-working Mexicans, it just does not seem fair. So much for 1995; one wonders which country will be the next . . .

Finally, none of these world events have left the IMF with an untarnished reputation. It is still the law of the jungle in international trade where the weakest get hurt the most. Far from an 'orderly' world trading system, the IMF has been accused of administering a leech-like financial superstructure that bleeds LDCs of their resources. For the poorest, least-resilient countries in the world, such as in sub-Saharan Africa, it is only too obvious that IMF stabilisation policies cannot be implemented. The immediate social cost is too great. These nations need more help with their domestic finances; in implementing internal development strategies; in insulating themselves from external shocks and in gaining more preferential access to rich-world markets. But without a fairer, more active international policeman there is no guarantee that the next century will treat such poor countries any better than this one.

KEY WORDS

A balance of payments deficit occurs when a country's total earnings on foreign trade fall short of its total spending.

Capital flight is where worried private investors liquidise whatever capital they can and spirit it out of the country into safer havens where there is less risk of loss. Thus in addition to whatever official loans or payments are entering or leaving the country private capitalists may be flying out funds as fast as they can. Note that large private sales of domestic currency in the attempt to buy foreign monies may precipitate a collapse of the domestic exchange rate.

Debt–service ratio Debt service is the payment of capital plus interest charges necessary to pay off a loan over an agreed period of time. This sum can be expressed as a percentage of the debtor country's earnings on export sales: the debt service as a ratio of its income from trade.

The International Monetary Fund was set up in 1944 to underpin the fixed exchange rate system agreed in Bretton Woods (see last chapter). The IMF would supply short-term loans of foreign exchange to central banks of the developed world if this was required to protect them from a currency crisis. (Speculators might sell a country's currency if they feared a devaluation, but heavy selling would thus bring about the consequence that was feared. IMF funds could increase a central bank's financial power to resist such a move and successfully defend its fixed rate.)

The IMF was established at the same time as its sister organisation, the **World Bank** – which was charged with providing long-term loans to developing countries. The IMF, however, has been drawn more and more into administering help to LDCs since defending fixed rates has been unnecessary after the collapse of the original Bretton Woods system in 1971 and it has been the poorer countries in the world economy that have lately been in greatest need of short-term loans and financial crisis management.

Money illusion persists in the time lag between receiving increased money incomes and the realisation that prices have all gone up and the real value of money has fallen. If incomes have increased by 10 per cent, for example, and inflation rises by the same amount then people's feeling of well-being may at first rise due to the illusion of increased wealth, but this feeling will only last up until they realise their increased incomes buy no more than before.

The real rate of interest equals the money (or nominal) rate of interest minus inflation. If you borrow $100 and pay back this sum plus 10 per cent interest next year then you must pay $110. But if inflation rises by over 10 per cent, then – in real terms – if you pay $110 next year you will be paying back less than you borrowed. The real rate of interest is negative.

Stabilisation policies are those measures recommended by the IMF to restore confidence and stability in a country's financial affairs. They have been variously described as orthodox, conservative, right-wing and austere in that they usually recommend cutting money supplies, increasing interest rates, floating exchange rates, balancing government budgets and cutting back on subsidies and price/wage fixing so as to allow the freer operation of markets.

The terms of trade refer to the prices at which a country can sell its exports. It is calculated by taking an index of export prices and comparing this to the index of import prices.

Formally: $\text{ToT} = \dfrac{\text{index of export prices}}{\text{index of import prices}} \times 100\%$

For countries which export only a few primary commodities, such as cotton, copper, timber, etc., they may be particularly vulnerable to changes in Western demand. A slight change in demand may cause a substantial fall in their terms of trade.

QUESTIONS

1 What was the 'debt crisis'? How did it differ for (a) the international banks; and (b) the developing countries? Has it passed?
2 How did the international debt crisis occur? Could it have been prevented? Could it happen again?
3 Is it sound economic policy to rely on international banks for development assistance? Under what circumstances is it wise for an LDC to incur increasing debt; when is it unwise?
4 Explain the involvement of the International Monetary Fund in resolving the debt crisis. What were the rescue packages it recommended? Could they have been bettered?
5 'The international debt crisis exposed the weaknesses of unregulated market capitalism for the world economy.' Do you agree?

FURTHER READING

Hallwood, C. Paul and MacDonald, Ronald. *International Money and Finance.* Blackwell, 1994.
Todaro, Michael. *Economic Development.* Longman, 1994.
The World Bank. *World Tables.* 1994.

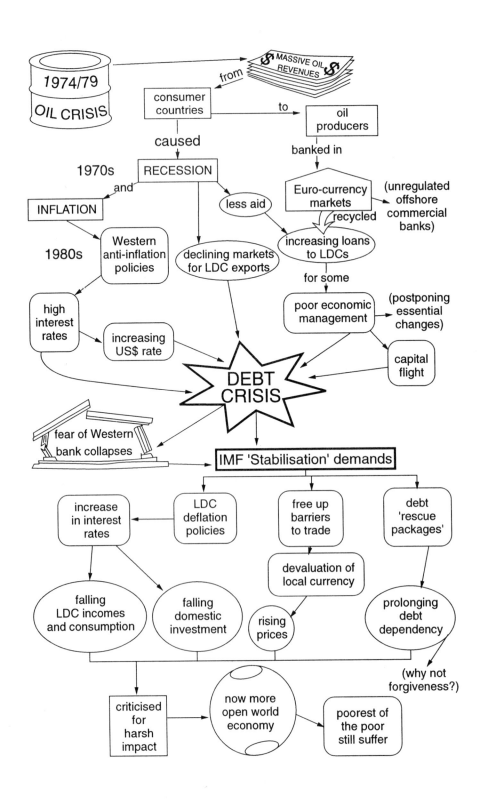

11 Development, growth and Asian dragons

Topics to be considered in this chapter

- Definition and measurement of development
- Strategies for development:
  i   primary product exploitation
  ii import substitution
  iii export promotion
- Theories of growth:
  i   Rostow's stages of growth
  ii Harrod–Domar growth model
  iii neoclassical growth model
- Experience of South Korea, Taiwan, Hong Kong and Singapore

INTRODUCTION

Wide disparities of income in the world have been a reason to turn to economics right from this subject's very beginnings – see Adam Smith, *An Inquiry into the Nature and Causes of the Wealth of Nations*.

Over two centuries later, however, modern economics still cannot make up its mind about the answers to this 'inquiry'. Surprisingly, there is not even agreement about how important the study of poverty and wealth is – are the problems of development and growth central to economics, or are they a specific branch or application of the subject?

A quick look at any introductory textbook seems to indicate that development economics is nowadays a somewhat low priority, end-of-book sort of topic. Since 'Development and Growth' is chapter 11 in *this* text also, maybe that is the impression given here as well. If so, take another look at the preceding pages. The philosophy running through this book is that national and international differences in poverty and wealth, rival theories and systems of economic organisation, are absolutely central to the subject. Moreover, no matter how extreme these differences appear to be, it is the contention here that the same economic forces are at work in all countries. Policy questions of demand-side and supply-side economics, budgetary and monetary control, free trade and regulation are debated in and out of governments all round the world, and if in the end different countries come up with radically different solutions, it is nonetheless maintained that the principles of economics remain the same.

Not all economists will necessarily agree with this claim. It can be argued that less-developed countries are structurally different from their richer neighbours and thus a very different analytical approach is necessary to understand them adequately. For example – growth theories that are appropriate to model the behaviour of rich, market systems are allegedly insufficient to satisfactorily encompass and explain the barriers to development encountered in many poor countries. Thus the notion of dualism – a formal, high-wage market sector coexisting but separate from the informal, poorer, traditional sector in LDCs – has been pursued both in conventional economics via two-sector growth models (earning the pioneering economist W. Arthur Lewis a Nobel prize) and also in more radical, Marxist interpretations that insist the poor are the inevitable residual left over after the rich have gained most of the spoils.

A little in the evolution of these themes will be discussed below. As before, the different theories and predictions derived are not just of academic interest – they have had and are having an enormous impact on government policy formulations and thus the livelihoods of billions. The most influential school of thought at present emphasises the relevance of mainstream, neoclassical economic theory – both in explaining the world economy's past performance and also in offering all countries practicable policies to enhance their future growth prospects. In these respects, although possessing numerous weaknesses (see criticisms throughout this book), neoclassical market economics claims to be more useful than rival interpretations of development theory.

MEASUREMENT

Any inquiry into the nature of development, however, needs first to identify what is meant by the term development, and how can progress in this domain be measured?

The first and most obvious criterion to consider is the real income enjoyed by the countries studied. The most frequently used measure in this regard is the Gross National Product per head of population. It is a crude but fundamental reference point that is relatively easy to obtain and is readily understood. The World Bank, for example, classifies low-income economies as those with a GNP per capita of less than US$676; middle-income economies are those with a GNP per capita between US$676 and US$8,355; and high-income economies with a GNP per head of US$8,356 or above per year.

In this example, all incomes are measured in 1992 US dollars – different world currencies being converted into dollars at the ruling market exchange rates. One difficulty with this yardstick is that current exchange rates are not a reliable means to convert dollars into all other monies – according to the imperfections of the exchange markets they may over-value some currencies and undervalue others. US$100 can often buy more goods and services in (typically) a poor country than in its richer neighbour. If this is so, then the local currency is undervalued at current exchange rates. GNP figures are thus made more accurate if dollars are converted into other countries' money via exchange rates calculated on a *purchasing power parity* basis – that is, exchange rates need to be adjusted such that an identical sample of basic goods and services costs the same in one country as another. (*The Economist* magazine has used a 'hamburger standard' as a quick approximation of this principle – if five dollars when converted into pesos buys a bigger hamburger in Mexico than in the USA, then the peso is undervalued, Mexico's GNP as measured in US dollars is undervalued, and these figures must be readjusted accordingly.)

Compare the figures below of GNP per capita, measured in current US dollars, with GDP per capita adjusted to purchasing power parity. Note that GNP and GDP are both measures of national income, but GNP differs from GDP in that the latter does not include a country's net income from abroad (a significant difference only for relatively small countries which have a high proportion of investments overseas, or have large foreign debt–service payments).

Although there are still wide differences between rich and poor nations, the use of PPP figures reduces the gap somewhat. The relative position of economies in this rank-ordering may also be affected (compare the change in the top four countries listed below if you compare incomes per head measured in current prices to purchasing power parities).

Table 11.1 Income per head, rank order of selected countries

	1991 GNP per cap. (current US$)	*1991 GDP per cap.* (US$, PPP adjusted)
Japan	26,840	19,390
USA	22,340	22,130
Canada	20,830	19,320
Germany	20,510	19,770
France	20,410	18,430
Italy	18,540	17,040
United Kingdom	16,530	16,340
Russia	3,290	6,930
Mexico	3,080	7,710
Brazil	2,920	5,240
China	440	1,680
India	330	1,150

Source: World Bank.

Even if adjusted to show national incomes on a purchasing power basis, however, there still remain a number of other criticisms of using GNP per capita to measure development. Many poor peoples may not be in close contact with the money economy – they may neither sell the product of their work, nor buy many goods or services. Much of what they consume might be provided by themselves or bartered for in unrecorded trade. Subsistence farmers fall into this category. Similarly, many participants in *the informal sector* – such as numerous street sellers, stall holders and those employed in small workshops – may be more integrated into the modern market economy but will rarely disclose their output or incomes. Calculating their economic contribution can be estimated via comparing the shortfall between the community's recorded incomes and recorded expenditures, but nonetheless considerable scope for underestimating the true national income of developing countries remains.

The methods used to compile GNP statistics in some countries can be very questionable. If output, expenditure and income data are surveyed with no great professional commitment to the exercise (e.g. by untrained assistants, part-timers, students, etc.) then many inaccuracies will be included due to errors and guesswork on the part of investigators, evasion and fabrication on the part of those surveyed. There may also be deliberate falsification of the results for political purposes.

But even if a country's GNP per capita data were 100 per cent accurate and included all economic activity without exception, it would still not necessarily be the best indicator of development. This is because it shows only a mathematical average income, and averages may conceal very wide income disparities between rich and poor. Plus the whole notion of development implies something more for a country than just a crude measure of monetary wealth. If a nation plunders its stock of mineral resources, desecrates its landscape, pollutes its air, exploits its uneducated workforce and mounts up enormous incomes for a corrupt few, it would 'enjoy' a relatively high GNP per head of population, but would it be developed? For this reason there have been many attempts over the years to define and measure development using a wider range of criteria than just income statistics alone.

A reporter once asked Mahatma Ghandi what he thought of Western civilisation; he replied: 'I think it would be a good idea . . . ' The notion that material wealth equates with civilisation was challenged.

Development implies that a country's living standards are improving for all; that there is a reduction in poverty, in inequality, an improvement in general standards of housing, diet, health and education. Apart from such socio-economic indicators, development can also be interpreted as including freedom from oppression and servitude, and freedom to create a greater cultural identity and sense of self-esteem. It implies that the majority of a country's peoples are actively participating in the development process and that no minority is being persecuted as a means to this end.

Defining development so widely leads to problems of measurement. The United Nations, for example, publishes a political freedom index that would rank some countries relatively lower in development terms than if purely economic criteria were used – e.g. China, Chile (under Pinochet), Indonesia, Saudia Arabia, etc. Concepts such as democracy, freedom of expression, the rule of law, etc. are embodied here.

Confining this study to economics, it can be said that rising average incomes are a necessary but not sufficient condition for development. Increased economic power may not lead to greater civilisation (consider Hitler's Germany), but no sustained development is possible without it. Economic wealth is power, and such power is necessary for the creation of good *or* ill.

The United Nations Development Programme uses GNP per capita data calculated on a purchasing power parity basis as a measure of incomes; life expectancy at birth as an indicator of health; and the percentage of adult literacy as an indicator of education. By weighting these three together, it comes up with a *Human Development Index* (HDI) on a scale from zero to one.

The nations shown in table 11.2 are ranked according to their income per head measured in 1987 US dollars at market exchange rates (column 2). Referring to the Human Development Index (column 6), however, the ordering of this selection of countries changes considerably. Contrast the positions of the United Arab Emirates and Chile, for example. Of the twenty countries sampled here, Chile improves from 14th position to 8th; UAE drops from 3rd to 14th – below Sri Lanka and not much higher than China.

The HDI is no objective measure free from criticism, however, because depending on how you weight the three indicators (featured in columns 3, 4 and 5) together you can come up with different results. Compare the findings on the USA and Spain, for example. A country over three times richer measured at market exchange rates and 1 per cent higher adult literacy is ranked lower on the HDI. There are grounds to question the methodology used here!

There have been many more attempts to capture the notion of development in measurable statistics than surveyed here, but there is clearly no single, objective indicator of such a value-loaded concept that is without its faults. Since it is differences in incomes that excite most commentators, however, and – as mentioned earlier – it is a popular and frequently published statistic, GNP (or where unavailable, GDP) per capita is used most often in this book as *the* yardstick of development (though its weaknesses mentioned above must always be borne in mind).

THEORIES AND POLICIES OF DEVELOPMENT

What are the economic strategies that a less-developed country can pursue to best secure its development? This is a concern that has only received

Table 11.2 Development indicators, selected countries

1	2	3	4	5	6
	GNP	PPP adj.	Life	Adult	
	p.c.	GDP p.c.	expectancy	literacy	HDI
Country	(1987)	(1987)	(1987)	(1985)	
	US$	US$	(years)	(%)	0–1
Switzerland	21,330	15,403	77	99	0.986
USA	18,530	17,615	76	96	0.961
Utd Arab Emirates	15,830	12,191	71	60	0.782
Netherlands	11,860	12,661	77	99	0.984
United Kingdom	10,420	12,270	76	99	0.970
Italy	10,350	10,682	76	97	0.966
Spain	6,010	8,989	77	95	0.965
Trinidad & Tobago	4,210	3,664	71	96	0.885
Greece	4,020	5,500	76	93	0.949
Argentina	2,390	4,647	71	96	0.910
Brazil	2,020	4,307	65	78	0.784
South Africa	1,890	4,981	61	70	0.731
Malaysia	1,810	3,849	70	74	0.800
Chile	1,310	4,862	72	98	0.931
Egypt	680	1,357	62	45	0.501
Sri Lanka	400	2,053	71	87	0.789
Pakistan	350	1,585	58	30	0.423
India	300	1,053	59	43	0.439
China	290	2,124	70	69	0.716
Bangladesh	160	883	52	33	0.318

Source: UN Development Programme, *Human Development Report 1990.*

serious attention since the 1950s. There was little interest in analysing the economics of LDCs in the nineteenth and early twentieth centuries – this was the colonial era when Europeans were more interested in action rather than reflection.

International trade in the nineteenth century was relatively simple. Finance was regulated by *the gold standard* and administered by what was in effect the world's central bank – the Bank of England. Thanks to continually improving transport technology, the world economy witnessed a gradual extension of markets that grew wider and wider around their basic centre in Europe. As was entirely consistent with classical economic thinking, colonies and ex-colonies had a comparative advantage in exporting primary produce, so Western capital was poured into plantations and mines, railways and shipping all round the world from Argentina to Indonesia, Kenya to the West Indies.

The LDCs thus entered the world economy as exporters of primary produce to serve Western manufacturers and consumers. Gains from this trade were enjoyed by both parties – the economies of poorer countries were transformed by Western capital and they could thus earn growing export revenues; meanwhile Europeans enjoyed cheap oil, copper, phosphates, rubber, sugar, tobacco, coffee, tea, etc. The distribution of these benefits – how much the colonies and ex-colonies gained in contrast to Europeans – depended on the terms of trade; that is, whether North American wheat, West Indian sugar and Malaysian rubber and tin could be sold in European markets for a high price or a low one. Some countries earned more and thus grew faster than others under this regime: Argentina, for example, was ranked as the eleventh richest country in the world in 1870.

The colonial era obviously brought economic benefits, but not to all people equally. Native populations of the LDCs had little choice in determining their destiny and many had not experienced the growth in incomes that they could see were enjoyed by a privileged elite. Analysis of the role of primary production as a strategy for development is inevitably coloured by this colonial experience, nonetheless underdeveloped countries of the world still today retain a comparative advantage in mineral extraction and agricultural exploitation and it is thus important to consider how far specialisation in primary production is a useful strategy for development.

Strategy 1. Exploitation and export of primary produce

There is no doubt that one of the earliest and seemingly easiest ways discovered to get rich quick is to go and find some source of great natural wealth and exploit it. Over the centuries, gold and silver from South America; spices from the East Indies; gold and diamonds from South Africa; cereals, cotton and tobacco from North America; and oil from the Middle East have all provided the means for some (not necessarily indigenous) people to accumulate wealth. Towns, cities and empires have flourished and declined according to the availability of such valued natural resources. Whether or not such resource exploitation leads to sustainable economic (and environmental) development, however, depends on the extent to which: (a) large surpluses can be generated; and (b) these surpluses can be productively invested in value-adding technologies in new industry. Re-investment is essential – clearly countries cannot go on enriching themselves forever simply by extracting more and more non-renewable natural resources (see chapter 13).

In fact, even if nations could go on and on plundering their natural riches, economic theory and history teaches us that the prices of these resources tend to be high for only relatively short time periods. Except in the extremely rare case of a natural monopoly, competition from alternative suppliers plus the price effect driving consumers to economise on demand tends to quickly bring down the revenues to be earned from the export and sale of scarce natural assets. (Having said that, however, the *rents* to be earned in the short-lived period when world markets are hurriedly trying to adjust can be substantial: for example, between 1963 and 1973 Saudi Arabian petrol prices averaged US\$4.6 per barrel and Saudi oil revenues averaged US\$1.39bn. Between 1974 and 1984 prices leapt to an average of US$27.6 per barrel and average annual revenues soared to US$53.05bn.)

Prices of primary produce can be volatile. Scarcity and inelasticity in supply means large incomes or *quasi-rents* can be earned for a short while but these surpluses inevitably drive the search for alternatives. Thus the competition between rival countries and mining companies eventually forces profits and prices down. Wars, panic buying or the introduction of mineral-specific new technologies (e.g. cars for oil; nuclear power for uranium) can bump up demand and thus prices for a while, only for the long-term downward price pressure to reassert itself afterwards. Less-developed countries that are *monocultures* – particularly if they are mineral resource dependent – can thus earn very unstable incomes (see chapter 10 on OPEC incomes, for example).

Who benefits from short-term bonanzas? It can be a local business community, multinational corporations or governments, depending on the structure of the industry employed in the exploitation of the natural resource, and the energy and efficiency with which the government can capture any of the rents earned. (Since the 1970s governments have become more adept at taxing and in other ways capturing a rising share of these rents without scaring away the business goose that lays the golden egg. This is true of all types of natural resource exploitation, but has been particularly noticeable in the case of oil.)

But whichever the institution that accumulates the wealth involved, it is the *proportion* of those surpluses earned that is invested in the economy and the *efficiency* with which they are employed in the promotion of diversification and growth that is the key to long-term economic development. Note, such inflows can come in the form of private investment or public investment; from local capitalists or from foreign direct involvement.

A problematic feature of mineral exploitation in particular is that such activity is often carried out on a huge, capital-intensive scale using expensive, imported technology and skills, with relatively little local labour absorption. Whether practised by foreign multinationals, by local private industry or state enterprise, the integration of these businesses into the local economy can be very limited. Dualism results – characterised by palaces in the desert, fortresses in the jungle, tower blocks above the ghetto, etc.

The stereotypical dualistic development pattern is of a small, modern, capital-intensive and innovative business sector which possesses good trade links with the developed world but which grows up as an enclave within a larger, relatively backward, labour-intensive and traditional peasant-worker economy. The level of communication and economic interchange between these two sectors is underdeveloped – indeed the gulf between the rich and poor communities within a LDC can be as great as the gulf between rich and poor countries as a whole.

The benefits of natural resource exploitation may thus not spread very far. This is not just the simplistic case of foreigners coming in like Pizarro to a poor country to plunder its riches and make off with them. (Though this has undeniably happened in the past.) Nor is it a case of corrupt governments and/or local capitalists expropriating riches and wasting them on conspicuous consumption and capital flight into foreign bank acounts. (This too has occurred.) It is just that it is the natural tendency of entre-preneurs anywhere and especially in developing countries to work hard to lift themselves out of poverty, to accumulate wealth and then to strive to protect it.

Lobbying governments to stabilise exchange rates at a high level can be instrumental in this process: it ensures high prices and profits for the export of the natural resource; it means the importation of foreign capital equipment and technology is cheap; so is the consumption of foreign luxuries like cars, fashion-wear, holidays, etc.; and domestic savings can be similarly cheaply converted into safe, hard-currency deposits. Unfortu-nately, traditional-sector industry and agriculture can be destroyed by high exchange rates: cheap imports compete away their domestic market and high export prices for their products mean they cannot find sales abroad.

An ailment known as *Dutch Disease* is a modern demonstration of this phenomenon. Exports of natural gas found in the 1960s caused the Dutch exchange rate to appreciate. Large revenues were devoted to improving social welfare, but with money supplies outrunning domestic production inflation began to increase. Meanwhile, traditional export industries were suffering from lost markets. Unemployment increased and growth rates declined. The gas bonanza benefited one industry, therefore, at the expense of all others.

The oil bonanza has had a similar effect on countries such as Nigeria, Mexico and Venezuela. In extreme cases there is even what can be called the Kuwait effect – i.e. where oil riches and exchange rates rise so high that almost nothing else in the economy can be produced and profitably exported. Labour forces may be made up entirely of foreigners and there is no incentive for the small, indigenous population to perform any work and develop any skills at all.

These are examples where national incomes are rising by depreciating the country's stock of natural capital. No or low re-investment is taking place. 'Development' is clearly unsustainable.

We can conclude this section by stating that relatively rich natural resource endowments are by no means a guarantee of economic develop-ment. Some countries can exploit and retain them productively (e.g. Canada, Australia); others may lose out (see table 11.3).

Gillis *et al.* (*Economics of Development*, Longman, 1990) cites Bolivia as an example of a mining country *par excellence*. After three centuries of plundering its mineral wealth it is still one of the poorest countries in South America.

Table 11.3

Country	Natural resource	Minerals as % of exports, 1990	% Growth of GNP p.c. 1965–90
Zaire	cobalt, copper	56	–2.2
Mauritania	iron ore	81	–0.6
Bolivia	silver, tin	69	–0.7

Source: World Bank.

This mixed development record of primary produce specialisation, the drive towards independence on the part of those colonised and the desire of many poor to emulate the economic success of the great powers were all themes that were current in the period after the Second World War when a new international order was being constructed. Academic thinking was inevitably affected. The economics of development thus evolved as a separate specialism at this time as interest grew in the theories and policies appropriate for LDC growth.

One of the most famous theories to emerge in this era was *The Stages of Economic Growth*, by Walt Rostow (Cambridge, 1960). Rostow identified five key steps or stages that all countries must go through to attain development:

1 *The traditional society*, where nearly all employment is in subsistence agriculture and low living standards prevent much saving and investment.
2 *Establishing preconditions*, where agricultural productivity rises and an entrepreneurial merchant class emerges.
3 *The take-off*, where increasing investment and growth in a leading sector in the country generates enough momentum to lift the whole economy towards:
4 *The drive to maturity*, where success is broadened to include other sectors such that the increased pace of investment and growth becomes self-sustaining.
5 *The age of high mass consumption* is finally achieved where living standards are increased for all.

Rostow's book contains a simple explanation for continuing poverty (see stage 1, above) – a vicious circle where low incomes prevent savings; no savings means no domestic investment; and no investment means no growth of incomes. In addition, it also provides a formula for success: establishing the preconditions in stage 2 leads on to stage 3, to stage 4 and thus 5.

The Stages of Economic Growth was descriptive rather than prescriptive, however. It gave no clear indication of the mechanism of growth and could not predict how such growth would proceed. The different stages involved seemed to follow one another automatically.

A theory of *economic dynamics* was necessary to explain more thoroughly how key variables such as the ratio of savings and investment should interact to produce growth. This was provided in the late 1940s by two economists working independently – Roy Harrod and Evsey Domar – in what has been called the *Harrod–Domar growth model*. Their work, along with Rostow's, inherited the dominant economic philosophy of Keynesianism (see chapter 3) with its focus on macroeconomic aggregates plus it was also witness to the economic power of Stalin's Soviet Union which had been built by massive increases in capital investment (see chapter 2).

The key to growth in the Harrod–Domar model lay in a country's savings ratio (s) and in its *incremental capital–output ratio* (ICOR, or more simply k). That is, the proportion of national income saved determines a country's flow of funds into investment, and the incremental capital–output ratio determines how much output will grow from this given increase in capital stock (i.e. investment). A country that saves 12 per cent of its income and has a capital–output ratio of 3 can thus have a rate of economic growth equal to $s/k = 12/3 = 4$ per cent.

Post-war development thinking was dominated by these ideas. Both Rostow's work and the Harrod–Domar model emphasised the importance of macroeconomic savings and investment ratios. Rostow's book was sub-titled: *A Non-Communist Manifesto*, and this indicates its genesis in the Cold War era, where the alternative model for developing countries was the evidently successful (at this time) system of massive, state-directed investment under communist central planning.

The appeal of political independence and, with it, more central government involvement in the management of economic growth was inevitable in this climate. Specialisation in primary product exports was associated with the colonial era and for LDCs emerging from the old European empires, farming and mining were therefore equated with backwardness and neocolonial dependence. Independence for many brought with it the insistence that it should be accompanied by industrialisation and economic self-reliance.

Strategy 2. Import-substituting industrialisation

The workings of an international market system dominated by the big Western nations were distrusted. Governments from Egypt to India, Argentina to Taiwan (then) were empowered to erect barriers against foreign imports, to channel funds into public and private enterprise and generally to promote the rise of domestic industry and skills (ignoring traditional agriculture). Foreign capital was still welcomed in many cases, but restrictions on its use were widespread. Charismatic, popular leaders like Nasser in Egypt, Nehru in India, Peron in Argentina, Sukarno in Indonesia and Mao Tse-tung in China came in on this wave of emerging nationalism.

The economic effects of this change in development strategy were beneficial at first. In addition to large public investments (in heavy industry such as iron and steel works, engineering, construction, railways, etc.), with restrictions on imports there is an immediate incentive for local entrepreneurs to provide all manner of goods and services to the domestic market. The 1950s and 1960s was thus an era of industrialisation, urbanisation, diversifying economies and generally rising incomes for the LDCs.

With internal markets protected, emerging infant industries are guaranteed sales. Employment is thus generated in an expanding range of domestic enterprises which fill the vacuum left by the absence of overseas competitors. The development impact can be very positive: there is much *learning-by-doing* as new skills, new resources and new products to the country are encouraged. Where foreign capital is employed this may be in the form of joint ventures of local firms with multinational corporations (MNCs). Both benefit: MNCs gain access to a protected market place; local businesses acquire foreign technology and modern managerial techniques.

There is theoretical support for import substitution stategies, too. Almost by definition, the typical less-developed country does not possess perfectly functioning markets that reach across the entire economy. Such market imperfections therefore imply that ruling prices cannot send correct signals to firms and consumers. There may be much latent potential in an LDC's capacity to supply relatively simple manufactured goods (such as basic clothing, food processing, low-tech. machines), for example, but such a comparative advantage may never be developed if LDC prices, market rates of interest and expected rates of return on investment do not reflect this. In particular, there are underdeveloped or missing markets for factors of production. Information for the efficient allocation of capital is lacking; land may be locked up in familial, feudal patterns of ownership; the emergence of entrepreneurs may be obstructed by traditional cultures resistant to change. Limited markets in which an unrepresentative sample of buyers and sellers come together cannot determine prices that allocate society's resources optimally. Profitable investment opportunities may go unrecognised; potentially productive resources may remain undeveloped – especially where substantial external economies exist. (No one manufacturing enterprise will set up in a poor area if local incomes are insufficient to promise many sales, but should a number of different businesses set up together they would generate rising incomes and sufficient trade for all – the employees of one firm becoming the customers of others.)

Price signals from international markets in these circumstances will override national ones. Without protection, with unrestricted access to highly lucrative overseas destinations, a poor country may lose to foreign employments those few resources that are emerging into the money economy. Valued personnel join the 'brain drain'; productive mineral rights are bought up cheaply by MNCs; accumulated savings go in capital flight to offshore financial centres.

The argument for protection, government intervention and regulation of the domestic economy is therefore justified. The conventional 'infant industry' argument (see chapter 5) can be generalised to the whole economy of an LDC. With astute government management a network of young industries can grow; management and labour skills can develop; home-grown technology can evolve until the industrial sector is strong and diversified enough to compete with MDC industry on its own terms – such that continued protection and government allocation of domestic resources becomes redundant.

Government intervention can secure such results, but it need not. Sensitively handled strategic trade policies have been productive in some cases (see chapter 5) but government failure in this regard is, unfortunately, far more common. Import barriers, protective legislation, hand-outs to local firms and direct public ownership and control of domestic industry have more often promoted not the growth of infant industries but their increasing *dependence*.

The absence of foreign competition ensures local businesses can make profits without being strenuously efficient. Worse, entrepreneurs learn that profits are made quickest not by raising quality standards to win sales in competitive markets but by lobbying public officials to get exclusive government contracts; to gain sole rights to import and distribute valued foreign manufactures; and to secure laws that increase protection and confer local monopoly power.

The domestic economy will thus grow and diversify under protection, but – as incomes increase – amongst the business class that benefits most there rises a powerful vested interest in the continuation of these detrimental (to the larger economy) policies. Infant industries therefore never grow up.

Where large state-owned industries make up the manufacturing sector, the pressure to maintain import restrictions and centrally allocated investment comes from within the public sector itself (e.g. in Egypt). Where private industry predominates there may be widespread bribery and corruption of government officials. More subtly, government ministers and top industrialists may graduate from the same restricted elite in society, do business regularly with one another and thus come to grant each other 'favours' on a reciprocal basis (e.g. in India).

The price structure of the domestic economy becomes distorted when government intervention is pervasive. Rather than improving the signalling mechanism, it becomes disabling. Tariffs, quotas and foreign exchange restrictions that are designed to shut out imports can lead to an overvalued currency. Governments subsequently come under pressure from the business class to formally fix the exchange rate at a higher than free-market level – this enables entrepreneurs to purchase cheap foreign capital inputs, yet their sales remain protected from imported consumer goods. Cheap foreign technology, however, means industry now has an incentive to employ more capital than labour. Capital-intensive industrial techniques are unhelpful in LDCs with labour surplus: it reinforces divergent dualism.

In India, for example, growth of industrial output between 1950 and 1970 far outstripped the rate of growth of job creation – the overall capital–labour ratio increased threefold. The efficiency of Indian industry did not similarly improve, however. With the allocation of investment directed by government planning and not via financial markets, industrial growth was the outcome of more and more capital inputs rather than the increasing efficiency of each unit. This Indian experience clearly parallels the dismal performance of Soviet capital as described earlier in chapter 2. Thus India's incremental capital–output ratio rose from around 4 in the early 1960s to 10.5 in 1975 – a damning indictment of its import substitution strategy.

Strategy 3. Free markets and export promotion

Precisely because it was a path-breaking theoretical work, the Harrod–Domar growth model was inevitably a simplification. In particular, reliance on the crude percentage of national income invested as the key to growth placed too much emphasis on the quantity of capital accumulation rather than its quality. As is evidenced above, after initial successes those nations that had barricaded themselves against world trade and resorted to substantial (and especially centrally directed) investment found their capital productivity falling and thus long-term growth more difficult to achieve.

Import substitution as a development strategy has another weakness too. It distorts internal markets in favour of industrialisation – suppressing farm prices in order to guarantee cheap food for urban labour forces and to divert investment away from agriculture and into industry. When the bulk of LDC populations work and live on the land, however, such policies seem distinctly perverse. Promoting urban industrialisation at the expense of holding down farm incomes is bound to cause dislocation and strife. Rural peoples are forced into the cities in search of better wages, only to end up in ghettos and shanty towns excluded from *formal sector* employment and straining urban public services beyond their limits.

The industrialisation bias in many LDCs is born of a pessimistic belief that traditional agriculture is inherently backward and has little attraction for modern investment. On closer examination, a number of studies have shown this not to be true. Under the right circumstances, traditional agriculture responds well to market incentives and opportunities for profitable investment are not lacking.

Results from South East Asia and Latin America have shown that in applying new technologies such as high-yield varieties of staple crops, fertilisers and irrigation – all capital-saving rather than labour-saving techniques – agricultural productivity can be rapidly increased. Where peasant farmers are not discriminated against by government policy-makers and where food prices reflect the real costs involved in their production, then the agricultural sector can become an integrated part of the growing LDC economy rather than a forgotten backwater in increasingly dualistic development.

The *neoclassical growth model,* first developed by Robert Solow in 1956, employs these principles mentioned above. The role of flexible market prices, free from any government intervention, is stressed as the prime allocative mechanism. Growth in production is considered as a function of both capital and labour inputs, though each in isolation is characterised by diminishing returns.

The production function illustrated here relates the amount of output per person in an economy to the amount of capital employed per person. As capital per head increases at a constant rate: 0, 10, 20, 30, etc. output increases rapidly at first but then progressively slows down: 0, 20, 35, 40, 43, etc. This is the principle of diminishing returns – the accumulation of capital becomes less and less productive.

Per capita output can only be improved in the long run by a shift upward in the production function. How is this possible? – by the invention and application of entirely new productive processes: technical change. Thus the production function shifts from P1 to P2.

Since increasing capital inputs secures steadily decreasing additional outputs, the neoclassical model therefore identifies *technical progress* as the only means to shift the production function over time. In addition, it should be noted that this model does not discriminate between agriculture and industry in their respective capacities to generate growth through the application of new technology. Both sectors are assumed capable of responding to new products and processes.

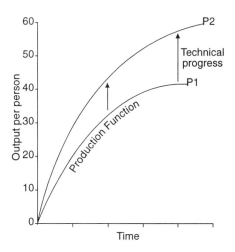

Figure 11.1 The slowdown of productivity over time can be shifted by technical progress

How technical progress occurs and why it is more productive in some countries than others is less easy to answer and has tested the minds of economists for some time. Recent thinking emphasises the need for investment in *human* capital – especially promoting education and the unrestricted competition in ideas and their application to industry. This has two implications: it brings the economics of growth theory closer to that of development; and, in embracing more variables in the neoclassical model, it requires mathematical analysis to pursue the study any further.

It should be noted that the neoclassical growth model was not formulated with LDCs specifically in mind and indeed, as has been argued earlier, many countries chose to ignore such thinking and follow a highly interventionist, import substitution strategy in the post-war period. Very few LDCs opted to go a different path – to promote an export-oriented economy with internal markets open to international prices. Neoclassical economists have claimed that those few nations that have embraced these policies gained the greater rewards.

THE ASIAN DRAGONS

It is argued that the remarkable economic successes of certain newly industrialising countries (NICS), and particularly the 'Asian dragons' of South Korea, Taiwan, Hong Kong and Singapore, illustrate the potency and relevance of this theory. There is no doubt that these four countries have an impressive growth record – how far this can be attributed to the pursuit of neoclassical economic policies, however, needs to be examined.

The average growth rates in per capita incomes in these four countries is given below for the period 1965–90. These figures show that these countries have now outperformed any other nation or group of nations on the globe for well over a quarter of a century.

These four 'dragons' have all since the 1960s followed a strategy of export promotion – actively seeking to exploit their comparative advantage in international trade in order to gain foreign sales for their expanding range of manufactures. Beginning with specialising in labour-intensive, relatively low-tech. products, all four sought to gain increasing investment in higher value-added production processes: exporting more and more sophisticated, greater income-earning goods and services.

Although the broad outlines of this growth strategy are the same for all four countries, the details differ. Consider firstly the characteristics shown in table 11.4.

Hong Kong and Singapore are both city states that act as offshore entre-ports and commercial centres for their surrounding regions. South Korea and Taiwan, in contrast, are altogether bigger countries with significant agricultural sectors. The development process in these two nations had therefore to take rural interests into account – and as a result they are more instructive exemplars for other LDCs.

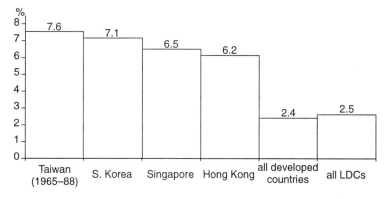

Figure 11.2 Average growth in GNP per capita, 1965–90
Source: World Bank.

Table 11.4 The Asian 'dragons': selected data

	S. Korea	*Taiwan*	*Hong Kong*	*Singapore*
Population (1992) (m.)	43.7	20.8	5.8	2.8
Geographical area (000km²)	99	36	1	1
GDP (1993) US$bn	360	217	110	55
GDP per person	8,090	10,388	18,390	19,166
Foreign trade as % of GDP	44	72	250	276

Sources: World Bank, Economist Intelligence Unit.
Note: Includes re-exports.

An agricultural transformation took place throughout East Asia after the Second World War with the implementation of various *land reforms*. Note that in all pre-industrial societies land is the major form of wealth and source of political power and prestige. Land tenure systems institutionalise the political, economic and sociological character of a country – determining the individual's rights, duties, liberties, the parameters of family life, the class system and the role of the state. Undertaking land reform, therefore, means changing all this.

Land reforms generally take place for political rather than economic reasons – in China it took place with a bloody communist revolution. In Japan, South Korea and Taiwan it followed American occupation as a means of dispossessing the Japanese ruling class which had supported the Imperial war against the USA. In the cases of the former Japanese colonies of South Korea and Taiwan, therefore, it brought about a major transformation from cultivation by poor tenants on large, Japanese-owned land holdings to a system of owner occupation on smaller-scale indigenous farms. Agricultural surpluses were now not transferred abroad to Japanese overlords but were available for domestic incomes, consumption and investment.

In *Korea* during the 1930s, two-thirds of all rice production was expropriated by Japan. This was indicative of the colonial structure of the economy up until the outbreak of the Second World War. Following the cessation of hostilities and the division of the country in 1945 into rival Soviet and American-supported zones, the southern half found itself with over 60 per cent of the population, 70 per cent of the rice-growing lands, much of the (then) light industry, but almost none of the heavy industry and power generation capacity. The one notable achievement in the politically turbulent period immediately following the war was the US administered land reform which redistributed cultivable land from large foreign and domestic owners to small (maximum 3 hectares) holdings. Scarcely had the US handed over control to a South Korean administration, however, when a new war erupted.

The Korean War lasted from 1950 to 1953, was fought mainly on southern territory and consequently left the south economically devastated. Half of the country's manufacturing infrastructure was destroyed. The country survived at first on US aid whilst it set about rebuilding. Imports were restricted in this period, exports were insignificant and confined mostly to primary products. Trade deficits were baled out by US aid but the currency became over valued and shortages of essential consumer and capital goods became more and more apparent. Agricultural output, however – based on the successful land reform – recovered rapidly to achieve historically record growth rates of 3.5 per cent p.a. from 1952 on.

The major change to an outward-looking, export-promoting economy took root with the incoming military administration of General Park Chung Hee in 1961. The Korean currency, the won, was devalued in order to cheapen the price of exports; interest rates rose (to encourage savings and limit inflation); and although a battery of import controls was maintained, exporters were given tax-free access to required foreign inputs.

South Korea grew up with a substantial defence force – essential for its security but a significant financial burden – and a military government that took an active part in all economic decision making. It was thus by government decision – not free-market forces – that Korea sought to promote a variety of export industries. Textiles, clothing and the assembly of electronic equipment can be argued as obvious candidates to exploit the country's comparitive advantage in relatively cheap, skilled labour industries. Shipbuilding, steel and high-volume car production, however, are heavy, capital-intensive processes that all grew from infant industries to become world beaters due to government planning and massive and continuing financial support.

Korea's rate of growth of income and rate of growth of manufacturing exports from the 1960s right through the oil price-induced recessions of the late 1970s and the debt-stricken 1980s is truly remarkable. It owes much to the country's ability to sniff out foreign markets and its flexibility to change products and destinations as world consumer demand shifted. Despite occasional mistakes, this ability was not found only amongst private entrepreneurs but also in government planners. The partnership between public and private sectors has been very successful in the South Korean case.

Taiwan's economic development was even more solidly based in agriculture than South Korea's. This was begun during Japanese rule in the 1930s when, with the purpose of feeding the Imperial homeland, much technical progress was achieved in agriculture – irrigated farmlands were extended; application of fertiliser became widespread and high-yield strains of rice and sugar cane were introduced.

The Japanese administration ended in 1945 and in the post-war period Taiwan received over a million refugees from the communist revolution in China. A sweeping land reform – as in South Korea – and the determined efforts of the new government to raise food production to feed the increasing population led to another leap in agricultural productivity. Annual growth rates reached 9 per cent in the early 1950s.

As a result of increasing agricultural output, rural wages rose faster than urban wages at this time. Industry specialised in dispersed, relatively small-scale labour-intensive enterprises. A growing agricultural surplus meant a healthy rural market expanded for industrial goods, meanwhile allowing labour and capital to increasingly transfer from the farms to the cities.

A cautious, protectionist regime dependent on foreign aid and traditional agricultural exports thus gradually came round to support a strategy of promoting manufacturing exports: the Taiwanese dollar was heavily devalued and foreign exchange restrictions eased.

Throughout the 1960s exports increased dramatically as manufactures were kept internationally competitive by the low cost of Taiwanese labour. This was ensured, however, less by the operation of flexible labour markets than by a dominant government determined to ban strikes and minimise protective labour legislation. The expansion of trade continued through the 1970s and showed – as in the case of South Korea – the country's ability to react quickly to changing world markets. As incomes rose, and richer countries protested about Taiwanese continued protectionism, the government instituted liberalising reforms – cutting back on tariffs and quotas – and encouraged more value-added, higher skill products. The economy remains diverse, integrated, internally and internationally competitive and responsive both to changing government and consumer demands.

Hong Kong and *Singapore*, while both island city-states which function as offshore industrial and financial centres serving regional and world markets, have a widely contrasting political economy. One is the product of an almost archetypal laissez-faire society – chaotic, vibrant and ever-changing – but with a future tied into the destiny of the communist-ruled Chinese mainland. The other is a very closely managed economy where the government intervenes in almost all aspects of social behaviour from the length of hair to the size of families and the freedom of foreign press. Both countries have little in the way of natural resources but have successfully exploited their geographical position and their native enterprise to achieve sustained economic growth based on manufacturing exports and re-exports and, increasingly now, financial services.

CONCLUSION

Is the success of these Asian dragons due to neoclassical economic policies, therefore? Not entirely. It is too simplistic to argue that growth is the natural result of liberalising markets. The unregulated price mechanism takes the underlying institutional structure of an economy as given, and in the circumstances of underdeveloped or missing markets, inadequate infra-structure and a grossly unequal distribution of wealth then implementing neoclassical policies can create more problems than they solve.

Free markets in LDCs can be characterised by *positive feedback*: the rich are able to reinvest their surplus income and thereby become richer; while poorer peoples are locked into a vicious cycle of poverty, insufficient savings and no growth. Only by direct intervention to remodel the economy's institutional foundations can the preconditions for free-market growth be established.

Putting productive resources at the disposal of local entrepreneurs who have a direct interest in raising outputs and efficiency will not happen through laissez-faire – it requires central command. This same principle applies to South Korean and Taiwanese land reforms as it does to the contemporary privatisations of East European state industry and Latin American pension funds. There is no ducking government responsibilities here – if the institutional transformation is botched, then the benefits will not accrue to the wider economy but to a privileged few who may have little incentive to spread the rewards any wider.

The provision of essential public infrastructure is, again, something the free market cannot provide. Road, rail and air transport networks must be provided by governments, as well as education and health services which all confer extensive external benefits. Where the supply of educated entrepreneurs is limited (especially in the earlier stages of development) then co-opting them to the service of the state in ministerial planning commissions has proved successful in Japan, South Korea and Singapore – though whether this is a recipe that will work outside of East Asia is uncertain.

On closer examination, therefore, the Asian dragons do not provide unqualified support for neoclassical economics. The direction of strong government has been much in evidence. But, having said this, *the direction in which all have moved has been increasingly to liberalise markets once the foundations for growth have been laid.* Ensuring realistic prices operate throughout the economy is the first important policy common to these countries. Three prices in particular deserve mention: the price of agricultural products, the price of labour, and the external exchange rate. These are essential to ensure the integration and not the dislocation of the farm sector, the application of appropriate capital-saving and not labour-saving technologies, and the international competitiveness of exports. Interest rates must be correctly priced too – to attract savings, discourage capital flight and to inhibit inflationary expansion of money supplies.

Economic development is not something that can then be left to laissez-faire. Sensitive management of a growing economy is something that will always be necessary – firstly, in parenting infant industries; secondly, in providing effective public infrastructure; and, thirdly, in policing fair and competitive markets. Resources are allocated between various employments and between a country's present and future needs according to the prices which rule. It is on this issue ultimately that a successful and flexible market economy is built.

It may be that in LDCs, markets are insufficiently, imperfectly developed. They thus send the wrong signals and, without corrective management, will promote sub-optimal, distortionary results. Monopolistic vested interests, a polarised society and a crippled economy can be the outcome. The solution here, however, is not to suspend the market system but to improve and develop it. What the Asian dragons have to teach us is that in the developing world what is required is not less market enterprise but more of it.

KEY WORDS

Economic dynamics studies the behaviour of variables through time – especially whether they move towards or away from a state of equilibrium. Dynamics can be contrasted with **comparative statics** which considers the balance of variables at a given time period, changes one key variable and then compares the result.

Formal and informal sectors exist in all countries and refer to those economic activities which are recognised by the state and those which are not. The former are subject to the law, official measurement, regulation, taxation and, in consequence, they figure in official statistics. They vary in size from small, one-person businesses to multinational corporations. Informal sector businesses are unofficial, they may or may not attempt to evade detection, they tend to be small, family-and-friends enterprises but can extend to large networks of contacts across a country and overseas. Informal sector enterprise ranges from subsistence farmers to urban stall-holders, workshops, repair services and drug-running cartels. Such operations can be very productive, extremely economic in their use of capital and may offer much employment, albeit at low wages. The informal sector acts as a residual pool of resources to formal sector employment that shrinks in size as booming conditions mean regular businesses are looking for talent and then it takes up the slack in times of recession when formal enterprise is cutting back. (See also chapter 2.)

The gold standard   operated successfully before the First World War when trading countries fixed their currencies to a given weight of gold. Any country's citizen could thus convert their banknotes into gold on demand. In international trade, if a country suffered a balance of payments deficit it would pay what it owed in gold. The subsequent loss of gold reserves meant domestic money supplies would have to contract, otherwise the central bank would have insufficient to maintain convertibility and meet customers' demand. The automatic deflation of the economy this caused could be relied upon to cure the trade deficit. The volume and pattern of world trade in these days was relatively small and uncomplicated; supplies of gold were sufficient to clear the required sums of international indebtedness; and defending fixed exchange rates by forced deflation was not politically costly.

Harrod–Domar growth model   An early theory of economic growth derived from Keynesian analysis. It emphasised the importance of entrepreneurs' investment plans: if they guessed right it would result in a balanced rate of growth for the economy; if they guessed wrong it could lead to either spiralling inflation or deepening unemployment. There was no inherent tendency in an economy to attain balanced growth. Key variables in this theory were the *savings ratio* – which determined the flow of funds available for investment – and the *incremental capital–output ratio* which measured the increase in a country's output secured by a given increase in its investment. Both variables were assumed given by the nature of the economy.

Monocultures   describes economies that are dependent on the production and export of one principal good.

The **neoclassical growth** model differed from the above in assuming flexible savings and capital–output ratios, like all prices, according to the markets concerned. Economic growth is characterised by stable equilibrium, therefore, unlike the unstable knife-edge that predicts accelerating inflation or unemployment as in the Harrod–Domar model. A key finding is that the neoclassical equilibrium growth path can be shifted by technical progress.

Positive feedback   A term borrowed from physics where an increase in output reinforces the increase in input. For example, the richer you get, the more you can invest and the richer you get. This contrasts with *negative feedback* which would apply if governments could impose (successfully) steeply progressive income taxes – then the richer you get, the more you have to pay in tax and thus the growth in incomes of the richest slows. (If governments can redistribute tax incomes to the poor, the gap between rich and poor should narrow – and not widen – over time.)

Purchasing power parity   A way to measure the value of currencies that takes into account their real worth in the countries concerned – that is, in terms of what money can buy. For example, if one dollar can buy the same sample of goods and services in country X as 100 pesos in country Y then the exchange rate is $1 = 100 pesos measured on a purchasing power parity basis. The actual rate ruling in foreign exchange markets may vary a long way from this, according to the demand and supply of the two currencies concerned.

Quasi-rents   are rents that are comparatively short-lived, due to the rise – after a time lag – of other competing suppliers who bid prices/earnings down in their desire to get into the market and make the same surplus as the original seller.

Rent   is the income received by the unique owner of resources that are fixed in supply but much in demand. Although the term is commonly applied to payments made by tenants to landlords for the use of their property, in economics it is defined more narrowly as the surplus enjoyed above costs by the monopoly owner of any resource.

QUESTIONS

1 What is meant by 'development'? What may developing countries (a) gain; (b) lose in promoting rapid economic growth in pursuit of modern, Western standards of living?
2 What policies would you recommend to secure the development of a relatively poor but unexplored region, rich in timber and mineral resources and populated only by indigenous peoples?
3 Compare, contrast and evaluate the Harrod–Domar and neoclassical growth theories in terms of (a) what causes economic growth; and (b) what government policies they recommend.
4 What are the similarities and differences between the 'Asian Dragons' in the strategies they employed to achieve steady economic growth? Have they anything to teach any other countries?
5 Contrast the role of central government and free markets in promoting economic development. Which is more prone to failure?

FURTHER READING

Gillis, Malcolm *et al. Economics of Development.* Norton, 1987.
Harris, Nigel. *The End of The Third World.* Penguin, 1990.
Pomfret, Richard. *Diverse Paths of Economic Development.* Harvester Wheatsheaf, 1992.
The Economist, 4 January 1992 and 11 January 1992.

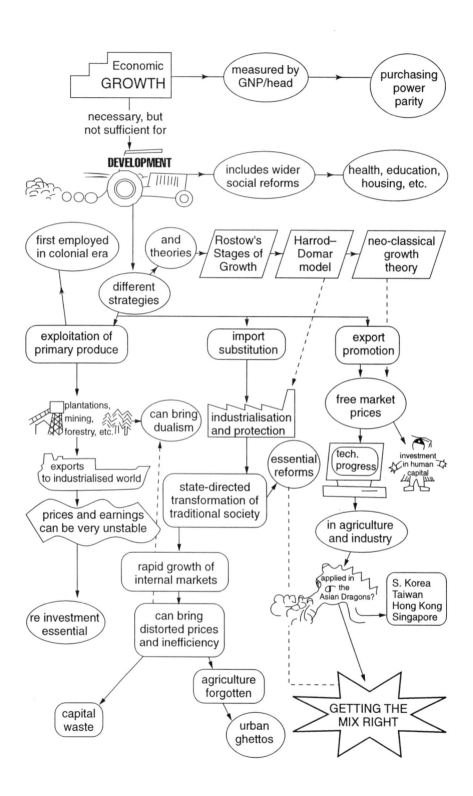

12 Environmental economics: sustaining spaceship earth

Topics to be considered in this chapter

- Economic growth and sustainable development
- Readjusting the price mechanism
- Optimal depletion rates of exhaustible and renewable resources
- Government policies to safeguard the environment
- Measuring the value of environmental resources

INTRODUCTION

If you listen to some people, in the future we are all destined to gloom and doom:

- Way back in 1798, Thomas Malthus predicted – on the observation of incompatible trends in population and food growth in the new American colonies – that humankind could not escape everlasting poverty.
- Some hundred years later, at the beginning of the twentieth century, it was predicted that at existing growth rates of horse-drawn traffic, central London within thirty years would be knee-high in manure and all transport would come sliding (ugh!) to a halt.
- In 1972, D. H. Meadows and others published *The Limits to Growth* in which it was claimed that at existing rates of exploitation the world would run out of oil, other essential minerals and thus the basis for continuing growth by the year 2000.

All these predictions were based on observable growth trends of their time and all have been proved wrong. Why? Because extrapolating existing trends always assumes that things do not change ... and of course they always do. Like the wedding speeches of Hollywood film stars, economists should bear in mind Sam Goldwyn's maxim: 'Never prophesy; especially about the future ...'

Experience shows that the price mechanism can provide an effective means to protect the environment. Take the issue of allegedly finite oil reserves. As was shown in chapter 9, when economies grow the demand for energy and oil-based products (such as plastics) will grow with them. Increasing demand for scarce supplies will force up prices – at an accelerating rate as stocks are depleted. This will cause consumers to modify their demands and simultaneously make it profitable for producers to seek out alternative energy supplies. The history of oil prices and outputs shows that, despite the imperfections of this particular market place, increases in prices *do* call forth greater efforts to search out new oil fields; more efficient and less wasteful technologies to produce oil; increased consumer concern to economise on fuel use; and increased research and development of alternative energy supplies, battery-powered cars, solar-heating panels, etc. Current oil prices towards the end of the 1990s are lower in real terms than they were twenty years earlier, indicating less relative scarcity now. Although a potentially exhaustible natural asset, oil will continue to be an important energy source long into the twenty-first century.

The most important single reason why certain doom and gloom predictions about the environment have therefore failed to be realised is that the market system employs a remarkably sophisticated and flexible control mechanism – prices – that urges people to change their (environmentally damaging) practices.

The most important single reason, however, that there *is* a growing environmental crisis is that not all natural resources have a market price. Many environmental goods essential for a decent quality of life have *no* price – they are *free goods* – and are thus being used to excess. There is no market incentive to economise on their use. For those natural assets that have no price (e.g. clean air, including the ozone layer) we can predict they will be used up and/or polluted the fastest. Other resources (e.g. fossil fuels, whales, hardwoods) possess positive market prices which are too low, reflecting only private costs of production and not their full environmental and social costs (such as the need to clean up oil spillage, conserve rare species, protect unique and fast-disappearing habitats). In these cases, rates of exploitation will be greater than the environment can sustain.

This point needs emphasising. Provision of most goods and services involves costs to the producer which are internalised in the prices they charge in the market place, and costs to the society at large which are external to this process. For example, in an unregulated market system car users will only pay directly for those internal costs such as fuel, depreciation and the loss of time and energy involved in driving. They will not pay for most of the damage inflicted on others by increased pollution, traffic jams, road accidents and the replacement of rural areas by the ugliness of motorised landscapes. These are the external costs imposed on society. And they will continue to rise so long as market prices fail to reflect this important component of real costs.

ADJUSTING THE MARKET MECHANISM

It is because in the past market systems have failed to value natural resources adequately to include all external, environmental costs that economic growth – especially of the most developed nations – has been seen as at the expense of the long-term health of the planet. Some critics have argued, therefore, that growth and the capitalist market system that drives it are to blame. But, on the contrary, if we are underpricing our valuable natural assets then this is an argument for more market operation, not less. (There is plenty of evidence from Eastern Europe and the old Soviet Union that the opposite extreme from the free-market economy – command systems – are far less environmentally friendly. See the example of Chernobyl in chapter 1.)

Economic growth need not impoverish the planet. Increased awareness of the interdependence of all living things and the fragility of this relationship is urging the pursuit of *sustainable development* – where we pass on to future generations at least as much environmental wealth as we inherited ourselves.

The analysis of sustainable development requires us to widen and to redefine our understanding of the economic process. For example, in neoclassical theory, economic efficiency is at the heart of the subject. This can be defined in terms of maximising profitability in the production process and maximising utility in consumption; subject in both cases to budget constraints. Thus efficency is gained in the market economy if producers switch to processes that yield more per dollar spent on inputs and if households switch purchases to commodities yielding more per dollar spent on consumption. That is, if you have only a fixed amount of money at your disposal, spending any of this scarce resource on items that yield less rewards than others is uneconomic. It is through the measuring-rod of prices that you can determine more efficient, less wasteful allocations of your resources. Producers will decide which are the most cost-effective raw materials and technologies to employ; consumers will decide which combination of goods and services yields most satisfaction.

The problem with the traditional, neoclassical outlook is that it takes no account of the long-term sustainability of this economic process. US economist Kenneth Boulding wrote a path-breaking essay in 1966 in which he argued that the West should stop acting as if it were in a cowboy economy with limitless frontiers and start behaving as if we were all passengers on spaceship earth where maintaining its life-support system is of paramount importance.

The signalling price mechanism needs to embrace not only private profit- and utility-maximisation but also environmental sustainability. Standards of living can only be guaranteed in the future if rates of growth of production and consumption do not exceed the environment's capacity to support them.

Readjusting the price mechanism to reflect humankind's multi-dimensional relationship with the environment is a complex business. Consider the following model:

1 Economic activity begins with primary industry and the creation of resources direct from the environment – mineral extraction, farming and fishing.
2 These resources are processed in secondary or manufacturing industry and converted into finished goods and services which are then distributed to the market place for final consumption.
3 Consumption of goods and services provides utility, which leads to increasing standards of living.

1 RESOURCES → 2 PRODUCTION → 3 CONSUMPTION → UTILITY

At all stages through this process there is the creation of waste. This occurs in many forms: 1a in primary production with oil spillages; slag heaps; the burning of agricultural stubble, and the discarding of non-commercial animal and fish products; 2a in manufacturing and distribution with spent materials, exhaust gases and depreciated capital; 3a in consumption with the disposal of rubbish and the generation of litter.

As final products yield their utility over time they are all eventually wasted – some more quickly than others. A newspaper becomes waste paper after a day or so; a car passes more slowly over the years into burnt rubber, scrap metal and carbon monoxide. Thanks to the first law of thermodynamics we can say that the sum of waste products at each stage of the production/consumption process above precisely equals the total value of the original resources:

$$RESOURCES = WASTE = 1a + 2a + 3a$$

What happens to the waste? Some of it is recycled. This depends on technological abilities and thus the commercial viabliity of recycling. We can predict that if resources become scarcer and more expensive and technology cheaper then the percentage of waste that is recycled back into production will increase. But according to the second law of thermodynamics we can never approach 100 per cent recyclability since a fraction of energy and matter will always be dissipated in any production process.

Much waste is destined to be dumped back into the environment, therefore. Crucial here is the environment's capacity to assimilate that waste. If waste accumulation exceeds this *assimilative capacity* then we shall damage the environment. Rivers will become polluted, the air foul and the landscape littered.

This decreases our utility directly since people derive pleasure from the natural world – in leisure pursuits, sightseeing, just sitting in front of the television or reading books about it – and it also further impairs the environment's productivity in generating future resources.

We can thus devise a closed, interactive environmental model to replace the neoclassical view of economic activity. According to this model, the environment is linked to the economic system in three ways:

- as a supplier of resources;
- as an assimilator of waste;
- and as a provider of aesthetic utility.

Economic growth needs the environment and can only be sustainable in the long run if mechanisms exist to restrict economic activity that is

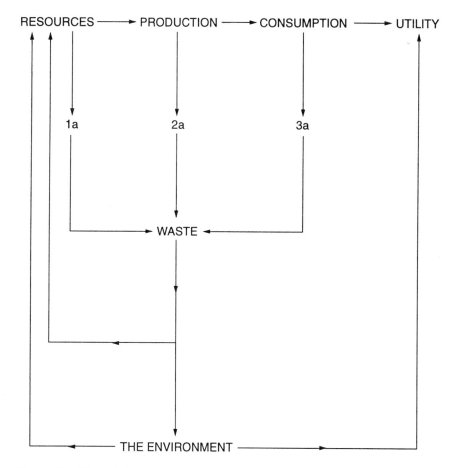

Figure 12.1 The relationship between economic activity and the environment

harmful to it and promote such activity that is beneficial. Before looking more closely at policies to adjust the relevant mechanisms, however, we need firstly to consider what we are trying to achieve: which activities are environmentally acceptable and which are not? How exactly do we define sustainable development?

SUSTAINABLE DEVELOPMENT – HOW MUCH CAN THE EARTH TAKE?

The Brundtland Report for the World Commission on Environment and Development (1987) defined this as 'development that meets the needs of the present without compromising the ability of future generations to meet their own needs'.

A number of implications follow from this statement. Firstly, waste generated from the production/consumption process must be kept at a level equal or below the assimilative capacity of the environment. Secondly, the rate of use or harvest of renewable natural resources such as forest hardwoods, fishing stocks, etc. must be equal to or below the *natural regeneration rate*.

It should be emphasised that these assimilative and regenerative rates are not constant. Atmospheres, seas, rivers and landscapes have a tolerance threshold which can lower over time. Alternatively, such capacities can be augmented by the application of man-made capital: fertilisers improve land productivity; air and water can be cleaned. In any equilibrium between economic activity and the environment, therefore, constant monitoring of rates of assimilation and regeneration is necessary and waste disposal and harvesting rates should be adjusted accordingly. Analysis of what constitutes an acceptable harvest rate of renewable resources is explored in more detail further below.

A third consideration is exhaustible resources. Differentiating between these and renewable resources is easy enough in theory but in practice the margin between them is blurred. Mineral resources such as oil and coal are the product of geological processes over millions of years and are clearly exhaustible and non-regenerative in human time-horizons. But what about native habitats like wetlands or tropical rainforests? Forests can be harvested and are renewable, but to what extent is the extraction of hardwoods, even at tolerably slow rates, destructive of a unique natural habitat? A precious ecological balance can easily be disturbed and thus permanently impaired. There are grounds for treating certain such habitats as exhaustible resources.

It is important to emphasise, however, that *all economic activity is to some extent dependent on the use of exhaustible resources*. The evolution of humankind and civilisation has been fuelled by them. If sustainable development is defined as maintaining the same physical stock of earth's resources into the future it therefore means exploiting no further non-renewable assets. But this means no more economic development is possible today, nor – by the same argument – will it be possible tomorrow.

Clearly this is too excessive a requirement. It is hardly consistent with 'meeting the needs of the present'. Exhaustible resources are indeed environmentally irreplaceable, but they are irreplaceable also as supporters of *human* environments. Coal and oil provide essential energy; land is used for housing; forests are cleared for agriculture. Each economic act destructive of the environment yields benefits as well as costs.

Insisting on maintaining a constant natural capital stock into the future ignores, furthermore, the possibility of substituting renewable for exhaustible resources; man-made capital for natural capital.

Consider an example: I am reminded that Roman roads through the English Lake District follow the mountain ridges. Why is this? Why do they not follow the valley bottoms like modern roads? The Romans built their routes on the mountain tops – at considerable expense we can only guess – because it was even more difficult to navigate the valley bottoms which were then carpeted with thick forests. (Exactly the same economic practices were followed over a thousand years later by the early settlers in New England, USA.) Native forests are an exhaustible resource. They have been replaced in their entirety in the UK by town and village, farmland and open moor. The former are undoubtedly an irretrievable loss, but the latter are not without attraction, as any visitor to the Lake District will confirm. In the meantime, the exploitation of native forests throughout the UK helped transform the country into the world's first modern, industrial economy.

The important conclusion from this example is that as exhaustible resources are depleted their reduced stock can to a considerable extent be compensated for by increases in renewable resources and man-made capital.

Finally, technological progress is directly concerned with getting more from less – on economising on the use of our natural inheritance. Engines are more and more fuel-efficient in our cars, homes and power stations. Energy can be generated far more cheaply from clean gas than coal and far more efficiently than from burning the wood and charcoal that led to much of Britain's deforestation in the past. Today, countries use far fewer exhaustible resources to produce one unit of GNP than they did a century ago and they will no doubt use far less in the future than they do now.

All these considerations indicate that preserving the existing physical stock of natural resources for future generations is neither practicable nor appropriate. Sustainable development must always involve some consumption of exhaustible resources alongside continuing technical progress and increasing substitution of other assets.

The relevant questions to ask are, therefore, what rates of exploitation of natural resources are acceptable? How much do we want to raise GNP now as compared to the future? At what environmental cost? Or conversely, how much do we want to conserve the planet? At what cost to our current versus future needs?

Before analysing these issues related to the rates of exploitation of renewable and non-renewable resources, there are a number of reasons for proceeding with extreme caution when attempting to value natural assets:

- *Irreversibility* There is the possibility of doing irreversible damage to the planet – for example the destruction of habitat; extinction of species; desertification and climate change. If we make a mistake, very often we do not know how to reverse it. The costs involved here are large and stretch over all time. They involve not only what is lost but also the forgone opportunity of what might have been.
- *Uncertainty* The distinctive feature of natural environments is the wealth of interconnected detail – such that a small change in a fragile ecological equilibrium can have a myriad of unpredictable outcomes over space and time. Our scientific knowledge is limited and the natural world reminds us that it will ever be so. We are uncertain as to the role of the ocean currents in climate determination; we cannot safely predict all the environmental effects of constructing dams and redirecting waterways; it is impossible to trace the final destinations of all waste materials disposed. The borderline between sustainable economic practices and tipping the balance over into cumulative environmental degradation can in practice be difficult to detect until too late. And note that the unpredictability of outcomes can impact on areas far removed from the scene of the original activity: smoke from British chimneys kills fish in Scandinavian lakes; Syrian dams deplete Iraqi waterways; northern hemisphere pollution holes Antarctic ozone layers.
- *Increasing public concern* Over time, as nations develop and incomes, education and public consciousness improve, so demands for environmental protection and conservation increase. The controversial fact here is that environmental degradation is only a cost if people *care* about it. And wealthier nations care more in the sense that they are willing to pay more for conservation. (See later on evaluation techniques.) The costs of exploiting natural assets are greater in rich countries than poor ones (cutting down the forests may be a matter of survival – in Brazil today as it was in Britain of yesteryear), and, with increasing economic growth, will be greater for future generations than for those today.

Summing up, the combination of irreversibility and uncertainty, with effects spilling out locally, globally and intergenerationally, all urge us to err on the side of caution when calculating the costs of environmental exploitation.

DEPLETION OF EXHAUSTIBLE RESOURCES

Supplies of exhaustible resources are not fixed, they become available to the market as a result of a three-stage commercial process:

1 Exploration and discovery. Considerable effort and investment are devoted to the search for and identification of profitably recoverable deposits. Despite enormous technological advances, there is an irreducible element of chance here.
2 Development. This is the thorough investigation and preparation for extraction of an identified source. Once the relevant capital equipment is in place, there then remains:
3 Production and distribution. The exploitation of reserves involves ongoing investment in extraction and transport techniques in order to guarantee the required depletion rate to satisfy market demand.

The speed at which such reserves can be made ready for market and the speed at which they are then consumed by society are both related to the price of the natural resource in question. These rates of depletion/consumption are of paramount importance – too quick and future generations will inherit less and less; too slow and current generations may be paying too high a cost of sacrifice. (If the price of energy is too high, many people may be denied heating and transport. In the extreme, some may die of hypothermia, or inability to reach emergency services in time. These are clear examples of where current generations and thus unborn future generations are paying too high a price.) The issues involved here are thus of *intergenerational equity* and an *optimal depletion rate* – that is the rate of resource extraction that is 'best' for society.

Economic theory has much to offer on these points. In a perfect market the price of an exhaustible resource indicates its relative scarcity and its environmental importance. Moreover, the optimal depletion rate for any such resource is that where its price is induced to rise at a rate of growth equal to the rate of growth of all prices, i.e. the market rate of interest.

Consider the following example: a community which owns certain reserves of, say, crude oil is sitting on a valuable capital asset. Should it extract and sell this resource now, or wait and sell it at some time in the future? If oil prices are appreciating rapidly this implies the market views future scarcity as the more serious. The community now has an incentive to delay drilling while their asset is steadily increasing in value. If current oil supplies are plentiful and prices are flat, however, then rates of return on alternative investments in the market place will offer a better reward. The community maximises benefits by selling now and thus investing their oil revenues elsewhere.

We can conclude that if prices of and revenues from natural assets are projected to grow less fast than the market rate of interest then resource exploitation should increase. Current generations are sacrificing more than future ones will. Conversely, if future revenues are likely to be greater than interest rates then current extraction is too greedy and should cease.

If current resource exploitation increases, then that which remains for the future is depleted – sooner or later prices will be forced to rise; conversely, if exploitation ceases and supplies are conserved for future generations then prices will at some time come down and thus prompt renewed extraction.

The optimum rate of depletion for any exhaustible natural asset thus evolves as that where the rate of growth of prices and revenues just equals the market rate of interest.

HARVEST OF RENEWABLE RESOURCES

Farming, fishing and forestry represent use of renewable resources. Sustainable harvesting of the land and seas can thus be determined in relation to the rates of regeneration involved. If the seas are fished, for example, at a catch rate equal to the rate of growth of the existing fish stocks then clearly this resource can be left at a constant size for the future.

Growth rates for renewable resources differ for each one involved. Cattle reproduce faster than blue whales; pine forests faster than tropical hardwoods. Growth rates for a given resource also differ according to its stock size or population density.

This latter point needs further elaboration. Take the case of elephant herds in certain parts of Africa – there is a *critical minimum size* (cms) below which reproduction rates are insufficient to guarantee survival. Above this, however, the herd grows first at an increasing rate – where the natural habitat is underpopulated and can thus support higher densities – then the growth rate slows, declines and finally reaches zero where the environment supports the *maximum carrying capacity*. The herd cannot grow beyond this size because death rates rise above birth rates as food supplies become insufficient.

The graph below plots the stock size of a given renewable resource against its natural regeneration rate. Given no interference from humankind, the natural equilibrium population is at the maximum carrying capacity (mcc). If for some short-lived reason (say, a year of good climate and improved food supplies) stocks should grow beyond this point then deaths will eventually exceed births and the stock must shrink. Conversely, if the population is reduced, births would outnumber deaths and growth would resume (see Figure 12.2).

The regeneration rate of the resource is the key concept since this indicates the environmentally sustainable harvest rate. As illustrated, the rate of growth of any renewable resource varies with its stock size, the maximum sustainable yield possible being indicated at msy.

The actual harvest rate that will be practised by those exploiting this resource depends on the costs and revenues involved. Generally speaking,

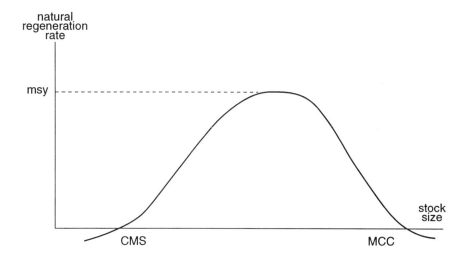

natural
regeneration
rate

msy

CMS

MCC

stock
size

Figure 12.2 How the rate of regeneration of a species varies with its
population/stock size

the cost of exploiting a renewable resource will rise as the stock size
shrinks. In fishing the open seas, for example, harvesting costs may rise
prohibitively for some species as their numbers are reduced, the possible
locations which they might inhabit are diverse and their market price is
relatively low. For large, easy to hunt species such as African rhino and
elephant, however, costs of poaching may be low, the gain from sales of
rhino horn or ivory may be high and thus stock sizes in these cases may be
driven below their critical minimum size (cms) where extinction becomes
a real threat.

To conclude the analysis of renewable resources, we return to a consideration of interest rates. How much foresters want to fell virgin hardwoods
and hunters prefer to exploit scarce species such as whales, rhino or tigers
now rather than at some time in the future depends on their *rate of time
preference*, or discount rate. The greater the preference for present rather
than future consumption, the higher their discount rate – that is, we say
that their future benefits are heavily discounted. For peoples and societies
with uncertain futures – for example very poor peoples or tribes in less-
developed countries; criminals and poachers – and for peoples living in
fast-growing economies where alternative investment opportunities offer
high rates of return, then there is likely to be a high premium placed on
present rather than future benefits.

This means, therefore, that where access to the resource in question is
open (like virgin forests, or the high seas) or impossible to police (like
some very large African game parks), where harvesters' discount rates are
high and where the costs of depletion are relatively low, then species

extinction is at serious risk. Harvesting will inevitably take place at a rate faster than the environment can sustain.

PUBLIC POLICY

Confining economic activity to the sustainable limits we have now identified must be the goal of all those interested in conserving the environment. The market economy must be adjusted such that all commodities and economic practices are priced in accordance to the full (i.e. external + internal) costs incurred in their production.

If those overexploiting exhaustible and renewable resources had to pay the price of the damage they inflicted on the environment they would conserve more. If polluters had to pay for their thoughtless disregard of others they would think more and pollute less. Inevitably, as industry's costs rise they would pass on some fraction of this to consumers in the form of higher prices, but this is how it should be: more environmentally damaging produce would be more expensive and consumers would thus buy less of them.

What are the ways that can be used to internalise in market prices all external, environmental costs that societies suffer? Firstly, it can be demonstrated that a free-market society based on *private property rights* can for many natural assets achieve sustainable development. Property holders have a vested interest in protecting their resource and they can force polluters, poachers and all violaters to pay through the courts of law for any encroachment they cause.

The classic case was given by Ronald Coase (1960) in which he described sparks from a passing steam train setting fire to a farmer's field. The farmer can sue for compensation and in so doing external costs (to the farmer) are internalised to the producer (the railway company). Profits of the enterprise hence fall and this will prompt a cut-back in economic activity and/or more careful conservationist practice. Alternatively, instead of cleaning up its act the railway producer can opt to purchase the property rights of all offended parties. Either way, costs and benefits are adjusted through the free market to internalise the externalities involved. Equilibrium is secured in this case without recourse to government intervention, other than in the institution of property rights in the first place.

This equilibrium, however, is subject to two conditions: (a) it requires that the resource in question is capable of exclusive private ownership; and (b) it assumes that transactions costs are not prohibitive.

(a)   as has already been observed, many vital resources have *open access* (e.g. whales, clean air) so no proprietor can prevent others' exploitation. True, for some common properties, e.g. fishing in a remote beauty spot, negotiated agreement between self-enlightened users can be possible, but there is always the temptation for one party to cheat (the *free-rider* problem).The larger the resource, however – such as a national park – the less exclusive it can be and the huge number of users precludes any effective free-market agreement. Government controls become necessary.

(b) Even where property rights are enshrined and enforceable in law, the *transaction cost* of suing for damages (especially where the transgressor is a big, powerful enterprise and the transgressed are many, small, non-organised property holders) may simply be too great an obstacle to overcome. An unscrupulous profit-maximiser may exploit its power, pay minimal lip-service to environmental causes and get away with it. Multinational mining companies working in LDCs have at times been accused of such practice.

Despite this, environmental pressure groups such as Friends of the Earth, Greenpeace, etc., are effective in the unregulated free market. Well-publicised campaigns against environmentally damaging operators, be they private or public enterprises, do succeed at times (e.g. against Exxon corp. in the Exxon Valdez disaster of Prince Edward Sound, Alaska). There is evidence, therefore, that sustainable economic activity can be controlled through the free market.

One-off successes are not enough, however, to permanently safeguard the environment from exploitation and degradation. Comprehensive adjustment of the price mechanism is not attainable by such an *ad hoc* approach. Government regulation of the market system is, in the end, indispensable.

There are a number of public policy instruments that can be employed; one extreme is to dispense with any adjustment of market prices and go straight for *direct controls*. Legislation can be passed to outlaw certain environmentally harmful practices. This can certainly be effective, and for some situations it may be the most efficient means of government intervention – for example, where clearly identifiable behaviour is considered harmful and must be totally prohibited, not just reduced, and where prompt and substantial changes are called for. This might include banning all construction in an area of outstanding natural beauty, or to outlaw hunting/fishing of a threatened species. In neoclassical terminology, such government action may be justified where the value of the resource is deemed to be so great that its 'price' must deter all consumption.

Direct controls, nonetheless, are too inefficient a mechanism to employ in many cases. Public regulatory agencies must firstly set up laws that are responsive to changing environmental circumstances; must catch private operators who break these laws; compile evidence to prosecute them, bring cases to court and then succeed in gaining effective penalties. The transaction costs of devoting resources to this end may be more wasteful than allowing the accused to get away with it in the first place!

Taxation can do the same job of environmental control, in most cases more dependably, effectively and economically than legislation. A carbon tax levied on the emission of exhaust gases, for example, will limit over-rapid exploitation of fossil fuels and, by the argument given at the beginning of this chapter, thus promote research and development of alternatives. Although not costless – it requires a technology applicable to energy-consuming equipment from car engines to thermal power stations, as well as a bureaucracy of tax inspectors – it is an automatic system that penalises carbon-users on a rising scale appropriate to their environmental impact.

Subsidies are appropriate to encourage conservation and recycling activities that have environmental and social benefits not recorded in unreg-ulated market prices. If it is justifiable to tax the production of socially costly practices, by the same argument subsidies should be awarded to bring down the market prices of those products and processes with a high net social benefit and which deserve patronage. Note that subsidies alone are insufficient in themselves to deter environmental degradation – they are relevant to encourage good practice but cannot prevent that which is harmful.

Pollution permits are a novel way of internalising external costs and making the polluter pay. The regulatory agency decides on the acceptable level of pollution (or, say, access to a specific natural resource) to be allowed. A batch of permits is issued authorising just that given amount and these permits are then offered for sale in the open market. Prices are determined by demand and supply. The more cars that want to pollute a certain com-muter route, the more factories which wish to belch out smoke, the more walkers who want to tramp over a certain mountain, the more they have to pay. Higher prices will shift demand to lower-use days and locations.

WHAT PRICE THE PLANET?

Each of the policy instruments above has its advantages and disadvantages; some are suited to some applications, others to others. All, however, share the need to evaluate environmental resources accurately and to adjust market prices accordingly.

The whole notion of calculating just how much certain resources are worth, and the extent of any damage that might be done to them, however, is fraught with difficulty. How can you measure the costs involved when they are controversial, uncertain and in some cases irreversible? How much is a beautiful view worth? What price clean air, or peace and quiet? What is the environmental cost of burying nuclear waste? But however difficult such questions may be to answer, something must be done. This issue is just too important to leave to uneducated guesswork or to the influence of powerful vested interests. Some rational, scientific means of measuring the impact of humankind's activity on the planet is essential if we are to amend the price mechanism, reduce environmental degradation and promote sustainable development.

Two basic techniques can be identified in assigning monetary values to environmental resources. One involves measuring various costs as indirectly recorded through existing market places; the other involves questionnaires asking respondents what values they assign to, or are willing to pay for, specific resources.

Market surveys

Private property has a market value related to the benefits enjoyed from its use. A significant part of the utility derived from any piece of land is directly related to environmental quality. Thus degradation of a certain locality will result in a measurable fall in property values.

Statistical surveys of a large cross-section of diverse properties at any one time can help isolate the change in valuation attributable to specific environmental degradation. Properties, of course, vary in price for a variety of reasons: the size and state of repair of the property itself; closeness to facilities, etc. After taking into account all these variables, however, the impact of, say, noise and air pollution is calculable. We can relatively accurately approximate the value of clean air, and of peace and quiet, therefore.

By the same process, reductions in farming, forestry and fishing yields can be traceable to the impact of pollutants; the social costs of traffic congestion can be measured in terms of the loss of time and thus outputs of city dwellers; injuries and deaths can similarly be costed (note that insurance companies put a price on people's health and life all the time).

There is an important distinction here, however. There is a difference between someone's or something's exchange value and their/its intrinsic worth. In a market society some people/items have a greater exchange value than others – the death or injury of an average managing director represents a greater loss to the market place than that of the average student. (Terrorists know this – they can demand higher ransom demands if they capture top oil company executives. That is why businesses employ bodyguards in Bogota . . .)

The notion of intrinsic value is nonetheless important. The fact that the market places a high value on some businessman but a much lower one on the salmon he is trying to kill or the stream that he may be dirtying is at the heart of the environmental movement's criticism of the market system. Some fanatic 'Greens' have even argued that businessmen should hunt each other rather than wild geese, deer or fish, since there is nowhere a shortage of the former, whereas the latter cannot defend themselves and are in danger of dying out in some places! This is a rejection of the market values placed on the resources in question. Some natural assets have a higher intrinsic worth than is recognised by the money economy, it is argued. Market survey procedures as outlined above are thus insufficient to capture how far an increasing number of people value the environment. Other techniques are necessary.

Questionnaires

Economics now recognises that the value of a specific resource includes:

- that which is revealed through existing markets by those directly or indirectly involved (e.g. the value of clean rivers to anglers, walkers and research biologists who splash in them);
- the value placed on the asset by those who might one day be involved and who thus wish to retain the option of using it untainted at some time in the future;
- the value placed on a resource by people who never intend to use it directly but appreciate it for its own intrinsic worth, or existence. (You may live in the centre of Africa, the USA or India and never intend to sail the oceans, but you might nonetheless insist that whales have a right to swim in them undisturbed.)

The total economic value (TEV) of a resource therefore equals:

TEV = Actual use value + Option value + Existence value

It is possible to gain empirical estimates of these values by using questionnaires – asking people to record their willingness to pay for environmental conservation and/or their willingness to accept compensation for its loss.

Construction of the relevant questionnaires is inevitably difficult. They contain biases for a number of reasons: firstly, respondents may conceal their true preferences (this is the free-rider problem met elsewhere); secondly, they may be influenced in their willingness to pay by the surveyor/ nature of the questions asked; respondents may be willing to pay more in one form (e.g. taxes) than others (e.g. entry fees); and they may value gains and losses asymmetrically. That is, people may be prepared to pay more to prevent further degradation than to secure environmental gains. For all these reasons, therefore, studies come up with different evaluations for the same resource, depending on how the questionnaire is designed.

Research in this area is still relatively new but, despite the difficulties involved, this questionnaire technique – the contingent valuation method (CVM) – remains an important and in many cases the only method of estimating important but elusive *option and existence values.*

Examples of CVM studies reveal interesting valuations. For the Grand Canyon, USA – quoted by Pearce and Turner – existence values were measured as 66 times more important than user values. People valued this resource highly for its own intrinsic worth, not because they wanted direct access to it for themselves. (This is undoubtedly because of this resource's uniqueness as a national asset.) In Norway, respondents were asked how much they were prepared to pay to stop acid rain. The study came up with 400 krona per person, or 2.5 billion krona in total. This was broken down into 1 billion user value and 1.5 billion existence value; although the willingness-to-pay technique here is almost certainly an underestimate. This is because most Norwegians view acid rain as a problem of imported pollution (from British and German sources, at least) and thus presumably would argue that other nations apart from themselves should pay to clear it up.

CONCLUSION

Economics sometimes gets a bad name from environmentalists who do not understand the subject. They believe that economists are only interested in calculating profits and promoting economic growth at the expense of the environment. This chapter hopefully demonstrates that economics is concerned with calculating *all* the costs and benefits involved in human activity. What price do you put upon a threatened species? a beautiful landscape? the inconvenience of photo-chemical smog? Economics attempts to quantify these issues; make clear what assumptions are being made; minimise subjectivity and increase objectivity in the analysis of the balance of gains and losses. The market system can be made more responsive to these concerns and the discussion on sustainable development and policy instruments above shows what targets can be aimed at and how they can be hit. It has been noted that the possibility of doing irreversible environmental damage; the uncertainty of our impact on complex ecologies we imperfectly understand; and the rising value that societies ascribe to the environment as incomes rise all indicate the need for extreme caution. The premium for external costs that needs to be appended to many market prices may well be high.

The biggest practical problem this raises is finding the political will to implement these costs in the market prices we must all pay. If this is difficult enough in one country, the problem is far greater where environmental costs are spread across many nations – in the case of global climate change, for example. Voluntary international cooperation is necessary – here with the signing of a treaty on limiting greenhouse gas emissions. But even if vastly different countries' evaluations of the situation could be brought into agreement there is always the temptation for an individual nation to free-ride. Without a supranational government, how do you stop one state from muddying a common pool? International condemnation? Trade sanctions, maybe?

Malthus's predictions of population growth in 1798 were wrong. Planet earth has supported a much greater increase in our numbers at a higher standard of living than he thought possible. Whether the planet can continue to sustain our continuing economic growth and exploitation of the environment depends on whether or not we can continue to adjust and adapt the market economic system we have devised to provide for us.

Whatever the eventual mechanisms, a political way forward should be found to confront the economics of the environment. For what is certain is that if we do not pay the full price of plundering our natural inheritance today then our inheritors will bear the brunt of these costs in their future.

KEY WORDS

Free goods Those goods provided to us that involve no economic sacrifice in their production and consumption – sunlight, the air we breathe, a sparkling mountain stream. Free goods have no market price; in contrast, **economic goods** and services are all those that are the product of scarce resources and, even if they are subsidised or given away free, they are costly to supply.

Intergenerational equity Exhaustible resources can be used today or in the future: by ourselves or by our children. If we choose to consume them now we raise our standard of living, which our children will benefit from, but they will be denied future supplies of natural capital. Conversely, if we choose not to consume known supplies of exhaustible resources today there will be undoubtedly more available for future generations – although they will not inherit such a high standard of material wealth. The issue of whether to have jam today or jam tomorrow thus depends on how we value present versus future costs and benefits, and how we wish to spread them between ourselves and our heirs. An equitable decision distributes the costs and benefits 'fairly' between the generations.

Natural regeneration rate The rate at which a renewable resource regenerates itself in its undisturbed state. This will depend on the size of the resource in question in relation to its environment: a given animal population, for example, will have a *critical minimal size* – below which its reproduction rate falls lower than its death rate and thus it will eventually die out – and at the opposite extreme a *maximum carrying capacity* where (typically) food supplies cease to be sufficient and thus death rates again rise above birth rates and the stock size falls again.

Sustainable development Economic development that ensures that we pass on to our children the same quantity of environmental wealth that we inherited ourselves. Any depletion of exhaustible stocks should thus be compensated for by increases in renewable resources and man-made capital.

QUESTIONS

1 What is the relationship between economic growth and the environment? What are the consequences if we value (a) growth more than the environment; and (b) the environment more than growth?
2 What is meant by sustainable development? Can any depletion of non-renewable resources be sustainable?
3 How can economics predict which species are likely to be threatened with extinction?
4 What policies could be appropriate to preserve Brazilian rain forests? What are their costs and benefits?
5 How could you measure the value of clean air in the town where you live? Is it worth preserving?

FURTHER READING

The key analysis above is based on:

Pearce, D.W. and Turner, R.K. *Economics of Natural Resources and the Environment*. Harvester Wheatsheaf, 1990.

An easier treatment is found in:

Turner, R.K., Pearce, D. and Bateman, I. *Environmental Economics*. Harvester Wheatsheaf, 1994.

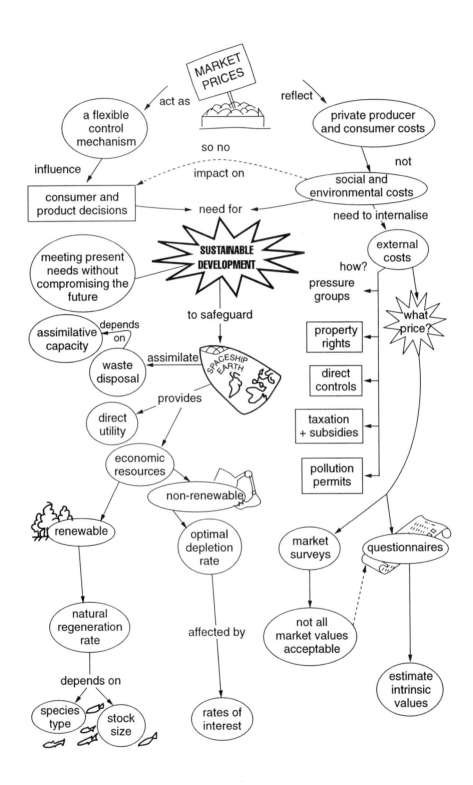

13 Conclusion: into the twenty-first century

As the 1990s draw to a close, what are the themes of most importance that we take into the next century?

Firstly, I hope it has been sufficiently demonstrated that the global economy *is* a global economy. The fortunes of all the passengers on space-ship earth are interlinked. Changes in the welfare of some citizens on one side of the world have their impact, sooner rather than later, on their distant neighbours a hemisphere away. Numerous examples have been illustrated and the reasons for increasing international interdependence have been analysed.

Trade joins all our destinies. Since 1945 there has been steady growth in world commerce and a progressive reduction in all sorts tariff and non-tariff barriers. The private, material benefits from free trade have been sufficiently persuasive to draw in increasing numbers of isolated and economically underdeveloped communities into international market-places. From smallholders in Taiwan to dockworkers in Poland and urban squatters in Latin America, all individuals have something to gain in joining the money economy, selling their skills and buying new products. Similarly, the fall of autarkic command economies was in part due to the pulling power of consumerist lifestyles embodied in a wide range of inexpensive foods, fashion-wear and popular music available in all countries outside the iron curtain. (Coke, Levi jeans and The Beatles were perhaps more influential than all the nuclear hardwear that threatened the communist regimes!)

More importantly, increasing economic growth of all countries, and especially that of the wealthy market economies, has required the un-restricted purchase of energy supplies and raw material inputs from all around the globe plus the simultaneous development of widespread export markets. The gains from free trade have also driven the creation of economic associations such as the European Union and NAFTA and, barring the resurgence of mercantilist rivalry, over time such groupings should deepen their integration, widen their membership and reduce their barriers to external parties. Other trading blocs can also be expected to follow these initiatives.

Growth in export sales has spurred the development of less-developed and newly industrialised countries and this process will no doubt continue – if it slows for some as they increasingly mature so it is likely that others will start along the same road. Increasing world competition, especially in the sale of manufactures, is not likely to abate, therefore, and the forces of creative destruction will become more widespread, impacting on all countries. As a result of all these pressures on resources, world energy prices must inevitably rise and this will set off another round of exploration and technological innovation.

Increasing competition in export markets is not constrained by a fixed limit to world incomes, as some have feared. Trade has brought rising incomes to all in the past, and if some countries persistently run export surpluses this is still feasible if, like Japan recently, they experience out-flows of capital – that is they recycle their export earnings abroad.

This leads us to the theme of the globalisation of finance. Commensurate with the steady growth of world commodity trade has been the recently accelerating movement in international money markets. Competition between rival financial centres has brought deregulated, liberalised capital markets in one country after another, such that funds can move across the globe out of one pocket into another in minutes and outside the reach of governments and their central banks. The telecommunications revolution has helped facilitate this international mobility of capital, plus it continues to broadcast all manner of financial information that communicates market worries from one side of the globe to the other. As a result we all now live in a world of fragile interdependency, uncertainty and risk where individual countries no longer have the luxury of being in control of the most important economic variables which influence their, and our, destinies.

With all our destinies so obviously interlinked now, we can expect increasing conflicts to arise over the distribution of global spoils. Poor people do not starve quietly when they see others enjoying lifestyles they are denied. Realisation that we are all passengers together brings with it economic responsibilities. Those that gain in the process of creative destruction should not and cannot now be uninformed of the social costs born by those that lose out. But apart from ethical considerations are there any *economic*, free-market reasons why winners should be concerned with the fate of losers? What does it cost to the inhabitants of Software Valley, Computerville if thousands are made redundant in Metal Basherstown, Labourersland?

So long as those whose incomes are growing rapidly possess short time horizons and are predominantly self-interested then any costs imposed on others will be heavily discounted. As is evident in free-market environments from Mexico City to New York, Rio to Rotterdam, wealth can live next door to poverty with negligible (or at best very slow-moving) mechanisms to bridge the divide and promote convergent growth. It has been mentioned before that winners have a natural incentive in market societies to identify with others of the same fortune elsewhere in the world and to lock their doors against losers in their own neighbourhood.

John Kenneth Galbraith warned as long ago as 1958 of the dangers of a world moving inexorably towards a destiny of private wealth and public squalor (*The Affluent Society*). Forty years later the same tendencies still exist, though the pace of change has accelerated and, if today the telecommunications revolution does not allow us to be ignorant any longer and brings the social costs of creative destruction into our living-rooms, so it also promotes everything else from mind-numbing game-shows to orgies of violence. Retaining sovereignty over our destiny remains as difficult as ever. The weaknesses of the market economic system (referred to in chapter 1) show no sign of diminishing.

Perhaps the most important development that takes us into the twenty-first century, therefore, has been the marked change in economic philosophy which now informs public policy makers. Keynes wrote that the ideas of economists and political philosphers are more powerful than commonly understood. As has been noted, since the 1980s the world seems to have rediscovered the vibrancy and relevance of free markets but with it has come an extreme ideological variant which – unlike in Keynes's time – now challenges the worth of government intervention in the economy. The ascendancy of neoclassical ideas is born of oil shocks, stagflation and the collapse of the command economic model. The economic consequences of the world supremacy of these ideas affect us all today and will continue to do so tomorrow.

It is with this issue – an examination of the appropriate role of governments in economic organisation – that this book started and will ultimately finish. If relationships between individuals, markets and governments are badly bungled then the next century will bring hardship for billions. The network of interchanges between these three parties, however, is so complex and the wealth of options in building a mixed economy is so great that, I believe, there are no simple formulas, no one right answer (like: 'take government off the backs of the people') that is appropriate for all countries, for all times.

The political imperative of our times, however, emphasises the need to reduce government expenditure, to reduce tax burdens, to accelerate the spread of privatisation and the deregulation of all existing markets. There is a falling commitment of governments to accept responsibility for unemployment, for improving public services and for rectifying market failure. Faith in government as an active and effective partner in the economy seems to have disappeared and instead there is the belief that the welfare state breeds a parasitic entitlement mentality.

This ideology has been articulated by the world financial community and promoted in the actions of numerous European, North/South American and Asian/Pacific governments. Its socio-economic costs, however, have

not been insignificant and indeed the polarisation of incomes, the environmental damage and breakdown of community and family life that have
been accompanying features of 'freer', more mobile markets are building
up severe problems for future generations.

There is no denying the power of self-interest in fuelling the free-market
engine, but equally there is no excuse for the pilots to abdicate responsibility
for where this motor is projecting our spaceship.

There is much that governments can, and must, do. If private markets
display high discount rates and blinkered vision then no one else other than
public servants can moderate recurring cyclical instability and promote the
long-run development of human resources, conservation strategies and
community support.

All the undoubted, and accelerating, scientific progress achieved over
the last hundred years and the sophisticated technological wizardry which
this has brought us only serves to emphasise how limited is humankind's
understanding of our own nature. 'Animal spirits' still seem to drive us
from boom into bust. Human memories remain as short as ever, and our
ability to hang together as a community – to make individual sacrifice for
the common good – seems more elusive now than ever before. There is
therefore no evidence to suggest that world markets can escape periodic
cycles of growth and recession in incomes, expenditure and employment
without the influence of government.

Unemployed people on their own are limited in their ability to move
with the market. They cannot acquire new skills without help and there will
be few private businesses that will take on this long-term investment since
they cannot guarantee the workers so trained will stay with them long
enough to pay back a market rate of return. Additionally, highly productive human resources are far more complicated and costly to identify and
develop than undersea oil reserves. How do you spot a potential genius
amongst the children of Calcutta's teeming millions or in the unemployed
of Moscow? Yet we all benefit if our neighbours are educated. This must
remain a responsibility of public authority since no profit maximiser will
undertake it.

The private market imposes no prohibitive costs on chopping down
trees to provide wood fuel, on dumping toxic wastes in the seas or on the
killing of rhinoceros to smuggle out their profitable horns. The fallacy of
composition ensures, however, that our spaceship will become impoverished – if not poisoned – unless we are persuaded to change our individually
destructive habits. It would be monumentally myopic of the dominant
species on this transport between the stars if we greedily exhausted all our
supplies in the mere minute or two of the geological timescale we have been
aboard.

By exactly the same argument, lack of awareness or concern about what
we are doing to *human* environments can even more quickly bring about
cumulative and irreversible decline. I refer here not so much to obvious

communal insanities like drug wars, arms races and nuclear sabre-rattling which are fed by unscrupulous sellers of cocaine and military hardware, but to the far more subtle, free-market necessity for mobile labour that rewards private interest but places a negligible, if not negative, return earned on constructing family and community stability.

Stability is important in all human affairs. Man is a social animal and economic philosophies must recognise this. For example, the development of human relationships in business can bring long-term profit. The decision whether to cut one's losses and sell out in a failing business project, or to put more money, time and effort into turning it around is extremely difficult but building up trust between management and workforces and promoting goodwill with customers has proven to be a sound investment particularly when the external economic environment turns nasty. (This is particularly true of businesses engaged in higher quality goods and services.) Wherever private rates of return fail to recognise this, however, then the market will opt to maximise short-term gain by selling out, liquidating capital and moving resources elsewhere.

The success of some European and Asian examples of relationship banking is causing some modern management to take aboard these ideas, but where is the private profit in promoting stable family life, deepening friendships and supportive communities? The emphasis on individual mobility and reward indirectly leads to the weakening of social ties, and with it increasing social costs such as a growing sense of isolation; rising stress and mental illness; more crime; increasing divorces; neglect of the weak, unfortunate and elderly. There are enormous external benefits to be earned in societies that are stable and healthy but the hand of government is necessary to guide markets to this end. A publicly funded welfare state is needed to cope with the problems of social breakdown and to identify policies to avoid them.

The conventional wisdom that government is the enemy of the market is a false dichotomy. Markets assume underlying social and power relationships as given and, with free rein, they may do little to help the disadvantaged. The Zapatistas of Chiapas have spoken for many inside and outside their country. Liberating the supply-side resources of a country requires microeconomic intervention to dismantle barriers, provide opportunities and promote entrepreneurship. Markets *need* government.

The future therefore requires a new political economy which is devoted to examining the relationship between individuals, markets and the state and to intervening where necessary to remove rigidities and to empower all to participate to the fullest. It should be operative at three levels: supranationally, nationally and locally.

The international debt crisis was a product of an unregulated world market system. It required, and still requires, supranational guidance to push wealthy, creditor nations to open up their markets, to limit their financial demands and to lead the poorest debtors out of a spiral of decline.

The major trading nations should be entreated to follow economic policies that, collectively, do not lead to overexpansionary growth or to beggar-my-neighbour protectionism. Global macroeconomic demand management is called for.

Similarly the environmental impact on the planet of localised consumption and production decisions – such as to cut down forests, or to pump out toxic exhaust gases – not to mention the global reach of multinational corporations and certain politically ambitious governments, requires a world forum for discussion, regulation and enforcement.

Wherever the single nation-state is too small to tackle problems on its own then international agencies such as the IMF and the World Trade Organisation need to be strengthened and constitutionally charged to take the long view and safeguard world interests.

At a national level, the policing of competition, privatisation schemes, land reforms and the restructuring of taxes are necessary to engage all in the ownership and control of resources. A commitment to reduce unemployment and inflation requires analysis of their respective causes plus demand and supply-side intervention where appropriate.

Some nations have made a notable success of the strategic direction of their economies. This requires, however, a social structure that recognises the importance of state/industry partnerships, open government, rule-abiding businessmen and civil servants and a general willingness of all to contribute to the common good.

The effective operation of essential public services such as the police, health, education, and the caring professions is best managed at local levels where providers are in direct contact with their customers. Supply-side investment in human capital operates at this level. Identifying education and training needs, providing job information, promotion of native entrepreneurship all start with the individual – so too does the analysis of community and family dynamics, offering counselling services and recommending action to stabilise relationships, enrich lives and deepen human resources.

Over two hundred years ago Adam Smith wrote approvingly of the social benefits of the free-market system where, by an 'invisible hand', self-interested agents brought about the greater good for all. This was in a tightly homogenous culture where all shared the same value system and the state operated effectively to protect individual rights. In a fast-changing, chronically uncertain world where our economic and technological power to create or destroy embraces vastly disparate peoples and indeed the entire planet then it must be concluded that some rather more visible hands would be very welcome to guide the wealth of nations into the twenty-first century.

Index